Big Dog Breeds

Dan Rice, D.V.M.

Big Dog Breeds

Dan Rice, D.V.M.

Photo Credits
Kent and Donna Dannen: pages xvi, xvii, xviii, 2, 22, 30, 31, 32, 33, 45, 69, 91, 99, 108, 109, 112, 113, 115, 117, 118, 121, 126, 132, 135, 136, 137, 138, 139, 149, 151, 156, 157, 158, 164, 166, 167, 168, 170, 171, 172, 175, 177, 182, 183, 188, 196, 198, 201, 202, 203, 204, 206, 207 (top), 209, 214, 215; Norvia Behling: pages 13, 27, 47, 150; Tara Darling: pages 16, 34, 111, 114, 116, 122, 124, 125, 127, 128, 129, 130, 131, 133, 134, 140, 141, 142, 144, 145, 146, 147, 152, 153, 154, 155, 159, 161, 162, 163, 165, 173, 176, 178, 179, 180, 181, 184, 186, 187, 189, 190, 191, 192, 193, 194, 195, 199, 200, 205, 207 (bottom), 208, 216, 217, 218, 219; Pets by Paulette: pages 119, 210, 211, 212.

Cover Credits
All covers by Tara Darling

Illustrations
Michele Earle-Bridges

636.71
1446248

All inquiries should be addressed to:
Barron's Educational Series, Inc.
250 Wireless Boulevard
Hauppauge, NY 11788
http://www.barronseduc.com

International Standard Book No. 0-7641-1649-5

Library of Congress Catalog Card No. 00-063086

Library of Congress Cataloging-in-Publication Data
Rice, Dan, 1933–
   Big dog breeds / by Dan Rice.
      p. cm.
   ISBN 0-7641-1649-5
   1. Dogs. 2. Dog breeds. I. Title.

SF426.R54 2001
636.7′1—dc21   00-063086

Printed in Hong Kong
9 8 7 6 5 4 3 2 1

Contents

Introduction   xiii

Section One: Big Dogs

Chapter 1 Selecting Your Partner   1
The Right Breed   1
The Right Reason   2
Intelligence   3
The Right Season   4
Giant Gifts   4
Impulse Purchases   4
Which Sex Is Best   5
Where to Find   5
   Purebred Breeders   5
   Puppy Mills   6
   Backyard Breeders   7
Mixed-Breed and Crossbred Big Dogs   7
Best Age to Adopt   8
Birth to Eight Weeks   8
Three Weeks to Three Months   8
Choosing Your Puppy   9
Personality Testing   10
A Quick Health Check   10
Veterinary Examination   12
Completing the Selection   12
Older Big Dogs   12

Chapter 2 Preparing for Your Big Dog   14
The Neighbors' View   14
Head Collars or Halters   15

Insurance   15
Big Dog Puppies and Small Children   16
Big Spaces for Big Dogs   17
Security Kennel   17
Crate   18
Puppy-Proofing   18
Your Backyard Is Barney's World   20
A Safe Yard   20
Garage and Workshop   21
Boarding Kennels   21

Chapter 3 Greta's First Days at Home   23
Picking Up and Handling   23
Bonding and Socialization   24
Housebreaking   27
Crate and Pen   27
Stairs   29
Feeding Schedule   29
Too Much Exercise Is Hazardous   29
Exercise for Adults   31
Identification   33
Good Manners versus Vices   33
Training   34
The Name's the Game   35
Recall or Come   35
Sit   36
Correcting Vices   36
Separation Anxiety (CCD)   37
Jumping Up   38
Begging   39
Chewing or Mouthing   39
Coprophagia   40
Bite Inhibition   41
Roaming   41
Guarding   42
Leadership Training   42
Digging   43
Automobiles   44
Chasing   44

Chapter 4 Big Dog Health — 46

Your Veterinarian — 46
History and Physical Exam — 48
Ask Questions — 48
Laboratory Tests — 48
Prognosis — 50
Therapy — 50
Big Dog Problems — 51
Elbow Hygroma — 51
Calluses and Decubital Ulcers — 52
Tail Beating — 52
Obesity — 54
Epilepsy — 55
Heart Diseases — 56
Nephritis (Kidney Disease) — 56
Valley Fever — 57
Diabetes Mellitus — 57
Von Willebrand's Disease (VWD) — 57
Hypothyroidism — 58
Atopy — 58
Progressive Retinal Atrophy (PRA) — 59
Entropion — 59
Ectropion — 60
Big Skeletal Problems — 60
Joint Anatomy — 61
Ruptured Cruciate Ligament — 61
Causes — 62
Hip Dysplasia (CHD) — 62
Osteoarthritis or Degenerative Joint Disease (DJD) — 63
Elbow Dysplasia — 64
Osteosarcoma or Bone Cancer — 64
Miscellaneous Bone Problems — 65
   Osteochondritis Dissecans (OCD) — 65
   Genu Valgum and Genu Varum — 65
   Retained Cartilage Cores — 65

Chapter 5 Preventive Medicine — 66

Active Immunity — 66
Vaccines — 68

Passive Immunity   68
How Much?   68
When?   69
Boosters   70
Preventable Diseases   70
   Canine Distemper (CD)   71
   Canine Hepatitis (CAV-1)   71
   Leptospirosis   71
   Kennel Cough   71
   Parvovirus   71
   Corona Virus   71
   Lyme Disease   71
   Rabies   72
   Nosodes   72

Chapter 6 Emergencies   73
First Aid Kit   73
Average Normal Vital Signs   74
Barney's Vital Signs   74
Cardiopulmonary Resuscitation (CPR) and
   Artificial Respiration (AR)   75
Shock   75
Muzzle   76
Car Accidents   76
Heatstroke   77
Prevention   78
Poisoning   78
Poisonous Plants   78
Chocolate Poisoning   79
Wounds   79
Severe Hemorrhage   80
Tourniquet   80
Deep Punctures   80
Nosebleeds   81
Snakebite   81
Porcupine Quills   81
Skunks   82

Chapter 7 Gastronomic Tribulations   84

Quantity   84
Quality   84
Hiccups   85
"Garbagitis" and Pancreatitis   86
Impaction   87
Gastric Dilation and Volvulus (GDV)   87
    How Torsion Occurs   88
    Prevention   89
Air Swallowing, Belching, and Flatus   89
Vomiting   90
Obesity   90
Weight Loss   91

Chapter 8 Feeding Your Big Dog   92

Nutritional Terms   92
Dog Food Types   93
Canned Foods   93
Semi-Moist   93
Dry Foods   94
Water   94
Fat   94
Protein   94
Carbohydrates   95
Minerals   95
Vitamins   95
Supplements   96
Meat   96
Bones   96
Dog Food Labels   97
Feeding Trials   97
Safe Treats   98
Nutritional Influences   98
Overfeeding   98
Homemade Diets   99

Chapter 9 Breeding Your Big Dog   **100**
Dog Psychology   101
Big Dog Idiosyncrasies   101
Delayed Estrus   101
Delayed Male Maturation   102
Short Breeding Life   102
Uterine Inertia or Fatigue   103
Pseudocyesis (False Pregnancy)   103
Why Not Neuter?   104
When and Why to Neuter   104
Raising Puppies   104

Chapter 10 Short Lives of Tall Dogs   **105**
Short Tempers of Old Dogs   105
All The Wrong Reasons   106
One Legitimate Reason: Old Age   106
Euthanasia   107
Grief Support   107
What Dog Next?   108

Section Two: Purebred Big Dogs

Afghan Hound   111
Akita   114
Alaskan Malamute   116
Anatolian Shepherd Dog   119
Azawakh   122
Beauceron   124
Bernese Mountain Dog   126
Black and Tan Coonhound   128
Bloodhound   130
Borzoi   133
Bouvier des Flandres   136

Briard	138
Bullmastiff	140
Caucasian Owtcharka	142
Chesapeake Bay Retriever	144
Curly-Coated Retriever	147
Doberman Pinscher	149
Dogo Argentino	152
Dogue de Bordeaux	154
English Setter	156
Estrela Mountain Dog	159
Fila Brasileiro	161
German Shepherd Dog	163
Giant Schnauzer	166
Gordon Setter	168
Great Dane	170
Great Pyrenees	173
Greater Swiss Mountain Dog	175
Greyhound	177
Ibizan Hound	180
Irish Setter	182
Irish Wolfhound	184
Komondor	187
Kuvasz	189
Labrador Retriever	191
Leonberger	194
Mastiff	196
Neapolitan Mastiff	199
Newfoundland	201
Otterhound	203
Pointer	205
Rhodesian Ridgeback	208
Rottweiler	210
Saarloos Wolfhound	212
Saint Bernard	214
Scottish Deerhound	216
Tibetan Mastiff	218

Index   **220**

About the Author

Dan Rice

After dedicating the first half of his life to veterinary medicine in Colorado, Dan Rice has retired to fulfill a lifelong dream. He now writes about dogs and cats for Barron's, drawing heavily from his practice experience. He also has penned an anecdotal anthology of veterinary experiences, and is presently writing his second fictional book about Bigfoot. *Big Dog Breeds* is his twelfth book for Barron's. The others are *Bengal Cats, Complete Book of Dog Breeding, The Complete Book of Cat Breeding, Akitas, Dogs from A to Z (A Dictionary of Canine Terms), The Well-Mannered Cat, Brittanys, Chesapeake Bay Retrievers, Training Your German Shepherd Dog, The Dog Handbook,* and *The Beagle Handbook.* Not quite retired, Dan and his wife Marilyn now live in Arizona, where his reading and research keeps him in touch with his former profession and the dog fancy.

❋

Dedication and Acknowledgment

This volume is dedicated to the incredible big dogs and big dog lovers of the world. I had the honor of knowing, lifting, and examining thousands of uncommonly large and giant dogs during the years in practice and have earned my share of spinal problems to prove it! Oh, how I wish hydraulic exam tables had been available in those days! Putting together this book has been a rewarding task, and for affording me that pleasure, I wish to thank Mark Miele, Barron's managing editor, Anna Damaskos, editor, and the other fine Barron's people who made it possible. My gratitude sincerely goes out to Frederic L. Frye, D.V.M., MSc, Cbiol, FIBiol, RSMVC. His expert evaluation comments on the manuscript added immensely to its form and content.

Introduction

A bone-chilling wind howls across the heather, whistling through chinks in thick stone walls. The raging storm batters closed shutters and rattles loose-fitting windows; candle flames flicker and lean away from the whispering wind.

Clattering hooves echo across the drawbridge, followed by hammering on the rustic castle door. Players at a game of whist pause and quietly consider whom the intruder or visitor may be. All eyes turn expectantly toward the doorway; the four men replace their tankards of warm ale on the scarred table and reach for their swords.

Rising from his seat beyond the fire's crackling glow a portly, heavily robed servant leans a candle into the fireplace and with it moves toward the door. Two enormous Wolfhounds slowly leave the hearth to join him, striding purposefully on either side, their backs reaching well above the servant's waist. Colossal strength exudes from these regal dogs and fills the room, just as their bodies fill the doorway. Thick muscles tense and hackles rise; their gigantic presence calms the castle inmates as the massive latch bolt is drawn from the pounding door.

Your heart quickens. You wonder if an intruder will step through the door into the jaws of those great hounds. You try to imagine the expression of a friendly sojourner when confronted by this brace of four-legged behemoths. The television image fades to black; a commercial interrupts the movie.

Pouring a cup of coffee, you think about the imposing size of those dogs. You fantasize about their strength and wonder if they are really vicious guard dogs; they are so big, quiet, and act so gentle. Your curiosity is piqued as you contemplate those brutes, and you dream further. What would it be like to share your parlor with a pair of those enormous dogs? What would your friends think? Looking around your modest living room, you decide your hearth probably wouldn't accommodate two of the huge hounds, but maybe just one?

Why not? Welcome to the club!

Ownership of a giant dog carries a giant-sized obligation. You are responsible for the actions of your big dog in every case.

Before you read any further, consider the hurdles you must leap; owning a big dog isn't always easy. Don't take these obstacles lightly! More is said about regulations and responsibility on page 14.

For a multitude of reasons, more dog owners than ever before are selecting big and giant dogs. Large breeds have many and diverse appearances, taking every shape and color imaginable. Seen in a myriad of coat types, with widely differing temperaments, big dogs arose in all parts of the world at different times. The work for which they were developed varies greatly as well. There is practically no similarity or uniformity among the many breeds of big dogs. However, in the United States, a common thread runs through these dogs, and that is that the people who admire them own them *primarily because of their size.*

Some urban dwellers don't consider their homes complete without a Great Dane or Irish Wolfhound sprawled across the floor. A Saint Bernard or Newfoundland happily shares a small Arizona backyard with family and children. Content with their environment, they're unaware or don't care that their ancestors originated in cool Britannia, the snow-covered Swiss Alps, or the frigid waters of the Northeast.

Ask owners why they own a giant or large breed, and you'll get many answers, but most will end with, "There's so much more dog to love." Big dogs express themselves in a big way, and whether Anatolian Shepherd, Saarloos Wolfhound, Caucasian Owtcharka, or Tibetan Mastiff, they are loving companions and large enough to be partners with anyone who loves them.

At one time in history, household security was in the hands of a big guard dog. Every prosperous family owned a tie dog or band dog, collectively known as Mastiffs. Dating to the Assyrian times, terra cotta replicas of big dogs resembling modern-day Mastiffs have been found buried under porches, presumably to frighten away evil spirits. Molossus, an ancient Roman dog, was captured in stone by an unknown Greek sculptor. The statue depicts a giant, if legendary, canine of a type easily recognized as a Mastiff.

Big dogs are a part of legend and history of all times. It's not our intent to group them together under the name of *Canis grande* and try to make a case for commonality among all types of giants. However, big dogs have abundantly similar characteristics, many of which are related to their physical size alone. They share related health problems, neighbors' fears, liability concerns, and housing needs, all of which are amply covered in this book.

The last half of this book is devoted to big purebred dogs, with color photographs, the history, description, purposes, and the inherent personality traits of each breed. The first half is dedicated to big dog peculiarities, generalities, and information specific to large dogs.

If you love and admire big dogs, this is your book! Punctuated with bits of humor and personal reflections, it's easy reading. If you like the imposing size of a particular breed, or just admire big dogs in general, this is the book for you. For the sake of discussion, we define a big dog as one that stands 27 inches or taller at the shoulder.

Advice is offered on selecting your big dog, places to purchase it, necessary housing, exercise information (which may surprise you), and facilities needed, as well as the need to match the temperament of each big dog with that of the prospective owner. Puppy personality testing is discussed as well.

Nutritional idiosyncrasies and eating problems are discussed. Isn't it interesting that big, fast-growing breeds can suffer permanently from improper feeding? Skeletal problems related to their size and maturation rate are also addressed.

Medical and hereditary conditions common to large breeds are likewise covered. If you are considering a big dog, regardless of type, this book will appeal to you.

Routine obedience training, housebreaking, vaccination, grooming, and common canine diseases are amply covered in other Barron's books and are here discussed very briefly or as they particularly apply to giants. This volume is dedicated to those conditions and characteristics that are unique to or prevalent in big dogs.

Big Dogs

Selecting Your Partner

NOTE: The writer has made every effort to exclude sexist language in this book. Our dogs are named either Greta or Barney. The dogs' names and related pronouns are alternated between female and male in various chapters. Likewise, when the canine heroine of a chapter is Greta, her veterinarian, trainer, or owner is masculine. When Barney takes the starring role, his owner, trainer, or doctor is feminine.

As puppies, big dogs require many hours of your attention and time. Proper diet is critical throughout life, and nutritional quality must be changed periodically. As a puppy and adult, a large dog's exercise demands are much different from those of a smaller dog. Greta will grow faster and mature later in life than a smaller dog, and will exhibit aging changes long before her tiny cousins.

Choosing the particular canine partner that is most compatible with you is a major undertaking, and one that should receive an appropriate measure of forethought. You've decided to select a dog that will weigh nearly as much as you or your spouse and may consume more food per day than a human family member. Selection of this dog requires knowledge of many facets of big dog ownership to be sure you choose the correct breed and the best pup available. The goal of this chapter is to guide you along the path leading to the right partner at the right time!

> No two dogs are alike. Some grow more slowly, mature later, reach gigantic sizes, have different problems, and die younger.

THE RIGHT BREED

Protecting your dog should be given due consideration right after you've thought about protecting yourself. We aren't speaking of bodily harm to you and your family, but of the necessity for defending yourself against criminal and civil litigation. All big dogs aren't alike; some are naturally more aggressive than others. Don't overlook this factor as you search for the perfect big dog!

- Read all the facts about your breed of choice, and speak to at least a dozen owners of dogs just like the one you've selected.
- Begin early to teach Greta to treat everyone as a friend.
- As soon as possible, begin backyard dominance lessons and obedience training.
- Enroll her in puppy kindergarten classes to learn canine socialization.
- Never overlook her smallest aggressive tendency, and nip it in the bud.

Guide dogs must occasionally display intelligent disobedience.

THE RIGHT REASON

Why do you want a dog that stands 25 or more inches tall, and may eventually weigh more than 100 pounds? Is Greta's prospective role in your family that of your friend and companion, or is she to be relegated to status symbol? Does your neighbor have a yappy little terrier that you hate and want to dominate in every way? Many a giant-puppy shopper unconsciously discovers such motives lurking behind the desire to own a big dog.

Do you harbor an inadequacy or paranoia and hope that owning a large dog will create a safe zone around you? I once knew a lady who revealed her intention to buy a Newfoundland so she could record its bark on her telephone-answering device! She knew nothing of

Newfoundlands but assumed they had a deep bark. Although I agreed that the resonant canine voice might get the attention of unwanted callers, I doubted that it would discourage them from calling again. If these or other similar incentives are influencing your purchase of a big dog, please reconsider.

Occasionally, a person obtains a large-breed puppy based on size or appearance without regard to the breed's inherent characteristics. For instance, a Bloodhound or Black and Tan Coonhound may be purchased solely on the merits of its long velvety ears, wrinkly skin, laid-back personality, and sad eyes. These breeds are great when used for scenting and trailing game. For years they have been selectively bred to be superior trail hounds, with fantastic senses of smell. However, such a dog needs the place and time to pursue those vocations. You needn't enter hunting or scent trial competition to keep these hounds happy, but they should be given the opportunity to follow their noses on a regular basis.

Like any other pets, large dogs have personalities that must mesh with yours. They have demands that must be met. They are expensive to care for and require a great commitment from their owners.

You should proceed with selection only after you have determined that your reasons for owning a big dog are appropriate and logical. If you love dogs, want to share your life with a dog, can financially afford to buy and maintain a canine partner, and don't appreciate moderate-sized or small dog breeds because of habits or personalities, you are probably a candidate for big dog ownership. If you have available

> **Personality is partly learned, partly genetic, and includes the dog's psychology, biochemistry, experience, education, and conditioning.**

time to care for, train, and exercise your big dog, continue with the selection process.

INTELLIGENCE

Some archaic literature expounds the theory that dogs' actions are all hereditary, with no room for thinking or reasoning. Others argue that dogs are blessed with more common sense than humans, and that they obviously think and reason more clearly than their neighbors down the block. Somewhere in between is the truth. Dogs perceive and react to their environment in ways that are much different from humans. Greta's world contains fewer colors; dialogue and emotion aren't terribly important. Tastes, scents, and movements are more important.

> **Intelligence is partly inherited, but experience and training are equally important.**

Experts say canine IQ tests are valid only when comparing two dogs of the same breed. If Greta receives loads of attention and experiences many different situations, she will appear smarter than if she were treated to years of

indifference. Are trick dogs more intelligent than less clever pets? Not necessarily, but they do receive more attention, more training, and more human time than most pets.

Often, picking a single trait such as olfactory sense (smell) and testing accordingly skews IQ test results. Which dogs will quickly pop to the top? Bloodhounds and Black and Tans, naturally! Are they more intelligent than other dogs? Probably not if other aptitudes are sought and tested.

Other testing chooses environmental interaction as criteria, as in guide dog selection. The German Shepherd, Golden Retriever, and Labrador Retriever suddenly jump to the top of this heap, but are they perfect for everyone? Not necessarily!

Intelligence may be associated with trainability, which is difficult to define. It's the dogs' ability to focus on their trainer, to listen and watch carefully, and to perform for the sake of pleasing their owners. It's a personality trait

found in some dogs of virtually every breed and is seen regularly in big dogs.

More important than intelligence testing is to find the breed that satisfies your particular needs, then compare several litters, and finally, compare Greta with her siblings. If she selects you as her owner, you've found your big partner!

THE RIGHT SEASON

When do you buy your big dog? Anytime you want her, right? Not quite! Consider the season and weather. If you live north of the Mason-Dixon Line, wait until the snow cover is melted and grass has sprouted in your yard. As a puppy, Greta requires space, and it's difficult to supply the needed amount in a yard drifted full of snow. Housebreaking is a chore under the best circumstances. If a midnight trip to Greta's toilet area includes wading in a foot of slush, it's bound to be a serious stress on this budding relationship.

Prepare to spend countless hours with your new partner the first few weeks she's in your home. This means Greta shouldn't be obtained just before you leave on vacation, when you plan a business trip, or when you expect an invasion of guests into your home. Arrange to bring her home during a relaxed, quiet time for the entire family, when she can become acclimated to the environment and adjusted to the inhabitants without undue excitement.

GIANT GIFTS

How can you give Greta to your husband as a Christmas surprise? That's easy: don't yield to that inspiration! A good rule to follow regarding presents is simple. Never buy a living gift for anyone without the recipient's total agreement. The only notion worse than an unannounced gift of a puppy is the impulse to buy a large dog, anytime, without adequate thought and planning.

If a Christmas puppy is agreeable, be sure the entire family has duly considered sharing their lives and space with Greta. Assuming total accord has been reached on that subject, hang a picture and some puppy toys on the Christmas tree, and wait to collect her when the season's activity is stable. This will afford the time to make necessary housing adjustments before her arrival. Purchase her bed, bowls, and toys in advance; install puppy-proof gates on stairways, reinforce fences, and buy a pen and sleeping crate.

> Big dogs, like big cars, should be purchased only after a great deal of serious thought.

IMPULSE PURCHASES

To mall shoppers, pet emporiums are like magnets. Often, these attractive pet stores are scrupulously clean, odors are adequately contained, and clumsy, healthy-looking, sad-eyed puppies with enormous feet are enticingly displayed in plastic cubicles. Bookshelves abound with descriptions and pictures of dozens of large dog breeds. You remember a friend's big dog, and there sits a puppy of the same breed.

Collars, leashes, dishes, grooming tools, and dog foods are arranged for immediate purchase and delivery. Time-payment plans are available, and return privileges apply if the dog is proven to have hereditary faults. The big pup has been vaccinated, veterinary health certification is included, as well as American Kennel Club puppy registration documents, and sometimes even pedigrees.

The store takes plastic, and you happen to have your Visa card with you. How can you resist? This is one-stop impulse shopping at its best! If you have almost decided to purchase a pet shop puppy, please select her only after considering the following: In order to choose the most desirable puppy, you should be able to meet and handle Greta's parents, or at least her dam. Siblings should be present for comparison. Personality traits are more easily determined if you can see how other puppies behave in similar situations. Contemporary pet shops have come a long way in the past twenty years, but they still have a few disadvantages.

> The nature of dogs varies from breed to breed, and from individual to individual within a given breed.

WHICH SEX IS BEST

In choosing a big dog partner or companion of either sex, very little is sacrificed. If you are considering breeding Greta, entering her in field trials, or conformation showing, gender has more implications, as will be discussed later.

Don't get hung up on size alone. Stature is a poor criterion by which to select a puppy of either sex of a large breed. Greta is going to be big, but typically, females are slightly smaller than their male counterparts. Some owners believe females are gentler and less aggressive than males. That's not necessarily true and depends to a great extent on the breed selected. Before you accept that generality, discuss with a breeder the aggressiveness of both sexes of the breed you've chosen.

Most companion-dog partners are neutered or spayed before reaching physical maturity. A female may be spayed at about any age, and the cost of this surgery is usually slightly greater than the corresponding cost of male castration. Neither cost is exorbitant when prorated over the dog's life, and both add a number of advantages that are discussed in the chapter on health.

WHERE TO FIND

Considering your investment and all the ramifications of owning a big dog, you owe it to yourself to progress slowly and deliberately as you make your selection. Follow a logical, systematic selection process.

Purebred Breeders

- Don't assume your canine partner will become a famous show dog or an obedience trial champion, but use those achievements for comparison to begin the search for your chosen breed. Purchase a copy of one of the various dog magazines found in a bookstore. These magazines will list dog shows and other canine events in your area, and you should plan to attend one or more. Once there, buy a premium list that will tell you in which ring and at what time your breed will be shown. After you have seen the best of your breed exhibited, you can talk to breeders of that specific breed.

- Watch your breed participate in other canine competitive events such as agility trials, field trials, coursing, tracking, weight pulling, and fly-ball events. Watch your chosen breed's ability, training, and enthusiasm in these events. You can gain a great deal of information about your breed by watching its representatives in competition.

- Visit several breeding kennels. Never make a spontaneous selection from the first litter seen on the first visit to a single kennel.

Experience the personalities of as many litters as possible.

- Discuss with breeders the general personality and traits of your chosen breed. The habits of each pup are individual. Greta's disposition is malleable and will be influenced by her bonding with you and your attitude and ability to train her. However, you must be aware of certain traits inherent in each large breed.

- Ask owners, handlers, and breeders many questions to satisfy your information needs. Conscientious breeders will furnish printed information about their strain or bloodline of the breed. They will happily answer your queries and probably will ask you more questions than you're prepared to answer. They will have information about the proper age to take a puppy, and should reassure you of their puppies' socialization.

- Ask about purchase price, return privilege, guarantee, veterinary examination, and routine parasite control. You need to know as much as possible about each breeder's puppies before you commit to purchase.

- You may be asked not to touch the puppies if they are only a few weeks old. Don't be insulted; this precaution is to protect the valuable litter until first vaccinations have been administered. Be content to observe pups at play. If you think you've made a decision, ask the breeder to mark the pup for you. Usually, the toenails of a hind foot are painted with a certain color of nail polish to denote your selection.

Puppy Mills

You've no doubt heard of puppies raised by unscrupulous breeders who are producing puppies in great quantity at the expense of quality.

> **No excuse is good enough to patronize a puppy farm.**

- A puppy farm usually advertises in newspapers, but sometimes their ads are seen in dog magazines.

- Puppy farms never identify their enterprises as *puppy farms* or *puppy mills*.

- Mills can be recognized by the breeder's lack of interest in buyers' families and facilities. If you get the impression the breeder doesn't particularly care where a puppy goes, you will find few guarantees or assurances of health or quality.

- Usually, farm pups are available to anyone who has the purchase price, and often the price is negotiable if the pups are of notably poor quality or older.

- Mill owners usually offer little information about the breed, and often the litter is displayed in the absence of their dam.

- Mill pups' health often is suspect. Puppy farm inmates may appear bony, potbellied, and in poor condition. If seen, their dam may be thin with a dull coat, and lack luster in her eyes.

- AKC registry usually is offered for mill pups. Don't be fooled by puppy farm owners who declare their pups to be AKC registered, pedigreed, or from championship stock. The AKC has no inspection program, and registration has no bearing on the health or quality of puppies. Pedigrees can be copied on official-appearing forms on any computer, and unless certified by the registry, are only as good as the peddler who produces them.

- Inspect the facility and the puppies' kennel environment. Most puppy farm residents live in cramped and sometimes filthy quarters, enjoying a questionable diet, with little opportunity for regular exercise or socialization. They may be kept in pens with other breeds, and sometimes two or three litters of various ages may be housed together.

• Equally deplorable is disregard for the predictable personality of each puppy. Often, mill owners know nothing of the dispositions of either dam or sire, and have no record of accomplishments of previous puppies born to the same parents.

If you smell a puppy mill, beat a hasty retreat! Don't handle the puppies, and don't grieve the inmates of the mill. You're planning to gamble a significant amount of money and time that your big puppy will turn out exactly as you want. This means keeping the odds in your favor by paying a little more to get your pup from a conscientious breeder.

Backyard Breeders

In some instances, the owner of an AKC-registered bitch will breed her to a friend's unproven registered dog of the same breed. Are puppies of such matings likely to be satisfactory canine partners for you? The answer depends on the quality of each of the parents, not the cuteness of the puppies.

• If both dogs are fair representatives of their breed, have few hereditary problems, and demonstrate acceptable personalities, their offspring may suit your needs.

• However, if both parents are quite young when bred, and nothing is known about their ancestors' qualities, especially conformation and disposition, you're flirting with disaster! Genetic diseases may be first exhibited after several years of age, and these conditions may be prevalent in both the sire's and the dam's bloodlines.

These facts should make you wary of obtaining a backyard-bred puppy. Judicious advice admonishes you to buy soundness in a big dog, not cuteness. Look for the best pup, not the most available one.

MIXED-BREED AND CROSSBRED BIG DOGS

Sometimes, a big dog may be inadvertently bred to a neighborhood fence jumper. Will the resultant mixed-breed puppies fulfill your needs? Or, a bitch of one large purebred may be *purposefully* mated with a purebred of another large breed to produce crossbred puppies. What can we predict in such pups? Again, only the puppies in question and the people involved can answer these questions.

• Something can be said for the hybrid vigor (heterosis) of mixed-breed pups. Sufficient research hasn't been done to prove that the offspring of such matings are truly stronger or more vigorous than the progeny of purebreds. Commonsense genetics tells us mixed-breed puppies should have fewer hereditary problems, but the wider gene pool behind them doesn't assure that these pups will be free of all such problems.

• Crossbred offspring conformation is relatively unpredictable on the first mating. If a large purebred female is bred to a large purebred male of another breed, anything is possible, and few assumptions can be made about the variety of appearances or sizes of the puppies until the litter is several weeks or months old. Previous matings of the same two dogs may predict the size of these crossbred puppies.

• Often, personalities of mixed-breed and crossbred pups are quite attractive, but are probably less predictable than those of purebreds. Even though individual dispositions may vary, purebred puppies' characters are likely to be similar to those of their ancestors.

• If you aren't concerned about the definitive size or appearance of your big canine partner, and if you find a mixed or crossbred litter, go for it! If the dam is a big dog and the sire is of equal or greater size, the litter has an excellent chance of containing at least a fair percentage of big puppies.

- Little has been published about the success of some guide dog organizations that have purposefully crossed Labs with Goldens to produce superior guide dogs with fewer hereditary faults. It will no doubt require a few more years to prove this experiment a success or failure.

BEST AGE TO ADOPT

A fairly narrow window of opportunity exists as an ideal age to take a puppy from her nest and siblings, and transplant her to your home. Although rarely is this time met precisely, it should be used as a guide.

BIRTH TO EIGHT WEEKS

Greta's ability to identify and communicate with other dogs is among the valuable knowledge that is mandatory for a well-rounded canine partner. Nothing is quite as frustrating as owning a large dog that has no canine-to-canine communication skills, one that tries to bully every dog she meets. It's virtually impossible for a human to teach a dog to get along with other dogs unless other dogs are a part of her environment. Normally, this vital education begins at birth and extends until the pup is taken from its nest. This is the principal reason for waiting until Greta is eight weeks old before adopting her.

Canine socialization comes first, followed closely by human socialization.

Taking Greta home too early is a mistake, as is leaving her with her dam too long.

Greta is subjected to a constant canine communication experience during her early life with her dam and siblings. She learns to take advantage of nursing opportunities provided by her mother. She learns nest etiquette and to respect her mother. She learns about dominance among littermates and her place in the litter's pecking order. Her personality begins to form in the nest, and this period is critical for acquiring typical canine characteristics. Experience and knowledge is extended to include Greta's place in the breeder's family pack order, and is adjusted when she arrives in your home. Your housebreaking chores will be easier because of this eight-week doggy experience; puppies learn to remove themselves from their food and nest for defecation and urination.

Canine greeting techniques that Greta learns in her nest will be used the rest of her life each time she meets a strange dog. Body language or postures and sounds are learned that will make life easier in your home and when on walks. She'll be taught by her dam and siblings how much aggression is tolerated, how rough she can play without retribution, and how to win another dog's friendship. She will learn submission techniques as well as challenge postures. Canine body language is innate, but final polishing of these techniques is learned and experienced in a litter environment.

THREE WEEKS TO THREE MONTHS

This period of life is the optimum time for human bonding. Pups that are frequently and gently handled during this critical period will adapt quickly to new people and human environments. Conscientious breeders recognize the added importance of handling big dog puppies during this time. It is a human socialization period, the time in which Greta should not only be petted and handled as often as possible by humans, but also taken to your home. If for some reason you can't take Greta home between eight weeks and three months of age, ask the breeder to take her into his home to socialize, and collect her as soon as possible thereafter.

Human socialization is important for Greta to experience her place in her human family, to learn that she will be loved, petted, and rewarded for correct actions, and ignored when she acts inappropriately. It is the time when she will most easily bond with you and your family. This early bonding period is doubly important if you want the most fruitful partnership to form between you and Greta.

> You've reached the stage that will establish a lifetime friendship. Consider it well!

CHOOSING YOUR PUPPY

You've identified a conscientious breeder who has a litter of big puppies, and you've visited them several times. You stopped by the kennel a few days ago and took a large towel, often referred to as a *momma towel*, and the breeder promised to put it in the litter's box. The litter has reached the age of eight weeks, and today you are going to make your final selection.

- Take a final look at the litter from a distance. Having already decided that your partner won't be shown or bred, you are principally interested in matching a puppy's personality with your own. Color and sex aren't of primary importance. You watch their playing and clumsy posturing. You want a puppy that isn't afraid of its shadow, but not a super aggressive one, one that likes you and will be easy to bond with.

- Don't immediately pick up any puppy.

- Take an empty soda can into which you have dropped a few marbles before taping the hole shut. While the litter is busily engaged in tumbling about, roll the can across the floor, but not directly at the pups. The noise probably will startle the pups, and one or two will run and hide (timid pups). Note the puppies that stop their play, then after a moment's thought, begin to investigate the can (curious pups).

- Wad up a page of paper, cluck to the pups, and toss the paper wad away from them. Note the pups that bound after the wad (retriever prospects), and particularly note the puppy that picks it up, looks around, and brings it toward you (definite retriever prospect). At least one or two of the litter will chase the pups that are chasing the paper, and tackle one of their siblings (aggressive pups).

- Sit on the floor and pick up each of the puppies that have caught your interest. Pet the pup; scratch behind its ears and note the interest it displays in licking your face and hands (socialized and ready to bond).

- Stand with the pup, take it into another room, and again sit on the floor with the puppy on your lap. Turn it belly up, and rub its tummy. Extend and stroke each leg in turn. If it doesn't strenuously object to this treatment (trusting pup), place it on the floor beside you. If it immediately attempts to climb back on your lap and lick your face (affectionate pup), you've probably found a match.

- Walk to the door. If the pup is following at your heels (bonding pup), you're getting close to a good choice of a lifetime partner.

PERSONALITY TESTING

Professional aptitude and personality testing is available in most parts of the country. Unfortunately, the testing isn't perfectly standardized and tends to vary depending on interpretation of the tests. Usually the tests are conducted by a third, disinterested individual and consist of a series of nonspecific exercises similar to those described above. The tester holds Greta on her back for several seconds to see if she trusts him and submits to such handling. Excessive petting is tried to see if Greta is socialized, and she is held tightly to indicate her submission to restraint. Other tests include walking away to watch for following, and kneeling to see if the pup wants to socialize with the tester. Greta's response to each test receives a numerical score from which interpretation is made.

Professional testing is a good but imperfect indication of Greta's personality and partner potential. Since this book deals with all types of big dogs from all the specialty groups, specific personality testing will be left to those owners who desire this added evaluation. Your veterinarian should be able to give you the names of behavioral experts in your area who are doing personality testing.

You should critically evaluate your own personality before you choose a pup. If you have a dominant personality, select a breed with a personality that matches. If you have a retiring, soft-spoken manner, you should select a more sensitive breed and individual with similar attributes. Athletic persons should acquire athletic, sporting dogs. Nonathletic people are usually happier with the laid-back big dogs. Outdoors people who like to walk a lot often are best matched with scent dogs that are happy to walk in the woods, sniffing game trails. Competition-minded people might be happiest with herding dogs and those on the lower-height end of our big dog definition.

A QUICK HEALTH CHECK

A few general health questions can be answered while you're handling your new partner. Open Greta's mouth and inspect her bite. Dogs of

most large breeds should have a scissors bite. This means her front teeth (incisors) should barely touch as the uppers slide over the lowers. Underbite is the condition in which the lower incisors protrude in front of the uppers. Overbite is equally bad, and is the condition in which the upper incisors protrude in front of the lowers. Either deformity, as well as twisted teeth (wry mouth), should be called to the breeder's attention. Although bite faults don't necessarily imply poor health, these hereditary deformities often mean disqualification in conformation shows.

Run your fingers over Greta's abdomen. An umbilical hernia will be indicated by a soft swelling at her navel. If you feel a bubblelike soft mass the size of a small marble, it's probably a hernia. Usually, hernias will disappear when she is turned on her back and reappear when she is standing. Hernias may be inconsequential or they may require surgical repair in the future, usually when Greta is spayed.

If a male is chosen, his testicles should be descended into the scrotum by weaning age. If you can't feel them there, call this deficiency to the breeder's attention and discuss it with your veterinarian when the pup is given his prepurchase examination. Often, big puppies' testicles are found in the scrotum one day and aren't there the next. Apparent appearance and disappearance of testicles may be normal until the puppy is several months old. However, if you are purchasing the pup as a show or breeding prospect, be sure both testicles are in the scrotum, and if in doubt, have him examined by your veterinarian.

Use the breed standard as a guide for selecting of your puppy, but regardless of Greta's quality as a show prospect, she should

Before it's too late, critically evaluate your partner's health.

be *your* pick of the litter! She should have normal colored pigment in the rubber of her nose, and her skin should be smooth and supple, even though it seems to be too large for her frame. Her toes should be collected and not show evidence of splaying, and her wrists should be upright and more or less vertical to the floor. Usually, her joints will be slightly out of proportion to the bones of her lower leg.

Never buy a sick or lame puppy. Lameness in big dog puppies is often associated with rapid growth and nutritional imbalances. Don't accept any lameness with the breeder's guarantee that Greta will be normal in a few weeks.

If she shows signs of coughing, or has a nasal discharge, pus exuding from her eyes, or a noticeable skin rash, tell the breeder you will take a rain check and return when she's healthy.

Diarrhea may simply be a sign of overeating or ingestion of some foreign substance. However, diarrhea may be a sign of parasites or other disease. Don't take a chance; return after a few days and collect your puppy only if her stool is normal.

Often, normal big dog puppies are clumsy, out of proportion, and have large abdomens, but if Greta displays any skin inflammation, scaling, redness, irritation, or itching, look elsewhere for your companion. Her skin should be clean and have no evidence of unexplained scars or blemishes.

She should have boundless energy and a desire to play when approached, and fall into a deep sleep when tired. Don't take her under any other conditions.

VETERINARY EXAMINATION

If you've had previous dogs, you may already have a veterinarian with whom you are well satisfied. If not, shop around, but never choose a veterinarian from an advertisement in the Yellow Pages before speaking to him and his staff. This is even more important with your first veterinary experience. Listen closely to what he says, and if necessary, take notes.

Ask the breeder to allow your veterinarian to check your new partner for heart problems as well as other hereditary conditions that affect her general health. Greta's nutrition should be part of this discussion as well. This examination will probably cost the price of an office call, although many veterinarians will provide an initial prepurchase examination free. Many conscientious breeders will agree to transport Greta to your veterinarian's office to assure both of you that she is healthy and normal at the time of purchase. Often, the breeder will split the cost of this examination, but regardless of the cost, it's cheap insurance for both of you. (See "Your Veterinarian," page 46.)

COMPLETING THE SELECTION

Once you've selected your pup, complete the purchase by reading and signing the contract, including the guarantee specifying whether your return privileges include your money back or the choice of another pup, and the conditions under which this guarantee will be honored. Other papers may include the AKC puppy registration and the pedigree. Another important paper is the health certification properly signed by the breeder's veterinarian. A statement should be included listing the date Greta was last wormed and when another fecal sample should be checked, as well as the names of vaccines that have been given and the date the next is due. You should receive a written statement of the quantity and name of the food being fed, and the number of times being fed per day.

For the purpose of transporting your canine partner to your home, it's usually best to take along a friend to drive the car while you attend to Greta. Be sure the breeder hasn't fed her for at least two or three hours before your journey. As you leave the breeder's house, collect the momma towel you previously left, and hold the puppy on your lap on the towel. If Greta is older, or seems to be quite nervous and upset, it may be best to place her and the momma blanket in a crate purchased for the trip.

OLDER BIG DOGS

Puppies are wonderful. Everyone should experience the challenge and satisfaction of successfully raising a puppy to adulthood. Watching the development of a puppy's intelligence, teaching the puppy to experience and adjust to human culture, and seeing the product of your efforts will be extremely gratifying. However, many families haven't time to devote to the idiosyncrasies of puppies. Perhaps we think we're too old to meet the demands of a young puppy, or we have too many other responsibilities to devote the necessary time to train a young dog. Although risks abound when adopting an older dog, this option is open to most of us.

Agencies specializing in the rescue of many different breeds are available across the country. After deciding on the breeds of big dogs that you might consider, look on the Internet, call a local all-breed club, or consult with your veterinarian. Find a rescue agency and put your name on the list. Agency personnel will interview you and ask many questions about you, your family, and your facilities before they will accept your name, but the chances of obtaining a big dog are relatively good.

Rescue dogs are often vaccinated, neutered, housebroken, and have stable personalities. The flip side of those desirable characteristics is that the older dog may have some personality quirk that hasn't yet surfaced. She could be a fear biter and this propensity will be seen only in some peculiar circumstance. She

might suffer from separation anxiety, have no respect for her surroundings, and rip your house apart the first time you leave her for an hour. She may be fine around humans, but superaggressive toward other dogs or pets. Some adult dogs have no respect for confinement and will leap over, tunnel under, or chew through the finest fence you can construct.

Dog pounds and shelters sometimes have large dogs available. Often, less is known about shelter dogs than rescue dogs. Most grown dogs in pounds have some reason or reasons for being there. Dealing with these dogs may be more of a challenge, but the outcome can be quite gratifying if you have great patience and some training ability.

When you make the decision to adopt an adult large dog, be sure you have a contract that allows you to return it within the first two or three weeks. Start out slowly, and if you find you can't cope with the problems, don't hesitate to take the dog back to the shelter or rescue agency.

A full-grown Mastiff and a full-grown Pekingese.

Preparing for Your Big Dog

Barney is coming home this week! You have a banner with his name ready to hang out, but what do you buy? What kinds of toys will he need? Can you expect problems related to his size? Will your neighbors object to him? In other words, how do the demands of big dog puppies differ from those of smaller dogs, and what preparations should you make in advance?

THE NEIGHBORS' VIEW

When the residents next door discover you've obtained a giant or big dog, there may be an immediate cooling of neighborly attitude. Unfortunately, many urban, suburban, and country dwellers consider big dogs to be big nuisances. Stories abound of big dogs' property destruction, aggressiveness, attacks on children, mail carrier confrontations, dogfights, small-pet deaths, and similar situations.

Some condo covenants restrict pets, but usually the law is on your side, and except in isolated cases, regulations don't prevent you from acquiring the dog of your choice, regardless of its size. Your neighbors have no legitimate objection, providing Barney doesn't break a nuisance law, so let them stew; do your own thing! You won't allow him to become an unruly rascal, so why is the homeowners' association circulating petitions? You'll prove their

fears unfounded, and then your neighbors will flock to your door to apologize for their distrust. Right? Not quite! Unfortunately this attitude doesn't do justice to a beautiful big dog partner, and doesn't aid accord either!

Big, untrained dogs can jeopardize neighborhood harmony. More than one home has been sold because a neighbor fears or distrusts a big dog. Whether this misgiving is based on fact or fantasy, you must accept and deal with it. Your best answer to neighbors' apprehensions is education. When you decide to acquire a big dog, don't keep your intentions a secret; address the issue before it becomes a blazing problem, deeply entrenched in nasty litigation.

> To minimize neighborhood conflicts, be positive, but also be responsive to your friends' apprehension and to legal restrictions.

- Call city, county, and state legal-aid and advice agencies. Ask if ownership of any particular breed is restricted in your community, and have the restrictions explained. Ignorance of dog laws is no excuse for violations. In some communities certain breeds are outlawed, and others may not be exercised out of your fenced yard off lead.

- Ask for friends' and neighbors' advice.

- Show them how you've prepared for your new partner.

- Take your friends with you when you begin to shop for a pup.

- Ask them to accompany you to dog shows and other events where big dogs are exhibited, and let them see how a well-trained, well-behaved large dog acts.
- After Barney has been with you for a week or so, invite the neighbors to bring their children to visit. Introduce them carefully and let them see how gentle and friendly a giant puppy is.
- As you train your new partner, exercise him in the neighborhood on leash for all to see.
- Teach Barney to sit each time he meets a friend, and encourage neighbors to stop and pet Barney.
- Quickly curb any sign of aggressiveness Barney displays toward people or their pets.
- Never allow your big dog to run loose in the neighborhood!

HEAD COLLARS OR HALTERS

A recent advance in dog equipment, the web head collar is entirely humane, more so in fact than chain or leather choke collars, and ranks worlds above the prong-type training collars. Head collars are halterlike contrivances that control your big partner by gripping his muzzle while applying pressure behind his ears. The halter applies physical control to his entire head, not to his neck alone. If Barney displays even a shadow of aggressiveness, or even if he doesn't, try a head halter for training and when he is among uninformed neighbors. If he accepts this technique, let your friends know why you are using the device and what it's meant to accomplish. They might be alarmed if they see you on a walk with a muzzlelike gadget on his head, but when they realize you are critically interested in Barney's control and discipline, they will be duly impressed.

> In most instances, head collars have been shown to dramatically improve a big dog's behavior.

INSURANCE

Most big dogs are quite docile and rarely cause damage to people or property unless they are abused, neglected, or allowed to run loose. As you look into Barney's big, soft eyes, it's hard to believe he might cause you or your friends trouble. Still, perhaps the most important preparation you can make is checking your liability insurance to be sure your homeowner's policy adequately covers your dog's actions. Advise your agent of your intention to own, train, and maintain control of a big dog, and follow standard insurance company advice about coverage. About 500,000 to 1 million dog-biting incidents occur annually in the United States. Liability claims involving dog attacks reach $250 million to $1 billion per year. Dog bites now are the second leading cause of emergency room admissions, according to the Centers for Disease Control. Don't join these statistics!

More owners are choosing big dogs, with big space needs, and too few big dogs are understood, properly socialized, and trained. Unlike a grouchy Chihuahua, a cantankerous big dog isn't satisfied to bite children's shoelaces and fingers; it can cause head, neck, and body injuries. Most of the approximately twenty annual dog-bite fatalities in this country involve children under the age of ten. All this information should cause you to *train and control your dog* from the very first day! You have absolutely no reason to harbor a dangerous dog of any size that might purposefully harm anyone.

Some insurance companies have blacklisted certain breeds, including many big dog breeds. Other insurers require certification of the nature and personality of your big canine partner by a veterinarian or animal behaviorist. Such experts can't be expected to furnish certification without proof of Barney's training as well as his peaceable personality. Other companies require certain good citizenship training certification. Whatever restrictions are imposed, meet your insurance company's requirements gladly. If you've met those requirements, a bundle of cash may be saved, but more importantly, you have a trustworthy dog that your neighbors can appreciate.

BIG DOG PUPPIES AND SMALL CHILDREN

Big puppies are easily injured. Young children may think big puppies are tough enough to tolerate rough treatment, but they aren't! Children less than about ten years old should always be observed closely when playing with a big dog puppy. These recommendations for children and big puppies may prevent injury to a pup and the accompanying veterinary bill.

> Don't keep Barney a secret from your homeowner's insurance company.

- Be gentle. This puppy is only a few months old and must be treated much the same as a human baby.
- Sit on the floor with the pup; never take it onto your lap while sitting on a chair or sofa.
- Never try to carry the puppy from place to place.
- Don't load the puppy into a wagon or carriage and take it for a ride.
- Never attempt to correct the puppy's mischievousness. Call your parents for help.
- If the puppy is observed beginning to mess on the floor, call for help; don't try to take it to the yard by yourself.
- No wrestling allowed—wait until the pup is older and sturdier.
- Never play tug-o-war with the puppy.
- Don't feed the puppy anthing, not even little treats, without your parents' knowledge.
- Don't play with the puppy with your toys; only use approved puppy toys.

BIG SPACES FOR BIG DOGS

In size and strength, big dogs' living quarters differ dramatically from those of smaller dogs. If your yard fence is 39 inches (1 m) tall, it can't be expected to contain a dog that stands more than 25 inches (62 cm) at the shoulder. Such a fence is usually an adequate barrier when Barney is a puppy, and it works when his human family is present, but it's no challenge for a strong, athletic adult big dog that wants to leave!

When Barney arrives at your house as a puppy, he should find a yard surrounded by a sturdy chain-link fence of approximately six and a half feet (2 m) in height and well anchored to the ground. The yard needn't be huge, because regardless of yard size, the amount of exercise a dog takes depends on his owner. Exercise is *afforded* by a spacious yard, but is *initiated* by Barney's human family.

SECURITY KENNEL

Even if your home has an adequately fenced yard, you might elect to construct a special run to provide more security when friends with babies or small children visit. It's also handy to use when the backyard gate must remain open for access by service people. A kennel run is an excellent place to confine Barney while a family barbecue is being cooked and goodies are placed on Barney-height tables.

Build Barney's kennel in a secluded corner of your yard, preferably in a place where the ground slopes downward from front to back. The run should have a packed sand floor and be as large as practical, keeping in mind that he won't use the run for exercise. A 6-foot (2-m) chain-link fence placed in the

> **Boredom or loneliness will make a fence jumper from an otherwise contented dog.**

shade of trees will suffice. It serves as a refuge or den when he seeks a place away from small children and as a place in which he can be safely housed when you go shopping.

Equip the run with a platform to lie on, a weather-tight doghouse, and a bed with washable blankets. Barney's doghouse can be constructed from wood, or if you prefer, it can be of molded fiberglass. Fiberglass doghouses are not terribly expensive, even in giant sizes that will fit your partner as an adult. They have convenient removable floors to facilitate cleaning. Some are insulated to remain cooler in the summer and warmer in the winter.

A wooden platform or porch is essential if Barney is to be kept in the run for any length of time, and should be large enough for him to stretch out. It should extend under and in front of the doghouse and be high enough to keep him out of the mud. If you live in an area where snow or rain prevails, build a weatherproof cover over the platform. The cover will give Barney shade during the heat of the summer as well as some protection from the winter elements. Often a big dog will use his doghouse only in inclement weather and prefer to lounge about on his platform most of the time. Lying on stone or concrete surfaces may cause damage to his elbows, wrists, and hips. See "Calluses and Decubital Ulcers," page 52.

Barney's food and water dishes naturally should be the largest available stainless steel bowls, preferably fitted into racks that prevent

> **Stealing steaks from backyard barbecues is a world-famous trait of all big dogs!**

If Barney gains access to the household supply of chemicals, ascertain what objects or chemicals he may have swallowed, and carefully read the labels. These labels will give you antidotes if they exist, and may save your puppy's life. Follow label directions, watch Barney carefully for the signs of illness described on the label, and then call your veterinarian for specific advice.

spillage. Both dishes and racks are available at pet supply stores. These bowl racks should be secured to a bench that can be increased in height as he grows. Elevating Barney's food and water bowls to the height of his chest serves several important purposes that will be discussed later. See GDV on page 87.

CRATE

Fiberglass shipping crates are available in huge sizes, but owners often cringe at the thought of crating their big dog, even as a puppy, arguing that such confinement is inhumane. Not so! If used prop-

Buy the largest fiberglass crate available, and be sure it has adequate ventilation.

erly, a crate is an excellent accommodation to manage Barney for a short time while he's a puppy or when he's full grown. Most dogs of all sizes enjoy the cavelike atmosphere of a crate when sleeping in the house, and a crate often makes the difference between yes and no when staying in motels with your oversized partner. Don't make the mistake of buying a crate that is too small for Barney as an adult. See "Crate and Pen," page 27.

PUPPY-PROOFING

Mischievous puppies are everywhere at once. Big dog puppies appear clumsy and uncoordinated, but when it comes to getting into trouble, they take no backseat to their agile little terrier cousins. Objects that are safe for other family members present some degree of danger to a new puppy that's constantly seeking a new toy to chew or pull. If a particular room contains attractive items needing protection, fit the doorway with a childproof gate. The same applies to stairways, which should definitely remain off-limits to your new partner. Look around for some of the following puppy hazards:

- Cords of all types. Spiraled telephone cords hang invitingly from

walls, and appliance cords peek over counters, daring Barney to jump. Massive tangles of computer cords are attacked recklessly much to your dismay and the detriment of your P.C., printer, scanner, and monitor. If a cord is plugged into a wall outlet, Barney might be electrocuted, or at least receive severe mouth burns.

- A cord that is unplugged may be less electrifying but is no less attractive to a pup. Dangling cords attached to appliances should be coiled and put out of sight.

- Vertical and venetian blind cords are also quite tempting and may be pulled across the room, leaving a trail of expensive window coverings in the wake.

- Containers of oven cleaners, pesticides, and numerous other toxic household chemicals should be kept out of Barney's reach. Soaps and cleaners of all types are frequently kept in the cabinet under the kitchen sink where they are easily found by a big puppy marauder.

- Pan scrubbers, with or without soap, provide a few moments of chewing enjoyment for an energetic puppy. Sponges and plastic or metal scrubbers may be swallowed and require surgical removal.

- Potted plants usually end up as an unrecognizable pile of green mush when attacked by a determined pup. As if the mess isn't bad enough, you must also decide which plants were eaten because some common house and garden plants are poisonous, and can cause serious illnesses in dogs.

Before you bring Barney home, you should survey your property to be sure it will present no dangers to your new partner.

- Artificial foliage is often put together with tiny wires that may be swallowed and cause major gastrointestinal problems.

- Books in Barney's reach may become expensive leather and vinyl chew toys.

- A great variety of hazards are housed in children's rooms. Foam rubber balls and soft plastic toys are especially dangerous. A sponge-rubber jacks ball may be harmless in a toy box, but if Barney swallows it, it could require surgical removal. It's best to keep the doors to kids' rooms closed.

- Coffee table scarves hanging over table edges provide a moment's entertainment for Barney. Unfortunately, priceless knickknacks are sacrificed in the skirmish.

Puppy-proofing a home isn't easy; sometimes it's impossible. As an alternative plan, confine Barney to the yard or to his run, or provide a safe, attractive play area in the garage. He will gradually outgrow his need to seek and destroy!

Infant gates are inexpensive and easily installed to close off a room or two for Barney. A tall portable dog pen will serve the same purpose. Pens are available from pet supply stores and are much less expensive than the valuables they protect. Crating the pup is another way to control his actions when you can't watch him.

Establishing a dog-proof yard is only the beginning. Play with Barney frequently. Groom him. Begin training sessions as early as possible. Spend time with your partner; he needs reassurance of your friendship as often as possible.

YOUR BACKYARD IS BARNEY'S WORLD

Escaped from my yard? Impossible! Are you sure it's my dog? Why would he want to leave? How could he manage?

Stories of yard escapes mar the histories of those masters of decampment, the impish little Jack Russell Terriers. You will soon learn that absconding isn't limited to small breeds. Quite the contrary; big dogs will escape if they have any notion they are being ignored. Boredom is the number one reason of all breeds for escaping their confinement.

You might think a fenced yard is the perfect place for a pup to spend the day. After Barney has finished his lunch, destroyed a rawhide chewy, and taken a nap, he looks around for his human partner and doesn't see her. He may become worried and decide to find you. If the fence doesn't extend several inches into the ground, he may elect to dig out. If the bottom of the fence is anchored in concrete, he may climb over. He might squeeze through an inconspicuous hole in the fence fabric after he has worked at it until it is large enough to accommodate his frame.

A SAFE YARD

Keep your backyard safe for Barney's arrival! Weed killers are dog killers. Fertilizers are harmful and can be deadly. Chemicals recently applied to the lawn or garden should be watered well into the soil to prevent him from contaminating his feet, then licking off the toxins.

When watering the lawn after chemical application, be sure Barney doesn't drink from pools or puddles on sidewalks. Keep him off treated lawns for forty-eight hours.

Yard sheds are filled with hazards. Puppy teeth can puncture garden hoses if they are not hung out of reach. Insecticides present major problems if left unguarded. Bags and boxes should be kept on high shelves. Insect

Labels on each garden product plainly state the danger to dogs as well as people.

sprayers should be hung up to prevent Barney from chewing on the hoses.

When Barney comes into contact with any chemical, call your veterinarian immediately. Provide the package label ingredient list and the amount consumed, if it can be ascertained. Don't attempt to treat him unless you're unable to reach a professional right away. The danger of poison is increased when ingested by a very young puppy because of his rapid metabolic rate.

GARAGE AND WORKSHOP

Keep the floor and driveway clean and free from engine fluids that may drip from your car. Virtually all automotive chemicals are hazardous to Barney's health, especially antifreeze, which may contain a kidney toxin that can kill. Ethylene glycol has a sweet taste that attracts dogs, and unfortunately, treatment for antifreeze poisoning isn't very effective. Keep antifreeze out of reach of all pets. In the event that poisoning is suspected, waste no time in obtaining professional help. Alcohol-containing products such as windshield washer fluid are equally dangerous.

Shelves in your workshop harbor more hazards. Paint removers are particularly dangerous, and even a quick investigative lick can cause severe tongue burns. Barney might trip over a can, and soak his feet with the caustic stuff. In such an event, rinse his feet immediately with gallons of cool water. Then wash them off with soap and water and call your veterinarian. Keep paint, turpentine, thinner, and acetone-type solvents well out of Barney's reach.

If you have a swimming pool, consider it a hazard as well. All dogs can swim, but pools

> **If Barney has access to your garage, clean it up before he arrives!**

may have escape ladders constructed for two-legged swimmers. If you have such a pool, provide a means of escape for him. Show Barney where the steps are, and teach him to use them. Swimming pool chemicals are dangerous and should be kept under lock and key.

Before bringing Barney home, walk around your yard. Inspect it from his view; look for attractive, chewable, and poisonous items that are stored within his reach. Remember that boredom will cause him to investigate things that would be safe from his sharp teeth if you were with him.

BOARDING KENNELS

Early in your puppy-planning activities, you should consider who will care for Barney when you travel and can't take him with you. A business trip or a vacation to an area that doesn't have canine accommodations may dictate that you leave your big partner behind. Often, big dogs don't adapt well to boarding kennel living and isolation from their human families. In these cases, kennels should be used only as a last resort. Some hunting breeds and many sled dogs are more accustomed to tethering or kenneling, and these dogs are less apt to suffer the loneliness characteristic of other big dogs. Plan ahead for the necessity of leaving Barney behind; identify friends who will help, and contact them before they're needed, but don't expect anyone to accept responsibility for Barney without adequate compensation.

- If you have a good friend who has experience with dogs, encourage her to make friends with Barney long before your absence. She can play with Barney frequently, take him for walks, feed and water him, and act as his surrogate partner.
- Call Barney's breeder. A person who raises big dogs usually has facilities for one more. A breeder is familiar with Barney's temperament, exercise requirements, and diet, and can furnish all his needs for a reasonable time.
- Contact an acquaintance from puppy kindergarten, obedience class, or breed club who has a dog of similar size. Perhaps she might be able to take Barney home for a while.

- If those options fail, the next best plan is to find a well-recommended boarding kennel that specializes in housing large dogs. Visit the kennel personally to see the accommodations. Be sure the kennel has rules that allow you to furnish Barney's bed or at least the blankets from his bed. Don't leave him in a kennel in which dogs must lie on concrete floors. Be sure that the indoor kennel is large enough to allow Barney to stretch out and that the outside run is spacious. He will take very little exercise, but he should be able to get out and about, leave his eliminations outside, and keep his inside space clean. The kennel should have veterinary service in case Barney suffers too much from your absence.

Use a boarding kennel only as a last resort.

When all these preparations have been made, it's time to collect your big dog partner and bring him home. Barney is going to be a lot of trouble for a few weeks, but he's well worth it!

Greta's First Days at Home

Arrange to collect Greta from the breeder at a time when you'll be home continually for several days. Once there, she'll explore your house except for those areas you have already partitioned off. She should be fed regularly and taken to the toilet area of your backyard as often as possible. Yard exploration should also be encouraged. It's extremely important to spend an abundance of time with her during this period; Greta must receive your love and petting any time she comes to you.

PICKING UP AND HANDLING

Pick up Greta as infrequently as possible, but spend as much time as you can sitting on the floor with her. Watch her and learn her likes and dislikes; respond to her need for love and petting, but don't rush to her side every time she whimpers. A whiny big dog is a king-sized nuisance, and if encouraged, it's a habit you'll regret.

Handling a big puppy isn't much different from picking up a smaller dog, except for Greta's weight and strength. Before you begin to carry her about, consider what you're starting. Picking up a large dog puppy and carrying her from place to place soon becomes a weight-lifting exercise. If you are a big husky guy, it's possible to lift your partner for a little cuddle on your lap now and then, but don't

> Common sense should govern your actions during your big puppy's first days in your home.

make a habit of it. Big dogs belong on the floor for several reasons.

Greta's weight makes her more susceptible to injury if she should be dropped, even from the height of a child's waist. Even as a puppy, she has amazing strength and may wriggle and try to jump from your arms; if you catch her by a hind leg, her weight is suddenly suspended by a foot. Greta may suffer sprains, torn ligaments, or worse. Be aware of this possibility, and establish a hard and fast rule prohibiting any child from trying to pick her up. Instruct the younger members of your household and their playmates to get down to her size and pet and play with Greta on the floor or lawn. If they never lift her up, she'll never injure a joint in a fall. If they always reduce themselves to her size, she'll never jump up on them.

If you or another adult needs to carry Greta, kneel down, place your right hand and forearm under her belly and chest, gripping her forelegs between your fingers. Then put your left forearm in front of her neck so that her head is cradled in the crux of your left elbow, holding her back securely with your left hand. Then stand and walk with her. When you arrive at your destination, kneel again, and reverse the process. Don't let her jump from your arms! Carefully set all four feet on the floor. Obviously, it behooves you to teach

Proper method of carrying a big puppy.

For the first weeks of life, Greta's highly structured nest environment was limited in scope. Born to these surroundings, she easily recognized familiar sounds, smells, and canine friends. This microcosm of life was all she knew. After a few weeks, she was taken from the nesting box to play with the breeder's children every day or two. Later she was allowed to romp in a tightly fenced play yard for an hour, then returned to the security of her nest.

Now she is abruptly removed from this safe environment and brought to your home. Her limited experience is suddenly swapped for a whole new world. She's suddenly associated with a different place that seems enormous. She smells new odors, hears different sounds, and sees tall strangers doing different things at different times. Big feet clomp around her, surprising and frightening the inexperienced puppy.

Significant shock is associated with these changes. At a total loss, Greta will seek some stabilizing factor, an inviting personal touch and friendly voice. You must be ready to supply this need. The greatest flaw in bonding with your big dog is a lack of frequent, personal, reassuring physical contact. Bonding is easiest when Greta is less than three months old. It can begin long before she leaves her dam and siblings if you visit her, cuddle her, pet, and make a fuss over her before she leaves the nest. If that opportunity wasn't an option, make up for it now!

Bonding is the term used to describe the blending of a canine's personality with that of

Greta to walk on lead very early in her life.

As an adult, Greta should be lifted by kneeling and placing one arm behind her, positioning that arm between her hocks and her bottom so she is literally sitting on your arm. Place your other arm in front of her chest and bring your hands together, with your arms encircling her body. Join your hands if possible, and hug her to your chest. Then, if you have the necessary strength, stand and place her on the veterinarian's table or whatever your target might be. While she is on the table, lay your hand firmly on her withers or neck to reassure her and prevent her from jumping down. When this exercise is finished, take her from the table by reversing the process. Don't allow your big partner to jump from any table to the floor.

> **Big dogs belong on the floor or ground. Take caution! A human back is at risk when lifting more than seventy-five pounds from the floor, and the risk is multiplied by the dog's wriggling while you are lifting.**

the owner. These first days in your home come around only once and should be used to your advantage. Greta is ready; she's been transplanted into a totally new environment; she's begging to be influenced by your character. Don't miss this wonderful opportunity! Big dogs bond quickly and easily. If you encounter a bonding problem, the solution probably will be found in your lack of understanding of the dog's nature.

Bonding, like any other mutual endeavor, requires a significant amount of human time. The relationship that develops between Greta and you is an invisible but obvious mutual attachment, one that will withstand every test, providing you spend the necessary time to encourage it. This doesn't mean you shouldn't teach her right from wrong! It means your soft voice should be heard frequently and your instruction should always be positive. Bonding is a highly personal process. The following suggestions address her puppyhood, training period, and the rest of her life. Bonding begins early and continues forever.

- Each time Greta comes to you, regardless of the reason for her action, praise her, pet her, and make her aware of your approval. Make her believe she is always right.
- When she deposits her elimination in the correct place in the yard, praise her.
- When she urinates in the wrong place, or conducts herself in an inappropriate manner, ignore her actions by turning and walking away without scolding or reprimanding.

> **Bonding with your dog is perhaps the most meaningful responsibility of dog ownership. This bond will be a joy to both you and Greta, and will assure a compatible relationship with your big dog. Don't fail to give this important subject your undivided attention.**

- Earn your partner's confidence. Be consistent in all things associated with her new environment and training. Dogs don't adapt quickly to changes. If you start off in the correct manner and persevere, bonding will be simple.
- Talk to Greta at every opportunity. Encourage her to listen for your voice; make it easy for her to focus on you and what you say. Devise games in which she must look to you for direction. Fetching, hide-and-seek, playing tag, and other simple exercises are among the many that encourage Greta to focus on you.
- Don't delegate her feeding to another person; do it yourself! This will impress your dog and make her see *you* as her benefactor, the individual who always supplies her major needs. As she learns to depend on you, the bond between you will strengthen.
- Groom her regularly; grooming sessions take five minutes a day, and the grooming experience is pleasant for both parties concerned.
- Even though your spouse and children may play with Greta, you should never forget to personally initiate a game with her regularly, preferably at the same time every day. She will soon look forward to your playtime with anxiety and enthusiasm; your time of arrival will be happily anticipated.
- Teach her something every day. Big dogs have great need for schooling. It's been proven that dogs bond better and more quickly with their trainers. Work with her every day on

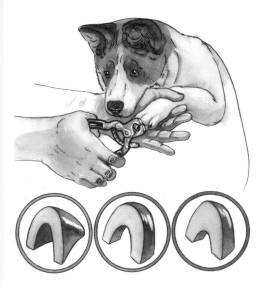

- When she doesn't understand a lesson, or gets mixed up, ignore her error and gently move ahead to the next lesson, or reverse your direction and repeat yesterday's lesson.

- Insist that she complete some training exercise properly before you reward her with a tasty treat. That is, never reward a task that is done halfheartedly or almost right. If she doesn't grasp what you ask of her, stop that exercise, and revert to another that she does know. When she completes it correctly, reward her appropriately. Quitting is something she won't understand; her goal is finishing and being rewarded for a task well done, and pleasing you.

- Often, big dogs are quite sensitive, and nagging them is a sure way to diminish the bond between you, sometimes stretching it to the breaking point. Some people use an iron hand when dealing with dogs of great size; don't fall into that trap! Never raise your voice, and don't scold or nag.

- Greta's size is no excuse for abuse! Under no circumstances should she be whipped, kicked, spanked, or physically struck. Dogs have wonderful memories. If Greta is given a command and struck if it isn't performed properly, she will remember your unexpected violence that accompanied the command. Her error won't be understood, but the whack you doled out will live in her memory forever. In the future, the command will be associated with your punishment, not her incorrect performance. A dog that has been struck or severely scolded during training may develop a trainer's nightmare known as fear aggression, which includes cowering, growling, and even biting.

- When Greta doesn't grasp what you ask of her, check your training technique. Maybe you aren't presenting the task in such a way that is easily understood. Most training errors fall into your court, not Greta's!

some exercise, even if it's nothing more than a review of an earlier task. When she's a bit older, and you're both bored with simple training exercises, try out for a fly-ball team. Training for agility trials is another superb method of playing with your partner while teaching her something fun. Winning agility dogs demonstrate excellent trainer focus and are usually happy and content. Who knows, Greta may be a competitive performer. Attend a trial, talk to contestants, buy a book, and try some of the obstacles in your backyard.

- Big dogs should receive no less than basic obedience instruction. This might take the form of formal obedience classes, but the primary training effort could be the Canine Good Citizen Certificate (CGCC). Training will be much easier if you begin this instruction after gaining her confidence and her focus on you. Greta may be a big pussycat, but she is perceived as a giant threat by unknowing people who come in contact with her. Dedicate yourself to dispelling this idea by training your big partner to always be on her best behavior.

HOUSEBREAKING

Most breed books and other pet books cover this topic, and there is very little difference between housebreaking a huge dog and housebreaking for a toy. The quantity of feces produced is roughly proportional to the quantity of food eaten. Therefore, it becomes quite important to be sure Greta is well housebroken; the amount of waste produced by your big partner may be monstrous.

We once owned a delightfully independent little Yorkie who ate only a tiny portion of food half a dozen times a day. Rowdy naturally drank water and urinated occasionally throughout the day as well. She was never housebroken. The thimbleful of urine she left could hardly be detected on the carpet, and more often than not, she waited until she happened to be outside for defecation. I suppose we could have crated her more hours to complete her housebreaking, but it was easier to ignore it.

> **When you're well trained, Greta will be trained as well.**

At the same time, my son was raising a big Malamute with a beautiful, thick, carpetlike coat. Flash disdained the house in favor of the great outdoors, the snowdrifts, and even her kennel. She usually ran loose on our acreage, playing with our sons, and was confined to a large kennel and run when her playmates weren't home. Her times spent in the house were short and infrequent, but housebreaking became an accelerated venture! When she urinated on the floor, a roll of paper towels was needed to soak it up. A Malamute-sized pile of feces couldn't be ignored; the odors emanating therefrom demanded immediate attention. Keep these factors in mind when you begin housebreaking your big dog!

Training Greta to empty her bowels and bladder in a designated place in the yard is simple enough. It will happen about as quickly as you can train yourself. If she's a house dog, you must take her to the toilet area first thing after she wakes, last thing every night, after every meal, and in between times if she begins to circle or show other signs of imminent elimination.

Prepare an attractive, easily cleaned toilet area for her by hauling in a few bags of sand and placing it in a pit in the chosen area; the texture will encourage her to use this area for her eliminations. Confine her to her crate or pen when you can't watch her. Praise her correct actions, and ignore her mistakes.

CRATE AND PEN

Buy a big crate, one that will allow an adult Greta to stand, turn around, and lie down comfortably. Crating works especially well for apartment giants and is also a boon to keeping your puppy in one place in inclement weather when she can't be outside. First, put in an old sock or some other article of your clothing that has been worn and hasn't been laundered.

Canines usually have foot fetishes. Strangely enough, they are attracted to the smell of our feet! Baiting Greta's crate with a smelly sock might make the difference between her loving the crate and hating it.

Place the crate in the room where you are. A rawhide chewy or a nylon bone is used to make the crate more attractive, and sometimes a treat is added. Lead Greta in, close the door, and walk away. If she whines or barks, ignore her; if she persists, respond with a sharp "no," and continue with your work. Confine Greta to her crate for short periods of time in the beginning and take her out of the crate frequently, gradually increasing the time she is confined.

Crates aren't punishment chambers! The crate or pen shouldn't be used to negatively reinforce some housebreaking or training error. Never scold your partner when crating or penning her. Give a special treat when she enters the crate and another little bite when she is released. If you make crating a positive experience, she won't resent it.

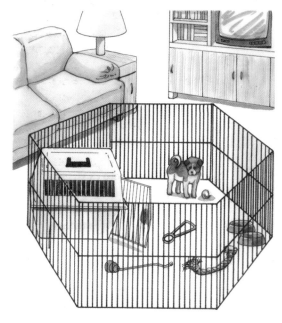

Greta will soon realize the crate isn't such a bad place; she's always praised and rewarded when she enters and exits the crate, and she's never made to stay there for long periods. Leave the gate open and periodically put a chewy in the crate when she isn't confined. Soon she'll use the crate as a den for naps or when household activity becomes hectic.

A crate is also handy when housebreaking Greta. When so used, it should be partitioned off to fit her size, so that the vacant space won't be used for a toilet. A wire pen can be used interchangeably with a crate, but large dogs quickly outgrow portable pens.

STAIRS

During puppyhood, stairs should be gated to prevent Greta from using them. Descending stairs takes better coordination than climbing, and tumbling down even a few steps could result in ligament, tendon, or bone injuries. For this reason, don't allow her on the second floor unless a gate is installed at the head of the stairs. An infant gate installed on stairways will serve a dual purpose. She can't fall, and she's confined to a smaller space where her actions can be monitored more easily.

Confine Greta to a few rooms on one floor.

FEEDING SCHEDULE

Throughout her life, Greta's diet should be kept stable and simple. If the breeder furnished you with a feeding schedule, stay on it without change for at least a week. Unless advised by your veterinarian that a different schedule is needed, feed Greta four equal-sized meals a day from seven or eight weeks of age until three months. From three to six months of age, feed three equal meals, and from six months on, two meals are adequate. Although a single meal per day may be advocated by some, Greta will appreciate her daily diet split into two meals, and this schedule has a scientific basis as well. Smaller meals are more easily digested, are less apt to be implicated in gastric torsion and bloat, and usually will produce smaller volume stools.

Keep your big dog's diet simple.

Feed Greta first thing in the morning, and feed the last meal several hours before you retire for the night. Midday meals should be fed at approximately equal intervals between the first and last.

Fresh water should be available to her at all times throughout the day, but while house-breaking, the water bowl should be taken away when her last meal of the day is fed.

If you suspect Greta's diet should be improved, by all means do so. Make changes gradually, and be sure changes are motivated by better quality of food, and not by cheaper price alone. See page 92.

TOO MUCH EXERCISE IS HAZARDOUS

One of the joys and duties in your relationship with Greta is providing adequate exercise for her. Regular exercise aids essential bone and soft tissue development in pups and in older dogs, minimizes the effects of arthritis and aging of tissues. Exercise is vital for all ages and sizes of dogs for normal health, and will aid in successful puppy training, bonding, and production of strong bones and muscles. Exercise improves Greta's attitude, thinking ability, and experience and enhances her problem-solving capacity.

It's an accepted fact, however, that big dog pups are easily harmed by excessive exercise. How much activity is needed, how much is too much, and what is the appropriate amount of exercise at each growth stage? The balance between too much and too little exercise presents a problem for which there is no easy solution and is possible only by reading everything available on the subject and talking with people who have big dog experience. Before you progress from one type of exercise to another, or longer sessions of exercise, use your head! Evaluate Greta's development, her

structures are often injured. The problem lies in the weight of the dog compared with the strength and maturity of the structure involved. In other words, injuries aren't necessarily related to external trauma, but rather to the immaturity of tendons, ligaments, cartilage, and bone when subjected to the weight of a fast-growing large breed.

Recent research at the University of Georgia, Michigan State University, and the University of Pennsylvania reported in the September 15, 1999, edition of the *Journal of the American Veterinary Medical Association* seems to confirm what many big dog owners and their veterinarians have known or suspected for many years. Reported statistics indicate that young big dogs, having a body weight of more than seventy-five pounds at less than two years of age, were at the greatest risk for ligament injury. With few exceptions, breeds most often afflicted with anterior cruciate ligament tears were large breeds. (See page 61.)

This report supports the need for regular, supervised, but limited exercise for Greta, and this exercise control should be practiced until she is fully mature, probably more than two years old. This might mean delaying some of Greta's training in vigorous activities such as agility and obedience hurdle jumping. Even her retrieving play should be closely monitored if she runs with abandon.

Avoid activities that require running with sudden stops, pivoting on hind legs, jumping, and roughhousing. Greta will love tug-of-war toys, but the game that goes with them should be avoided. Often, yard balls that are

strength, her coordination, and her overall size and weight. Consult with Greta's breeder, trainers, and of course, your veterinarian.

Before bringing Greta home, you need to know about the potential detrimental effect of exercise on big dog pups. Too much too soon can be as dangerous as too little too late. Books related to raising and training dogs list the many advantages of regular exercise, but often fail to state that *repeated, early, vigorous, and excessive* exercise can be detrimental to big dogs' health. Overexercise is especially dangerous in giant breeds, where facts are well documented.

When young big dogs play and exercise vigorously before their bones, cartilage, ligaments, and tendons are fully developed, these

> **Supervised exercise should be encouraged, but excessive or strenuous activities should be curtailed. Safe exercise for a large pup includes controlled walks on a leash, controlled swimming, and simple games of hide-and-seek.**

batted about like soccer balls stimulate undesirable overexercise in a pup. If you elect to buy Greta a yard ball, give it to her while you can monitor her playing, and take it away if her activity becomes overly energetic.

Association with other dogs enhances a puppy's mental development. However, too much or too rough play with other puppies can be disastrous. Don't leave another young dog with Greta unwatched.

EXERCISE FOR ADULTS

Choose exercises to fit the breed you have. Working dogs such as Rottweilers and Bernese Mountain Dogs may prefer carting to any other type of activity. Malamutes may enjoy sledding or skijoring that exercises their tremendous hind leg musculature. Newfoundlands and Great Pyrenees sometimes exhibit great talent for competitive weight pulling. Scent hounds such as

> **Never exercise your partner alongside your car, bike, or horse.**

Skijoring is an exciting sport.

Bloodhounds and Black and Tans prefer laid-back exercise such as following scents in parks and woods for hours on end. Sight hounds such as the Greyhound and Borzoi are sprinters and enjoy a fast run across open fields in pursuit of rabbits, both mechanical and real. Herding breeds prefer sheep or duck herding trial competition, and sporting breeds usually enjoy hunting or field trials. However, puppies shouldn't be subjected to these activities until they are at least two years old.

As Greta's partner, you must judge the level of exercise she can handle to maintain an appropriate condition and prevent obesity. You should strive to balance her nutritional intake with her energy demand all her life, but especially during her first two years.

IDENTIFICATION

Greta represents an important investment in terms of your time and your emotional ties to her. Like other valuables, an investment of this magnitude has a price tag.

From the time she is able, Greta should wear a collar with an attached identification tag listing your name, address, and telephone number. A collar and tag will help honest people find her home in case she becomes lost.

Protect your investment!

Since a collar can easily be removed, have a microchip implanted under Greta's skin with similar information. This chip can be read by most veterinarians, using special scanning equipment. It can also be read by staff members at shelters and dog pounds. The microchip can't be easily removed, and offers more certainty of Greta's return if she is found. Microchip implantation may be scheduled for the time she is first taken to your veterinarian.

A third means of identification that is easily applied is a tattoo. A series of letters or numbers can be tattooed permanently on Greta's flank, an earflap, or elsewhere. Would-be thieves might pass her by in favor of another target when they see the tattoo. Tattooing also is done by most veterinarians and dog clubs.

Microchips and tattoos should be recorded by one of several agencies that register dogs' identities. If a dog is presented to a pound, is examined for tattoos, and is scanned for microchip identification, the agency is contacted and she is soon home.

GOOD MANNERS VERSUS VICES

All puppies have inborn traits that might be considered vices, and given the opportunity, other bad habits will be learned. Greta is no exception to this rule. The difference between big dog vices and those of modest-sized dogs

Well-mannered dogs.

is the amount of damage caused, both to your possessions and to the pup's body. Be prepared to face each new fault, have a modification technique ready, and act as soon as the wickedness presents itself.

Appropriate conduct is simply the absence of canine vices that are displayed in the human environment. Your big dog wasn't born with good manners. She has no inherited tendency to behave appropriately toward people, but she has an innate desire to please you. The key to teaching good manners is to use Greta's inborn desire to please her master.

> **Behavior is the act or manner in which dogs conduct themselves in human environments. If what your dog does is okay with you, it's okay with me.**

TRAINING

Good-conduct lessons include housetraining, correcting, minimizing or preventing vices, and a few lessons in comportment and behavior. Another important component of home schooling a big dog is leadership training. You should begin training of this sort the moment Greta arrives in your home, and give tune-up sessions for the remainder of her life. Behavioral problems are often associated with the dog's lack of confidence in the owner and a lack of respect for your person and possessions. Leadership or dominance problems are the number one reason for behavioral faults. This lack of respect sometimes can be reduced or eliminated in the following ways.

In this discussion, the term *reward* is used frequently. Reward means your approval, which may be shown by petting, ear scratching, voice inflections, or giving her some food. Big dogs have big appetites, and tasty tidbits are always appreciated.

Another bit of advice is to *say as she does*. Anytime you see Greta doing something that you realize you will be teaching her later or have taught, say the command immediately. Give her the impression that her action is always associated with your commands. If she sits, immediately give her the *sit* command. When she runs to you, tell her to *come* while she is in the process.

> **All training begins with focus. Your voice, your body, your hands, and your facial expression must become central, the focal point of your dog's attention. When you have accomplished that concentration, training becomes simple!**

THE NAME'S THE GAME

A major purpose in training is to get and keep your big partner's attention riveted to you. Begin on the first day by teaching Greta her name. Call her name frequently, and each time she responds to her name by looking at you or coming to you, reward that response with praise, petting, and a treat when possible. When she looks up from play with children or another pet and notices you, and her body language tells you she's ready to come to you, say her name distinctly and with excitement in your voice. Reward her amply when she arrives.

> **Become the center of Greta's focus!**

In the beginning, use tasty rewards to encourage her focus and response. Later, when she expects a reward, a kind word of praise or a quick ear scratch will satisfy her as well as a liver treat.

> **Take advantage of her normal reaction to seeing you. When she runs to you for any reason, tell her to come.**

RECALL OR COME

Come is an obedience command that should be taught as soon as Greta recognizes her name. Proper response to this command can save her life. It is undoubtedly the most important command you will ever teach your dog, and only when Greta responds automatically should she be walked off-lead outside your yard.

Prepare her food while she's in the yard. Step outside the door and excitedly say, "Greta." She will naturally look up at you. At that second, give her the command *come*. She will smell the food, recognize the excitement in your voice, and run to you. When she arrives at your feet, praise her, and show her she has pleased you by giving her the bowl of food. In a few days, she'll understand what the recall command means.

Come can be taught dozens of other ways as well. Various rewards can be used, such as tidbits, a game, a particularly desirable toy, or a walk around the block. Always be sure the command is followed by an enjoyable, memorable event. Never call Greta to you to punish her, and never attempt to punish her for not coming.

If she refuses to come to you, try running in the opposite direction. This will really confuse her, since she realizes that you want her but doesn't understand why you're running away. Rarely can a puppy resist chasing her owner. Once she begins to chase you, slow down, turn, drop to your knees, and stretch out your hands.

A long line on her collar may be used to encourage proper response at other times and under different circumstances. The result is the same. When she hears her name followed by the *come* command, she will run to you and receive her reward.

> **Big dogs have no behavior problems. People sometimes have problems dealing with natural, inherent canine behavior. Usually these undesirable behavioral traits have been created by domestication.**

SIT

Sit may be the second most important command you will teach your dog. *Sit* is an easy way to prepare Greta for other commands if you are inclined to go further into obedience work. Many trainers have argued the pros and cons of teaching this command with treats or by pushing the pup's bottom to the floor.

> ***Sit* is most important when your big partner meets and greets you.**

Each time Greta sits in your presence,

tell her *sit,* even if it isn't important that she do so. After she has taken the sitting position, reward her. She will be surprised by your approval, but soon she'll get the message that sitting pleases you and that when she pleases you, she's rewarded. She'll feel terribly clever each time she sits on command, and your household will benefit from this proper deportment.

Sit can be taught as an exercise by itself, but it can become a part of other exercises as well. If you want to cause her to sit, let her smell the tidbit you have in your fingers. Give her the *sit* command and extend your tightly closed fingers to a position slightly above and behind her eyes. She will look up as she backs up, and invariably will take a sitting position. When she does, give her the treat, your praise, and lots of petting.

CORRECTING VICES

After Greta reliably has learned to focus on you when she hears her name called, to come when you ask her, and to sit when she arrives, she is ready to learn more meaningful lessons. Many of these lessons are associated with what we want our dogs to do or not do. When correcting vices, remember that many canine actions are natural and aren't intended to irritate you. These activities may be softened, but it's unlikely you will totally eliminate the predisposition for them. Set your sights on adjusting Greta's natural tendencies, modifying them to fit your view of acceptable behavior in your household. Some of them are listed here.

- Predatory activities toward cats and other small pets is a natural extension of hunting, chasing, and feeding.

- Lifting the hind leg or inappropriate urination was once a method of marking territory.
- Pulling on-leash is part of a dog's hereditary desire to sniff and investigate trails of prey.
- Running, nipping, and mouthing is part of a dog's natural instinct to play with its siblings.
- Barking, chewing furniture, and other separation anxiety signs stem from the dog's instinctive attachment to the pack leader.
- Growling, biting, staring, and bristling back hair are signs of dominance aggression normally associated with alpha (pack leader) dogs.
- Shaking, shivering, tucking the tail, and laying the ears back are all signs of a frightened, submissive dog toward a more dominant one.

SEPARATION ANXIETY (CCD)

Technically known as Canine Compulsive Disorder (CCD), separation anxiety is a serious problem and is seen in an estimated 14 percent of all companion dogs. Frustration, mental discomfort, and escape attempts are part of this destructive behavior. When you leave Greta behind, she attempts to follow by any means possible. Scratching at doors, jumping through windows, barking, howling, drooling, defecating, urinating, and destroying personal property such as furniture all signify this problem.

A pound or shelter is often the next move for dogs suffering separation anxiety. Like other conditions, CCD is relative to the size and strength of the dog with the problem. Little dogs make little messes, whereas big dogs can demolish an entire house. Abnormal

Separation anxiety is seen in dogs that are particularly attached to their owners. Paradoxically, these dogs often end up in shelters.

bonding together and well-established household routines may be part of the separation problem.

Greta has bonded closely with her owner. She enjoys togetherness and considers her owner part of her pack. Mentally, she's fixed a regular routine that governs her daily life. When that pattern changes and she's left alone, even for brief periods, she feels left out and becomes frustrated and worried. This results in physical violence during which she may injure herself by jumping out of a window and running amok. During an episode, she may determinedly trash a room or an entire house.

Experts say that stress is associated with many cases of CCD, and that stress may be caused in part by the dog's inability to cope with changes in routine. Overbonding is thought by many to be at the core of this condition. Experts warn that bonding with your puppy is essential, but too much of a close relationship can be counterproductive if a sudden change in routine is necessary. Stress may be manifested by depression, loss of appetite, frequent yawning, restlessly changing postures, and lifting the feet as if marching in position.

You can attempt treatment on your own, but frequently behavioral specialists' advice and assistance is necessary. Sometimes, antidepressant drugs such as clomipramine are prescribed with success. If you decide to attempt treatment at home, your objective should be to break old routines and teach entirely new activities, then never let these activities follow a repeated pattern.

- If you've always taken Greta for a walk when you get home, exercise her shortly before you leave instead. This should relax her so she'll be ready for a nap.

- Take her out at odd times, and cook breakfast earlier or later than usual. Leave at different hours each day. Try never to establish habits that take place at certain times, with certain activities.
- Take Greta for walks of varying distances, in different directions, and at unexpected times; mix up your pattern.
- Keep Greta occupied with various, often changed, techniques. Use a feeding cube one day, such as a Buster Cube stuffed with kibble. The next day, try a Kong toy that can be filled with peanut butter. On consecutive days, give her a couple of chew-sticks, a pig snout, or a big raw knucklebone. Tempt her with a new toy each day, putting away the last one for future use.
- If possible, alter your time of departure from the house, and change the duration of time you're away from home. Begin on your day off by leaving and returning numerous times during the day and evening.
- Over several days, gradually lengthen the time away.
- Don't emphasize your return. Once in the house, go about your chores without making a fuss over Greta. Later, when she's settled down, give her a pat on the head and a treat.
- Don't give up! Have patience. Consider hiring a surrogate partner for Greta for daylight hours, or building her a house and run in the backyard where she will have more interesting, different scenes to view.

JUMPING UP

It's natural for a puppy to jump up on you; after all, you're her loving, equal partner,

Call a halt to jumping up before the habit becomes permanently engraved on Greta's dance card.

right? It's just her way of greeting you, like she might greet a sibling, right? Wrong, wrong, wrong!

Being greeted by your partner is always a joyous occasion, but you should insist on your proper place in the pack hierarchy! She can greet you with respect as her senior partner, like she might say hello to her dam. Keep this in mind as you wipe Greta's slobbers from your tie and attempt to brush her gigantic muddy paw prints from your new suit. Don't scold her. That would only defeat your purpose; you certainly don't wish to dampen her happiness upon seeing you.

Jumping up is equivalent to jumping from porches, playing tug of war, and other activities that can damage Greta's joints; it's hazardous to your dog's ligament safety as well as to your health and sanity. An example might put this subject in better perspective. An untrained, excited adult Jack Russell Terrier will jump up, snag your socks, inflict scratches on your shins, and possibly mess up your shoeshine. However, an untrained Mastiff adult will knock you over, bruise your spleen, destroy your shoes, shred your sweater, and slobber on your glasses, all in the name of greeting! Muddy footprints on your cuffs aren't desirable, but when they extend to your shoulders, it's time to reflect on Greta's puppyhood training.

While she is still a puppy and before she first jumps up on you, prepare yourself for dissuasion training by dressing in old clothes. While she's loose in the backyard, walk through the gate or out the back door. Approach her and speak to her excitedly, as if you have been away for a long time. She will run wriggling toward you with tail wagging, eager to display her affection. Just as you perceive she is planning to launch her leap, take several rapid steps backward, kneel down, and reach out your hand to her.

Her reaction to this unexpected tactic will be to hesitate for a millisecond, then start toward you cautiously with less exuberance. With your outstretched hand, pet her and gently place her in a sitting position. As her bottom meets the lawn, praise her and repeat the *sit* command. When she sits, lavish all the love on her that you can muster. Offer your face for her to lick, because if you don't, she'll surprise you with another lunge about the time you're off-balance. She's going to lick your face; you may as well take off your glasses, close your mouth, and prepare for it! When the greeting is complete, praise her soundly, offer a tidbit, rise, turn your back, and walk away.

At this time, you're more interested in survival training for yourself than teaching her the *sit* command. Your primary objective is to teach your big partner that running to you is fine, being eager to greet you is wonderful, her kisses are perfect, but reward and reciprocal praise is given only when she stops, sits, and allows you to kneel and place your hand on her.

Repeat this exercise as often as possible. She'll quickly learn that an excited Greta won't be ignored! You've used positive reinforcement to teach her that appropriate conduct is always approved. You haven't employed any negative action; however, Greta is still a puppy, and sometimes she will forget. When she jumps, even a little bit, don't reward her with kind words or petting. Instead, turn your back on her and walk away without a word. This will negatively enforce her understanding that to receive your attention and possibly other rewards, sitting calmly is the key. A strong part of this training is *never* to forget to kneel and reach for her each time she runs to you. Before long she'll be tall enough that you can show your affection without kneeling, but you should always reward her after she stops, sits, and allows you to reach out to her.

Begging at any time is nuisance behavior, a deplorable vice!

BEGGING

At mealtimes, take your partner outside or to another room and give her a chew toy. If she doesn't ever begin, begging will be foreign to her nature. Don't allow guests or family members to feed her from the table. Don't give her scraps of your meals that can be recognized by their smell. Once the tastes and smells of your dinner have gotten into her mouth and nose, the damage is done. Don't forget that what's attractive to a small puppy is more desired by an adult. When your partner is full grown, she'll be able to snatch a steak from the table with little effort, and that's a poor time to begin training.

CHEWING OR MOUTHING

Prepare for this natural canine habit well in advance. Sometimes chewing isn't as pronounced in large breeds as in terriers, but big dog pups are happy, inquisitive characters with active mouths. Big jaws filled with big teeth are part of big puppies; they can reduce a baseball glove to unrecognizable leather shreds in minutes! These sharp teeth will shorten the sleeves of your favorite jacket in the wink of an eye. Schoolbooks left on the floor quickly become wastepaper wads, and a briefcase loaded with important papers is turned into a sandwich before your very eyes!

Chewing doesn't represent maliciousness or a desire to displease you. Dogs investigate and experience their environments by mouthing; tasting is inherent and can't be stopped, but it can be detoured. Greta knows nothing of the value or importance of items left in her path. She chews them because they are there. They look different from her rawhide chewies, and she wonders how they taste. She has an inherent urge to taste something new and different, especially if your scent is on the object.

Buy Greta a number of different chew toys such as nylon bones, and a supply of chew sticks that are composed of bits of rawhide pressed together. These chewys should be presented at the times you want to reward her or when you leave her for a long period, and should be substituted for anything else you find in her mouth.

Never give her the opportunity to chew a shoe, glove, or other object that she might run across. Dogs don't comprehend the difference between new and old. They can't understand why it's okay to chew up one old soiled tennis shoe, but not newer, shinier model.

Pick up your personal belongings and store them out of Greta's reach. Teach your children to pick up their toys and clothes at the same time you're teaching Greta to restrict her playing and chewing to her own toys. When she makes a mistake, it will probably be your fault, but don't despair. With a firm vocal reprimand, take the shoe from her mouth; give her a chew stick or nylon bone, pat her head, and forget the whole episode. Don't make a big deal of it! Greta may develop a chewing habit to get your attention when she's being ignored. To make an issue of one instance will cause Greta to remember it and repeat it when she feels neglected. That is precisely *not* what you want!

COPROPHAGIA

One of the most disgusting habits your big partner may develop is eating feces. *Coprophagia* is the term assigned to this revolting idiosyncrasy. Why does Greta like to raid the cat box litter and eat cat feces? She hasn't lost her mind or developed a strange dietary deficiency. She probably just likes the flavor of cat manure! Why does she eat her own feces or that of other dogs when on a walk in the park? Theories abound, but regardless of the reason, experts all agree that coprophagia is probably not a good habit.

Correct this vice by placing the cat litter box where it is inaccessible to Greta. Sprinkle Greta's feces with cayenne pepper or some other product that's designed to stop chewing. Pick up her droppings and dispose of them as soon as her toilet area becomes soiled. Keep her on a leash when walking, and when she noses any animal's droppings, use the *no* command and the leash to control her actions.

BITE INHIBITION

In the nest, grabbing another puppy's ear or tail was acceptable to all concerned except the other puppy. The attacked pup probably pulled back in response, with or without a yelp, and a tussle ensued. If the dam's ear was grabbed, that action was followed by a quick snap of the mother's teeth.

- The first time Greta takes your finger or hand in her mouth when you are playing with her, don't impulsively yank it out. Stand or sit very still and let your hand go limp. Don't scream or yell, but say her name firmly to get her focus on your face and voice. Tell her "no" in a gruff, moderate tone. Then slowly remove your hand, turn, and walk away. Your action will be contrary to what she expects. Leave her wondering what she's done wrong. She first bit, and then you went limp and quit playing with her; that's what she'll remember. A few minutes later, offer her a chew toy and praise her when she takes it.

- The next bit of schooling is a type of dominance training. When she is quite young this bite inhibition exercise will be easily taught. While she's eating from her bowl, approach her from the front and extend your hand over her neck. At first, you shouldn't touch her neck or collar, but be sure she sees your hand suspended above her neck. With that same hand, drop a special food treat into her bowl. After you've used this procedure a few times, and after dropping the treat into her bowl, move your hand down to her neck, and grasp her collar. Don't pull her away from the bowl, just rub her neck under the collar. When she's become accustomed to this action, the next step is to lead her by the collar a few feet away from the food bowl. Allow her to return, and upon releasing her at the bowl, drop another tasty treat into her food. This training exercise teaches her not to fear or resent her neck and collar being handled while eating, that usually treats are added, and that a brief excursion from the bowl is okay. It's invaluable when Greta has matured to a hundred-pound adult!

> **Biting may be an unexpected act or an entirely predictable reaction.**

- Another similar program is to teach her that the food bowl isn't exclusively her property. While she is eating, reach toward the bowl. When your hand is an inch or two from it, toss a tasty morsel into the bowl. She won't challenge that action one little bit. Just before she's finished eating, repeat the procedure. After a few days you have demonstrated that you aren't planning to take her food. At this point, reverse the procedure. Instead of tossing a treat into the bowl, take a bit of food from the bowl each time. Then reverse again, putting a different treat into the bowl. Soon, she will simply watch you as you exchange food for treat and food for food, and she'll no longer be overly protective of her food. You can approach her while she is eating with no fear that she will bite or growl.

ROAMING

To correct the unacceptable habit of roaming, consider the cause. Why does Greta want to roam? Probably because she's founds friends in the neighborhood who feed her, pet her, play with her, and make her welcome. Perhaps she's discovered other dogs with which she plays, hunts, or scavenges.

> **Big dogs are fond of roaming about neighborhoods, which usually presents big problems.**

However, the answer to roaming can be found in the activities at your house. If she's subjected to daily neglect, only a strong fence will deter her wandering. To correct this problem, begin more training, more play, grooming, long walks, and other pleasurable activities. In other words, reflect on your earliest commitment, and get to work! If you fail to do so, you'll find yourself picking up Greta's limp body from the street, answering your neighbors in court, paying bills for her destruction, or paying a veterinarian for her gunshot wounds.

> Without training, big dogs, by virtue of their size alone, are a deterrent to anyone entering your property.

GUARDING

Guarding your property may have been one reason you purchased Greta. Territorial aggression is a dominant trait in a few specific breeds. Dogs with a working history, such as the Rottweiler and Doberman Pinscher, often are selected for their aggressive behavior. Excellent guards, these big dogs sometimes overreact to perceived threats. They snarl or growl at any uniformed person, postal employee, meter reader, census taker, and the like. When facing at close range a pair of lips drawn back displaying sharp teeth and raised hackles, those service people can hardly be blamed for using deterrent sprays.

Training with a positive approach is the key to discouraging this aggressive behavior. Ask a cooperative uniformed delivery person to help you. Fit Greta with a head collar, and while the assistant stands by, review some basic obedience commands such as *sit*. After a few minutes, the volunteer should kneel in front of Greta (not necessarily in a praying position), extend the back of his hand, and speak to her in a soft voice. After a few

instances Greta should relax. That's when you furnish your assistant with a handful of treats. When Greta is accustomed to receiving treats from the individual, tell him you will leave more in a covered plastic dish on your porch for him to give her anytime he is in the area, whether or not he is entering the yard. Many service personnel are dog lovers and may surprise you with their cooperation!

LEADERSHIP TRAINING

These lessons take no specific order of importance, but are simply suggestions to make your life easier with your big partner. The more attention you pay to this section, the happier you will be sharing your life with a dog that approaches your own weight and has twice your strength.

Use Greta's pack instinct to solidify your role as the boss, the leader of the pack. Dogs, as descendants of the wolf, inherently respect the alpha member of the pack, the leader or king. You must never allow Greta to bring about a role reversal. That's true for any dog, but it is doubly important for big dogs. Force or power is not the determining factor for pack leadership. In the wild, the toughest animals are eliminated from the gene pool by exerting all their energies toward bullying their way into the alpha role. Thus, while they fight and enforce their physical superiority, others are carrying on the reproductive and leadership roles by cunning and thinking.

Treat your big partner kindly and gently, and she won't strenuously object to anything you do. If Greta objects, that's an indication that more lessons are needed. Repeat some of these lessons daily at first, then several times weekly until she relaxes, expects, and accepts them. Once she has accepted your physical manipulations and you have the leadership role in her pack, you can repeat a lesson or two every month and continue these lessons forever.

Leadership training is essential for all dogs. From puppyhood onward Greta must recognize human authority and yield to your control.

- Never respond to Greta's commands. Except during housebreaking, don't jump up and let her out when she barks. Wait a few minutes, get a drink of water, pick up a newspaper to scan for a minute. Then open the door.
- Spend plenty of time playing with Greta, but *you* pick the time. If she demands attention, ignore her until you are ready to play. If she brings her ball for a game of catch, ignore the ball, pick up a brush, and groom her.
- If Greta nudges you for affection, ignore her for the time being. Later, toss her retrieving dummy for her. Give her an obedience command, and after she has correctly performed, reward her with your affection.
- Place puppy Greta on her back while sitting on the floor. Touch and gently flex each of her legs, and handle her ears, chest, and muzzle. When she grows tired of being held and begins to squirm, hold her for another minute. In a few seconds she will relax, and when she does, release her.
- With one hand, hold her muzzle gently but firmly closed for a minute.
- Open her lips and run your fingers over her teeth.
- Open her jaws and inspect her tongue and gums.
- Stroke her tail, and pick up and inspect each foot, spreading her toes. When she tries to draw the foot back, hold it firmly for a second before releasing.
- If she has a favorite spot on the floor, move her and sit on that spot yourself.
- Always feed her after the human family members have eaten.
- Never give her the opportunity to beg at the table!
- Occasionally ignore her when you return home, and give her the anticipated attention a few minutes later, when she least expects it.
- Don't allow her to sleep on your bed or living room furniture except when she has been specifically invited.
- Keep certain special toys out of her reach, reserving them for play sessions with you.

Persuade other adult family members to participate in this dominance training. If it is practiced with love and patience, and never with a heavy hand, Greta will accept her place in the pack and will rarely challenge your leadership.

DIGGING

Digging is a minor vice, but big dogs make enormous holes!

Perhaps the best method for correcting digging is to encourage it in an appropriate place. If you have a large yard, find a spot where you have no flowers, lawn, garden, or other living thing. Scoop out the topsoil and transfer it to your garden. Buy a yard of creek sand, and dump it into the spot.

Don't scold Greta for digging elsewhere, but encourage her to dig in the sand by hiding her toys just below the surface. Each time she begins to tunnel from the center of your lawn to the Orient, call her to the sandbox, hide a chew toy, and reward her heartily for digging it up. Soon she will catch on to the game, because she will be discouraged by your lack of attention when she digs elsewhere and will be happy to dig where the result is a reward.

AUTOMOBILES

Greta isn't likely to be afraid of cars—after all, she's nearly as big as a Volkswagen—but it's best to dispel any misgivings she may have about them when she's still a puppy. Condition her to the car first by lifting her in and starting the engine. Leave it running while you pet and make a fuss over her. After a few such exercises, try putting her in her crate in the car and driving around the block. Gradually increase the time and distance until she is comfortable with the experience. When you return home, reward her amply and play a game with her.

Decide where you want her to ride, and insist that she stay in the designated area. Pet supply stores carry dog safety harnesses that fasten into the automobile's seat belt system. Her fiberglass crate is the safest and most positive means of confinement, but it might not fit in your car. Big breeds deserve station wagons with the rear portion cordoned off with dog gates. Minivans are wonderful for taking your giant partner to the country. Pet supermarkets usually have a variety of car-riding equipment and barriers for you to chose from.

Sometimes dogs become ill when riding. Car sickness is accompanied by signs of abdominal distress, nausea, salivation, and vomiting. If Greta suffers from this malady, your veterinarian or pharmacist can provide motion-sickness tablets. The dosage will vary

Your big partner will lose fears for what she understands.

as she grows, and although most products are safe, check the dosage with your veterinarian. Greta probably will outgrow the problem, but until then, give a dose of the drug about an hour before your car trip. Greta will appreciate it, and it beats cleaning up a big dog mess afterward.

Other techniques to prevent car sickness include allowing no food for two hours before an automobile trip. If Greta has a sensitive stomach, consider using a high-protein paste as an energy substitute for food when traveling. Such products are available at most pet stores or veterinary offices and provide temporary nutrition without the bulk of regular dog foods.

Anyone who drives a pickup truck is bound to consider allowing his big dog to ride in the back. Pickup riding is harmless enough unless Greta sticks her nose around the cab to find new, interesting scents; her eyes will suffer various injuries when doing so. Riding in the back of a pickup also can be harmful if she decides to bail out while the pickup is moving. Practically every veterinarian has patched up a wrecked dog that jumped or fell from a truck. If no other means of transport is available, cross-tie Greta so it's impossible for her to leave the moving vehicle. This also might partially protect her from wind whipping her face. Then schedule a weekly consultation with your veterinarian to treat Greta's eyes.

CHASING

A chasing habit can end in disaster! It is an abominable behavior resulting in untold damages to both the chaser and the object being chased. The problems rarely relate to the chase, but become important when the catch is made! Of the many living and inanimate objects dogs chased, other pets are of the greatest importance.

Cats run, dogs chase. That's the way the world is structured. When cats don't run, dogs usually won't chase unless they've learned that chasing is okay. Big dog puppies are often too clumsy to catch an agile, athletic cat, but occasionally they get an advantage and catch the feline anyway. Usually they regret it! Follow these guidelines, and cat chasing won't become a problem.

Introduce the cat to the big puppy with one of the two securely confined to a crate. If the feline was in the home first, put Greta in her crate and bring the cat into the room to smell and investigate the new puppy. After a few such experiences, take Greta out of her crate on a leash and allow kitty to smell, hiss, and show her fangs. Then gradually allow more communication between the animals,

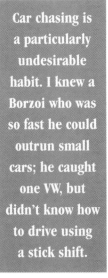

Car chasing is a particularly undesirable habit. I knew a Borzoi who was so fast he could outrun small cars; he caught one VW, but didn't know how to drive using a stick shift.

with Greta on-lead. When each pet realizes that the other has no ulterior motives, they should get along famously. Just for a precaution, provide escape routes for the cat. If possible, assure that each room has an upward escape plan available.

While accustoming Greta to the cat's presence, arm yourself with a goodly supply of tasty treats. When first she is allowed untethered communication with the cat, speak to Greta and give her a treat. Repeat this procedure as often as necessary. Soon the cat will become a welcome visitor, since Greta gets goodies when the cat shows up.

Big dogs seek comfort, food, water, shelter, protection, companionship, and a leader. All we have to do is provide these things, and our big partner will give us pleasure beyond measure!

Big Dog Health

Big dogs are unique in many ways. Their size alone often influences the outcome of medical conditions. When you choose your big partner's doctor, do so with knowledge and discernment. Veterinarians generally are trained similarly, but many have extensive experience with particular types of pets. This doesn't mean that you must seek a big dog specialist instead of a general pet practitioner, but neither does it mean that just any veterinarian will do. Look for a clinician with the facilities and ability to handle large dogs, one who doesn't shy from Barney and is comfortable with big dogs.

> **Veterinary medicine is a wonderful, satisfying profession, but not all veterinarians are created equal.**

YOUR VETERINARIAN

If we all had animal medical knowledge and experience, we could make our pet health decisions without help, but we don't, so we consult a veterinarian. Veterinary practitioners are women and men with years of education, a practiced eye, and an understanding of animal medical science. Most veterinarians didn't take up their profession as a second choice; they aren't physicians who couldn't get into medical school. They are dedicated to their careers and generally work very hard, studying constantly and forever improving their knowledge. While immersed in an extremely difficult but gratifying profession they provide valuable services to the animal-owning public. I've often heard that animal medicine is more difficult than human medicine because patients can't tell you where it hurts. Hogwash! A sick dog is honest. Usually, he displays his signs of illness straightforwardly and doesn't try to mask his pain or dysfunction.

Dogs don't drink themselves into oblivion or sniff compounds that create gross destruction of their brain and demolish olfactory cells. They rarely eat too much weird food or take a plethora of tonics to increase their awareness or stop the aging process. Dogs can't inject drugs that aren't digestible and won't voluntarily consume pills to make them sleep, keep them awake, get them high, or make them hallucinate.

Dogs don't drive cars, fly airplanes, or sail ships, all of which may cause anxiety or paranoia. They rarely climb mountains for sport, and although they enjoy romping with their canine friends in the park, they don't crash violently into one another merely to see a ball or puck sail across a goal line. Never involved in road rage, dogs have no need for guns or knives and rarely hold grudges. Domestic canines have no perception of time or money, no appointments to keep, no stressful businesses to run, and can't comprehend deadlines or payments. Their needs are simple;

their pleasures are inexpensive and enormously satisfying; they have few family disputes; and they can't understand lawsuits.

Compared with human medicine, veterinary medicine is much easier to practice. Big dogs are good patients, with few exceptions. They often have high pain thresholds that sometimes mask physical signs, but a knowledgeable veterinarian will realize this and will look for the nearly imperceptible signs of pain. Most big dogs act and react in time-honored, predictable fashions, and their medical signs are more diagnostic because they aren't ignored, faked, or exaggerated.

Enormous technological advancements have been made in veterinary medicine in the past few decades. Great varieties of diagnostics are available, leading to quicker diagnosis; new therapeutic techniques give big dogs a better chance for long, comfortable lives. Alternative medicine is available for owners who disdain the use of modern drugs and prefer homeopathic remedies.

Don't get the idea that Barney's future lies only in the hands of your veterinarian. It is you, the owner, who must make decisions. Just as you make decisions relative to your own health, Barney is your dog; take responsibility for his well-being.

Many people accept a veterinarian's diagnosis and prescribed treatment without question. A veterinary degree hanging on the wall doesn't mean the clinician is always right on target. The state license doesn't indicate that veterinarians are infallible; they aren't saints or geniuses. It's no insult to the veterinarian's knowledge to ask intelligent questions. Legitimate reasons for owner queries always exist, even when you have total confidence in the doctor's knowledge. A diagnostic consultation or therapeutic discussion should be a two-way communication between veterinarian and pet owner. It's an explanation of the professional's diagnosis and recommendations, based upon examination of Barney's physical and physiological signs (including laboratory results), coupled with your history of Barney's illness. You and your veterinarian are a team. Each of you has specific responsibilities. You are entitled to a scientific medical diagnosis and treatment options for *your* dog.

> **Perhaps a dog can't tell you where he hurts, but a thoughtful, professional examination will reveal an abundance of telltale signs that owners may overlook.**

HISTORY AND PHYSICAL EXAM

Most veterinary practitioners take a logical approach to diagnosis. The clinician usually begins by taking a complete history from the owner, including the length of time Barney has been ill. She will ask about his usual food as well as any changes in his diet, appetite, exercise, or work. Stressors including psychological and environmental changes should be discussed, as well as lameness and body attitude changes, vomiting, abnormal bowel movements, and salivation. His temperament, sleep habits, and activity level should be noted, with all changes pointed out. You are responsible for having and sharing this information with the veterinarian.

This history should be followed by a physical examination that includes no less than the following observations. The clinician may look into Barney's eyes, observing the color and texture of the cornea and the presence of abnormality of other ocular tissues.

Generally, his temperature is taken and his pulse is checked as well as the mucous membrane character and color of his gums.

Palpation may follow. During this examination, the veterinarian checks his limbs and joints for abnormalities, and palpates his

> **Only you are liable for your dog's care.**

> When you take Barney to a veterinarian for any health reason, courteously suggest that you wish to be included in each step of his diagnosis and treatment. If this proactive stance is frowned upon, you're in the wrong exam room!

abdomen, head, and neck for lumps, bumps, and organ pain.

When indicated, the exam also might include stethoscopic examination (auscultation) of his chest, throat palpation and inspection, an ophthalmoscopic (eye) exam, or an otoscopic (ear) exam. This physical exam needn't take more than a few moments, but is of tremendous value in guiding the veterinarian's diagnostic search. At that point, if the diagnosis needs support or is in doubt, laboratory blood tests, X rays, and other aids or referrals might be suggested.

ASK QUESTIONS

Your veterinarian may work quickly and seem to breeze through the exam, but there is always an opportunity to ask questions. Barney is your responsibility, and you must take this obligation seriously. Trust in your veterinarian doesn't include accepting everything said in the exam room without your complete understanding.

LABORATORY TESTS

Ask your veterinarian questions about laboratory error probability. Ask the purpose of each test being ordered, including blood tests, X rays, ultrasounds, or specialist referral. (There currently are sixteen different veterinary specialty organizations with specially trained, certified clinicians.) Ask what risk is involved with each test. For instance, are X rays or ultrasound imaging of pregnant bitches ever contraindicated? Is the accuracy and value of the examination worth the risk? X rays are diagnostic tools; if an X-ray image won't lend understanding to diagnosis and indicate a particular course of action, why is it taken?

Sometimes a battery of tests done on a single sample of blood is performed for a much lower cost than individual blood tests done separately. If such a blood profile is suggested, ask the veterinarian whether any test or tests will confirm a diagnosis, or whether the battery will be used to screen, searching for a clue. A blood profile may be an excellent way to ascertain internal organ health, even if a diagnosis has already been made by history and physical examination. The profile results may govern the course of treatment, or it may find weak organs that must be considered. However, the value of a blood test or a profile screen should be clearly understood and its cost should be specified before it is ordered.

When a diagnosis is made, ask if it is definitive (certain), presumptive (highly probable), or one of several possibilities that must be differentiated from one another by further examinations or testing.

If a definitive diagnosis is made by examination, and a clear course of treatment is indicated, is laboratory testing really necessary? For instance, if Barney has a face full of porcupine quills, some of which are dangerously near his eyes, and they can't be removed without sedation, should you agree to a blood profile before sedation is administered?

Some veterinary practices offer in-house laboratory diagnostic testing; others send blood samples to commercial laboratories. Modern technology may make either choice advantageous in terms of accuracy of results, cost, and speed. Ask where the lab work is to be done, how soon results are expected, and the overall cost. The tests listed here are only a sampling of those available, and none, by itself,

is absolutely diagnostic. Any veterinarian who's worth her salt won't substitute laboratory tests for a thorough history and meticulous physical examination, but biochemical profiles may support or differentiate between several presumptive diagnoses and may help determine the safest treatment.

- Alanine aminotransferase. Elevated levels usually indicate liver disease.
- Alkaline phosphatase. If elevated, this may indicate liver disease or Cushing's syndrome.
- Amylase. Elevated values point toward pancreatic or kidney disease.
- Blood Urea Nitrogen (BUN). If significantly elevated, kidney disease is indicated.
- Calcium. An elevation of the serum calcium usually indicates parathyroid or kidney disease.
- Cholesterol. Elevation of canine cholesterol may indicate liver or kidney diseases.
- Creatinine. If elevated, this test indicates kidney compromise.
- Glucose. A reduced level points toward liver disease, and a higher than normal level may indicate diabetes.
- Phosphorus. When higher than normal, this supports a diagnosis of kidney disease.
- Bilirubin. An elevation of this liver pigment in the bloodstream suggests bile duct obstruction.
- Total protein. When the total protein is increased in the blood, various

> When a test is suggested, ask why it is important and whether its use has a logical place in the diagnosis of the suspected disease.

> This sampling of common blood tests may be included in a blood profile screen.

organs may be compromised, including the liver, kidney, or gastrointestinal tract.

Other, more specific tests may be used either in addition to a blood profile or independently. Lab tests are invaluable in confirming a diagnosis. For instance, various blood platelet counts and clotting tests are often employed to aid diagnosis of von Willebrand disease and other hereditary bleeding disorders. Thyroid tests such as T3, T4, and THS (thyroid stimulating hormone) are used to confirm diagnosis of hypothyroidism. Plasma cortisol, before and after adrenal stimulation with ACTH (adreno-corticotropic hormone), is used to help diagnose Cushing's syndrome. These and other specific tests are needed by your veterinarian, and often are suggested after seeing the profile results.

PROGNOSIS

Prognosticate means "to foretell or predict"; *prognosis,* then, is the prediction of outcome and course of a disease and the probability of recovery. Although prognosis is no more than an educated guess by an experienced professional, it should be a part of your decision making process and should be considered before a course of therapy is accepted. Ask what the prognosis is if no treatment is begun, and whether the prognosis is expected to be the same if other, less costly drugs or techniques are used.

Prognosis is a decision-making tool provided by your medical adviser to give you, the owner, information about your canine partner's disease. It is an inexact science; in the case of a life-threatening condition, such as cancer, an experienced veterinarian will rarely predict the time remaining in a dog's life. This folly is usually left to new graduates and those who like to gamble.

THERAPY

We've now reached the stage of Barney's treatment plan. The very first question to ask relates to options available. Treatment options include everything from doing nothing to the most radical or expensive therapy available. When discussing your options, the veterinarian should explain the possibility of success (prognosis) associated with each treatment, as well as the expense of each. Ask whether treatment is expected to bring about cure and complete recovery, or is merely supportive. Ask whether suggested therapy can mask other important signs of the disease. In today's therapy strategies, a variety of drugs may be used to treat a disease, and one drug may work faster or more effectively than another; ask about this.

Will prescribed surgery or conservative therapy cure Barney's problem and return him to normal or merely make him more comfortable? Is the benefit of treatment dependent upon other factors? For instance, a joint injury is diagnosed and an injection of cortisone into the joint is prescribed. Ask whether exercise or rest is prescribed to enhance the effect of the injection. Ask whether there is some supportive therapy such as splinting or bandaging that could be employed as well. Ask about Barney's weight: Should he go on a diet, and if he loses weight, will that affect the prognosis? Ask about anticipated side effects: What can cortisone injections may cause? Will he need further injections in the future, and are more definitive

> Almost always, there is more than one approach to treating a patient.

> What is the expected outcome of this condition?

treatments available that may be less expensive or have fewer side effects over the long term?

BIG DOG PROBLEMS

A number of health disorders are more dynamic or seen more frequently in large dogs. Owners of dogs that sometimes weigh a hundred or more pounds should be aware of these conditions. In this section we will discuss miscellaneous ailments and metabolic diseases that don't fall into specific categories. Other health problems associated with bones and the digestive tract are found in the following chapters.

Regular home inspection is critical in big dogs.

ELBOW HYGROMA

Hygromas may form on either elbow, or on both simultaneously. The cause is blunt trauma, and is related to the surface provided for Barney to lie upon; concrete or wood floors predispose to this condition. Many big dogs assume a down position by first sitting, then dropping to their elbows.

Hygroma is a fluid-filled sac. It may be the bursa that distends with liquid and forms over a deeper bony structure—in this case, the elbow. Hygroma development, therefore, is an overreaction to Barney's environment and is associated with confinement to hard surfaces. This peculiarity is occasionally seen in medium-sized dogs, but big dogs' weight, and their habit of dropping to their elbows when they lie down, predisposes them to bruise and abuse their elbows. This abuse is accompanied by irritation, inflammation, and hygroma development. The pocket of fluid gradually becomes larger and larger as your giant partner's weight and habits continue to insult his elbows.

A typical hygroma appears as a painless, fluctuating mass, ranging in size from peanut to tennis ball dimensions. Initially it is sterile; the fluid within the sac has about the same composition and function as joint fluid. The sac forms immediately beneath the skin, which may be abraded or punctured, in which case bacterial introduction may follow and an infection result. If that happens, a new problem presents itself, which must be addressed posthaste.

To prevent this unsightly structure from ever forming, furnish Barney with a soft pad on which to lie. If he occupies a run and kennel, use soft sand for the floor.

When faced with hygroma, most veterinarians have a favorite treatment. Merely aspirating (draining) the fluid from the sac is usually futile unless some technique is used concurrently to prevent its refilling. Cortisone injection into the empty sac might help reduce inflammation, and bandaging the elbow will obviously help collapse the sac and discourage fluid accumulation. When this technique is used, it may hold for a short period, only to have the accumulation recur soon after the bandage is removed.

Bursas are natural, protective, cushioning structures that form over bony prominences.

Some veterinarians may dissect out the fluid filled sac, then suture and bandage the surgical site to protect it from further trauma. This may work very well, but only if Barney is prevented from taking the bandage off prematurely, and if the underlying cause of the hygroma is treated as well.

Another technique is to make a small incision into the hygroma at both top and bottom. A surgical drain is threaded through the hygroma from top to bottom, suturing the latex drain tube to the skin above and below the cyst. This allows the fluid to drain, and causes the hygroma to remain open so that scar tissue will heal it from inside out. Usually a bandage is used, and antibiotics may be administered to prevent infection that would complicate healing. This technique may work, but will often leave a pair of ugly scars that could work to Barney's disadvantage in the show ring.

In any case, an Elizabethan collar usually is placed on his neck, so that he can't reach the bandage to lick it. This apparatus looks somewhat like a giant, clumsy funnel that is secured to his collar, and it adds to the fun of owning a giant breed.

CALLUSES AND DECUBITAL ULCERS

Canine callus formation also is influenced by weight and your dog's habits. If Barney always lies on his left side, calluses will undoubtedly form on his left elbow, stifle, hip, and sometimes on the lateral (outside) of his left feet, wrist, and hock. Like hygromas, calluses form in response to the surface of the dog's resting place. Repeated trauma or irritation and friction cause hair to wear away and scar tissue is gradually substituted for the once supple skin.

Unsightly, hard, wrinkled, bumpy, hairless lesions, calluses are unappreciated by most owners. These thickened skin lesions have no significance unless they become ulcerated and infected. Even then, when they involve only the surface area, they rarely pose serious problems. Prevention is nearly impossible and

> **Human calluses often spring from hard work, but Barney's calluses are more likely associated with his laziness.**

would entail padding virtually all the surfaces that Barney chooses to lie upon. Treatment usually is unnecessary, but various creams and ointments may soften the callous skin and return it to nearly normal. Ointments containing aloe vera, vitamins A and E, lanolin, and other emollients have been used quite successfully when rubbed into the lesion frequently. Infected calluses must be treated by regular cleaning and application of drying agents, skin disinfectants, and sometimes, antibiotic creams.

Occasionally, the repeated trauma to a callus may cause ulceration in which the skin wears away and exposes underlying soft tissues. Infection may begin, and if the resulting ulcer doesn't receive medical attention, the infection can spread to deeper tissues and become a serious medical problem. Often an older dog condition, decubital ulcers are similar to bedsores that sometimes are seen in people who are confined to bed for long periods of time. Watch Barney's calluses carefully for serum oozing, tenderness, and swelling.

TAIL BEATING

Thank goodness the average big dog doesn't have an ambitious, rapidly wagging rudder like many of the small breeds. The maelstrom created by a few odd pounds of posterior flesh and bone can raise havoc with coffee table knickknacks, dishes, and table lamps. Anytime Barney changes direction, lightweight pieces of furniture are at risk. If you've ever inadvertently been struck with his caudal appendage, you know its power firsthand.

Knocking things helter-skelter is bad enough, but it's only a hint of a common, more serious problem associated with big dogs.

Suppose Barney stands 20 inches from the nearest brick wall and wags his 21-inch tail vigorously. You guessed it; the tip of his tail will beat against the wall unmercifully! His high pain threshold allows the damage to his tail to continue, and instead of stepping forward an inch, he continues to beat the appendage to a bloody pulp. Tail beaters are happy dogs that deserve a break, but what can you do?

Barney's tail should be licensed as a lethal weapon.

The callus that may eventually form in response to his tail beating only magnifies the problem. This thickened tailtip loses its former suppleness and becomes hardened and easily traumatized. Before you can say splat, the raw tail is oozing blood and serum, and his eagerness to see his friends results in a fine pink spray of serum that quickly stipples walls around the room. Everywhere he lies, his thumping tail embosses his signature on the carpet or tile. Barney is soon banished to the backyard, where the problem continues. Trees, garage walls, fences, and rock gardens receive new red paint instead of coffee tables, refrigerators, and stereo cabinets.

Once outside, the visible evidence is reduced, but his battered tail remains. This seemingly minor problem has little general health significance, but it has ruined many big dog relationships. Once your big partner is relegated to life in the yard, he's no longer a family member. His problems somehow seem less important. Your partner assumes an unwanted, unappreciated role. Big dog lovers, arise!

If you've ever tried to bandage the tip of a giant tail, you know the futility of the project. Occasionally bandages will stay on for an hour or two, but meanwhile Barney will continue pounding the bandage, tissues will seep blood, and before long the saturated bandage will shoot across the room, hitting the wall with a splatter.

If Barney is a pup, treating the tail tip with drying or toughening agents may mitigate the messy results. Consult your veterinarian for her advice about applying tincture of benzoin, tuff-skin, or other such agents. If this preventive care doesn't work, other techniques may be employed.

Finger splints are those tough little plastic, round-end devices that physicians put over the tip of your injured finger. Available in pharmacies, finger splints can be purchased in several sizes, one of which will just slip over Barney's tail tip. At a lesser cost, try a plastic hair roller. When you install either device, don't put it on too tightly; allow an air space between the battered tail tip and the protective plastic cylinder. Tape the splint to the hair of Barney's tail an inch or two above the bleeding wound, and don't cover the entire splint. Wounds heal more efficiently if air circulation is maintained. Consult your veterinarian about medication to apply directly to the wound. Sometimes it's best to use drying preparations, often it's better to soften the callous lesion, and occasionally, antibiotic creams will work best. Buy a supply of splints, and change the device every few days. When removing it, try to save as much tail hair as possible.

Barney probably won't beat his tail while on long walks, or exercising in the park, or during training sessions or other outdoor activities. Indulge him in such events for a few hours after the splint is removed. This will allow the tail's skin to receive more oxygen, and he will appreciate the freedom from splinting. When he is allowed inside, put on a clean splint.

An alternative technique might work. Simply secure his tail to his hock. He won't particularly appreciate having his tail tied down, but it will prevent him from beating it bloody. If you have any questions about this project, ask your veterinarian. Some tape is easier to remove from hair than others, and veterinary advice will help you in that regard as well.

Generally, the technique is simple. Use about 18 inches (.5 meters) of 2-inch (4-cm) wide tape. Stick the tape to the hair of the tail, attaching it circumferentially several inches above the raw tip. Stick the tape to itself, mastic side to mastic, for a few inches, then stick it loosely to the hair of his hind leg in a circumferential manner, just above the hock. After rounding the hock, stick the tape to itself again. The result should be a tail that can still wag, but with the end loosely tied to his hock. If this technique is used, switch the anchor from left to right hock every time you renew the tape, and move the tape up or down the tail slightly as well. Big dogs usually accept this restriction without too much objection.

Another option is to have Barney's tail amputated—not just the bloody part, but most of the appendage. This may seem radical treatment, which it is. A Wolfhound with a stubby tail is a tragic conversation piece. If only the tip is amputated, you're apt to discover that Barney stands closer to offending walls with the same result as before, except the surgical site is more easily traumatized.

Amputation isn't necessarily the best answer to this problem, but it works, and although Barney may resent the loss of his rudder for a while, amputation is a better answer than giving up your big partner or banishing him to his kennel.

OBESITY

Fat cells function in healthy animals to store energy until it is converted to blood sugar and used. In moderate quantities, fat is as important as any other nutrient, but balance must be maintained between the the fat that is needed for normal body function and excess fat that is simply stored in the body. Fat can be manufactured from carbohydrates, so feeding a low-fat diet isn't enough!

Big dogs have no greater propensity for obesity than small dogs, but in larger pets, overeating results are multiplied many times over. Big dogs' lives are at risk from obesity for several reasons. Anything that adds unnecessary weight to already stressed joints is detrimental to the dog's livelihood and comfort.

> **Fat big dogs are short-lived big dogs.**

Usually, obesity is diagnosed by rib cage palpation. Barney's ribs should not be seen, but easily felt with your fingers when petting him. When rib outlines are obscured by fat, obesity is present. Conversely, if his ribs are visible, he's probably too thin. Fat on his abdomen, and over his hips are other signs of obesity. If excessive fat causes a 15 percent increase in Barney's normal weight, the situation is dangerous and should be treated. Unfortunately, fat will be concealed elsewhere throughout his body, not just where you can see and feel it.

Barney's big carcass has big bones, but more than a heavy skeleton is required; he needs a great deal of muscle to carry it from place to place. His ability to get around comfortably and agilely depends on ligament stability, muscle flexibility and power, and tendon strength. These tissues must be well conditioned, which in turn depends on heredity, diet, and exercise. If you curtail his exercise, you must adjust his diet accordingly; failure to do so will result in weight gain and soft tissue weakness.

Obesity presents a vicious circle. When fat cells are stored internally, they infiltrate other tissues and reduce the effectiveness of tendons, ligaments, and muscle. Fat deposits weaken these locomotion structures, and discourage physical activity, which in turn adds to his obesity.

Fat adds to body weight, which means Barney must carry a heavier load everywhere he travels. The immediate effect of obesity might be lack of normal movement, but, the heavier load results in stresses on joint cartilage and eventually may cause remodeling of the surfaces of bones that form the joints.

Fat deposits surrounding vital internal organs can compromise the function of those organs. The heart, liver, kidneys, pancreas, and other organs do their work at less than full capacity when surrounded and infiltrated with fat cells. The result is premature aging of organs and an obese, inactive big partner.

Owners and veterinarians alike argue about the causes of obesity. Castrating of males may reduce their activity by giving them one less reason for running to neighbors' houses. Removal of the androgenic hormone, testosterone, may increase fat production and deposition, although this premise is questioned and rejected by many. Spaying females has no influence on fat storage and usually doesn't result in obesity. Obesity may have a variety of underlying causes, but in the final analysis, it is dependent upon caloric intake in excess of need. Dietary and activity management is necessary to control or cure this condition. Consult with your veterinarian about diets, and steer a logical reducing course. Inappropriate dieting can create a worse nightmare than obesity.

> Witnessing their dogs in seizures, owners often become hysterical and display some pretty weird actions themselves.

EPILEPSY

Spontaneous and excessive electrical activity of nervous system cells (neurons) within the brain initiate a seizure focus. As the abnormal electrical activity extends to other nerve cells in other areas of the brain, seizure occurs. Dogs rarely die during an epileptic seizure unless it is prolonged, which is known as *status epilepticus* in veterinary literature. This continuous state of unconscious activity soon becomes an emergency that must be treated quickly.

Epilepsy affects virtually all purebred dog breeds to some degree and a few mutts that haven't any particular heritage as well. For some reason, it is especially prominent among big dogs. Epilepsy may be associated with brain injury or disease, but sometimes it's known as *idiopathic epilepsy,* which means the cause of the seizures is unknown. Many authorities believe the predisposition for idiopathic epilepsy is inherited. The first seizure often occurs sometime after the third year, and they may take various forms. In the mildest form, Barney will merely act confused or disoriented. After a few minutes, the mild event passes, and he appears quite normal. A few weeks or months later, he may act bewildered, stagger, fall, and lie panting on the lawn. These seizure signs may progress to the point where his head is thrown back and his legs are paddling furiously. Epileptic seizures may become more frequent and more severe with time, and eventually, he may die in a seizure-induced coma.

In any event, if Barney begins to show signs of having a seizure, it's best to know what steps to take. Your initial response should be to note the time so you can report the duration of the seizure. In early seizures, he isn't apt to hurt himself or bystanders, but since his large frame is capable of striking objects or people with a good deal of force, you should pad his body with a blanket or coat.

Dogs can't swallow their tongues, so don't reach in his mouth for that or any other reason. His jaws may involuntarily clamp down, and you will suffer greatly from your folly. By the same token, don't try to hold a stick in his mouth, because he might bite it in two and the result could be worse than the seizure.

Talk to him in a soothing voice, and prevent him from overturning tables and chairs or hurting himself by falling into a tight place. Wait out the seizure, which will probably last only a few minutes. Allow him to rest for a reasonable time, then call your veterinarian for advice. Several different medications may be prescribed to reduce the severity and frequency of future seizures or halt them altogether. Currently, no cure for idiopathic epilepsy is recognized.

HEART DISEASES

Various types of congenital vascular and cardiac anomalies are seen in large dogs, and these will be found in the breed discussions in the second section of this book. Suffice it to say that the heart of a big dog may be overworked by virtue of the enormous capacity of his circulatory system.

Aortic stenosis is congenital cardiac disease seen in a number of big breeds. During gestation, a fibrous band develops below the aortic valve, which restricts the blood outflow from the left side of heart to the body. Severely affected dogs have a short life expectancy and risk sudden death. Blood flowing through the pinched aorta can be heard with a stethoscope and furnishes a presumptive diagnosis that can be confirmed with ultrasound or X-ray images. Surgical repair is possible, but should be done early in the dog's life.

> Big-hearted Barney may be at risk of heart disease.

NEPHRITIS (KIDNEY DISEASE)

Antifreeze consumption, leptospirosis, or bacterial infection may cause acute kidney malfunction, but the most common kidney disease is caused by old age. Chronic kidney disease, or nephritis, is manifested by frequent and increased water consumption with associated frequent and voluminous urination.

Appetite usually is depressed, weight loss and decreased activity are accompanied by strong ammonialike urine odor, and finally vomiting begins.

Incurable, chronic kidney failure is treated with various support techniques such as dietary change and medication that reduces secondary complications. Dialysis is possible at some veterinary teaching hospitals, but usually isn't a practical treatment. Chronic kidney disease is the cause of death in many dogs of all sizes, but is more common in big dogs. Dogs suffering from this chronic form should have access to unlimited fresh water and should be protected from stresses.

> Chronic interstitial nephritis is responsible for many older big dog deaths.

VALLEY FEVER

Big dogs are usually outdoor dogs. In the Southwest an endemic fungal disease is quite common in these dogs. Suppose you're traveling with Barney through Arizona, New Mexico, Texas, or parts of California. You may exercise him at desert landscaped rest areas. If he noses about, sniffing at all the interesting trails, he could be exposed to Valley Fever. By the time you reach home in the Northeast, you won't be thinking about the pretty Arizona rest stop, and your veterinarian may not consider it when Barney's symptoms begin.

Coccidioidomycosis is the name of this infection, and it's as bad as the name sounds. Fungus spores (reproductive elements) lie dormant in the soil and can enter Barney's body via his respiratory passages. The fungus grows from these spores and reproduces in the lungs, where its radiographic lesions simulate those of cancer. The fungus often spreads to other parts of the body, especially bone tissue.

Lethargy, appetite suppression, a low-grade fever, coughing, and breathing difficulty are common symptoms. If the fungus becomes localized in bones,the principal sign of infection may be lameness.

Usually diagnosis is made by a specific blood test and is commonly supported by chest and affected bone X rays. Treatment is possible, but must be continued for lengthy periods of time, sometimes six months or longer. No preventive methods are known for this disease.

> **Microscopic fungal spores cause more illness in outdoor dogs of the Southwest than scorpions and rattlesnakes combined.**

DIABETES MELLITUS

So-called sugar diabetes is a metabolic disease that can occur in all breeds, but large dogs seem to have a predisposition for its development. Diabetes may be caused by the weight of the large dog, and is seen more often in obese females, usually those past middle age. Its early signs are lethargy, excessive water consumption, increased urination, and weight gain. If untreated, the later course of the disease is marked by sudden weight loss, vomiting, and coma.

> **A metabolic disease, diabetes is all too common in large dog breeds.**

Diabetes mellitus involves an insufficiency of insulin, a hormone secreted by the pancreas that functions in glucose utilization by all tissues of the body. It's sometimes identified as an autoimmune disease, and its hereditary predisposition is well documented.

If you suspect diabetes in your big dog, consult with Barney's veterinarian. This disease is treatable, but success depends on early diagnosis.

VON WILLEBRAND'S DISEASE (VWD)

Hereditary bleeding or blood clotting disorders such as von Willebrand's Disease (VWD) and Hemophilia A are prevalent in many large purebred dogs. VWD is related to a genetic mutation that is thought by many to be brought about by inbreeding. The disease is manifested by a defect in the blood protein responsible for platelet formation and clot formation (coagulation).

A dog affected with VWD may suffer hemorrhagic episodes, or the disease may remain dormant for extended periods. VWD may first

> **Several blood diseases are prevalent in large dogs and believed to be hereditary.**

be identified at an early age, often during teething. Often, it is manifested by hemorrhagic swelling in and around joints, and if the dog bleeds into the thoracic cavity, abnormal breathing is seen. Diagnosis is made by specific laboratory testing, and treatment is basically supportive.

HYPOTHYROIDISM

The most common of all endocrine (hormonal) diseases having hereditary causes, hypothyroidism has been recognized forever. It is now commonly classed as an immune-mediated condition (lymphocytic thyroiditis). The thyroid gland may be attacked and destroyed by the dog's own immune system. This in turn reduces regulatory hormones normally secreted by the thyroid. The hormones thyroxine (T4) and triiodothyronine (T3) are needed for normal function of all cells of the body.

Hypothyroidism usually is seen between ages two and five, and is prevalent in many big purebred dogs, including Afghans, Doberman Pinschers, Golden Retrievers, Great Danes, Irish Setters, Irish Wolfhounds, Malamutes, and Newfoundlands.

Signs of thyroid compromise include lethargy, mental dullness, and lowered pulse rate and body temperature with concurrent intolerance to cold. Other signs include loss of hair on flanks and tail and behind the ears, accompanied by thickened, darkened skin that sometimes is scaly, oily, or waxy. Weight gain, and later, a

> **Atopy must be differentiated from other skin itching.**

reduced appetite are seen as well. Brood animals often fail to conceive.

Diagnosis of hypothyroidism is made by history and examination and is confirmed by blood testing. One blood test that measures thyroxine (T4) is somewhat diagnostic. Low T4 value may be further confirmed by using thyroid stimulating hormone (TSH) to indicate whether the thyroid gland is capable of producing thyroxine.

> **Hypothyroidism, one of the first recognized metabolic diseases, is now considered to be of autoimmune origin.**

In the absence of these and other specific diagnostic tests, when physical examination points toward hypothyroidism, the inexpensive empirical use of thyroid hormone sometimes is still used. That is, a course of thyroid hormone is prescribed, and the dog's physical signs are reevaluated several weeks later. In any case, oral, daily thyroid hormone is continued for life.

ATOPY

Predisposition for an allergic skin disease may be inherited, especially in large outdoor breeds. This condition is called atopy, and is manifested as a nonparasitic itch affecting young adults. It rarely is seen in older dogs. It may be seasonal in nature, being associated with grass or tree pollens. Exposure to the allergen is through inhalation, ingestion, or contact. The result is severe itching, redness, inflammation, and the resulting trauma from scratching.

Atopy is difficult to diagnose. Often owners fail to realize that an ingested or inhaled allergen may cause a symptom as dramatic as an intense itch. Logically, they associate the inflammation with an irritant that touches the skin of the feet, flanks, or armpits. Owner focus may be turned to grass or weed contact, and dozens of soothing and drying remedies are tried before professional help is sought.

PROGRESSIVE RETINAL ATROPHY (PRA)

Progressive Retinal Atrophy (PRA) is a gradual deterioration of the light sensitive posterior (rear) membrane of the eye. This hereditary condition is prevalent among many large outdoor breeds of dogs in which the central cells of the retina die, impairing the dog's ability to see fixed objects. Moving objects still can be seen by the peripheral portion of the retina. PRA may not be evident until the dog reaches about five years of age. If Barney has sired puppies in his first few years of life, and is affected, he may be responsible for perpetuating this disease.

Signs of PRA include fear of the dark or cautiousness when subjected to reduced light. Climbing or descending stairs often presents a problem, and bumping into chairs and other small objects becomes a daily hazard for affected dogs. Pupils often remain dilated as the disease progresses.

Although no treatment or cure is known, preventive measures are taken by having all propagation stock examined prior to breeding. A national organization, Canine Eye Registry Foundation (CERF) offers help in identifying affected dogs. When a dog is certified free from PRA by CERF, a certificate number can be added to his or her registration.

> One of the most publicized inherited eye diseases, PRA can be eliminated by eye examination and selective breeding of PRA-free brood stock.

ENTROPION

Entropion is a congenital disease common among large dogs with big heads; its signs gradually appear as the puppy matures. Especially prevalent in dogs with looser than normal head skin, predisposition is seen in Saint Bernards, Irish Setters, Bloodhounds, Great Danes, and some of the larger hunting breeds. Signs include eyelids that roll inward, and in the worst cases the lid and eyelashes come in contact with the eyeball. Usually the lower lid is at fault, but the upper eyelid may be involved, and in some cases, both are rolled inward. In mild cases, no symptoms are recognized except excessive watering of the eye, but in more serious cases, the cornea may ulcerate, and vision impairment and eventual blindness may result.

Surgical treatment produces a high success rate, and in most cases, a single correction is sufficient to last a lifetime. In a few cases where eyelids are especially loose, a second operation must follow the initial correction. If you suspect entropion, have the diagnosis confirmed and follow professional advice. In very young puppies, your veterinarian may prescribe protective ophthalmic ointments until the appropriate surgical time.

> If your big dog has excessive facial skin folds, he's a candidate for entropion.

ECTROPION

The opposite of entropion is ectropion, which is a hereditary drooping or rolled-out lid and is more prevalent in the lower lid. It is seen most often in Bloodhounds and other big dogs with loose skin about their heads. As a pup matures, mucous membranes of the lid's underside (conjunctival sac) are exposed and often become infected (conjunctivitis).

Droopy eyelids are the primary sign of ectropion.

Infection causes the dog to rub and scratch at the irritated eyelids, increasing the damage.

Surgical correction is somewhat standard procedure, but ophthalmic ointments or solutions are often used until the dog reaches maturity, when the eyelids are tightened to correct the condition.

Realistically, dogs' skeletons can support only a nominal amount of weight.

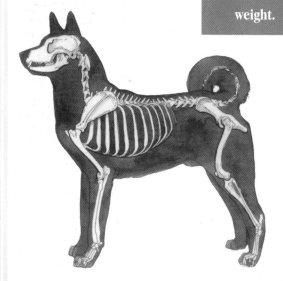

BIG SKELETAL PROBLEMS

An often-discussed theory relates to canines. If allowed to breed without human intervention of any kind, all dogs in time would appear much the same. The tiniest dogs wouldn't survive, and neither would the biggest giants. The hardiest males would mate with the strongest females, and eventually hereditary weaknesses would fall by the wayside. *Heterosis* (hybrid vigor) among the mixed breeds would prevail, and eventually a wide and deep gene pool would result in nearly perfect puppies. At that time, all dogs would become approximately the same size, their heads would be in proportion to their bodies, their muzzles would attain a moderate length, and their legs would be

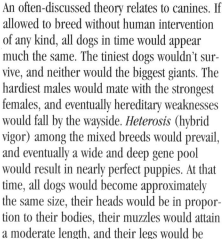

strong and well muscled. Their colors would be variable, but spots would dominate their medium-length coats. This similarity of type is observed in wild dogs and wolves.

Humans have manipulated the gene pools of their pets and have selectively bred dogs for human purposes. Occasionally, this manipulation has produced monsters when the appropriate ratio of body mass to skeletal strength has been sacrificed by selecting for body type or color. In other cases, proper angulation of joints has been forfeited in favor of some unrelated genetic feature without regard to function. If selective breeding has emphasized enormous body mass without regard to skeletal strength, problems surely will follow. Bone structure may be too fragile to adequately support body weight, and stresses are introduced into the skeleton, especially in joints.

Dogs bred with poor joint angulation, or weakness of ligaments or tendons, are predisposed to lameness.

JOINT ANATOMY

Barney's skeleton has hundreds of joints. Most of them aren't stressed by his considerable weight, but unfortunately a few are. A joint is made up of the ends of opposing bones, the surfaces of which are covered with cartilage and shock-absorbing cartilage pads known as menisci.

Joint cartilage is a slick, fibrous material that allows smooth movement between bones and prevents one bone from directly contacting another. Cartilage is of great importance in cushioning the impact between bones, but unfortunately it also has a built-in self-destructive factor. The joint capsule composed of strong fibrous material envelopes each joint and is lined with specialized secretory glands that secrete synovia, a highly efficient viscid lubricating fluid containing mucin and mineral salts. Synovia also nourishes the intra-articular (within the joint) structures. In an ill-fitting joint, the joint capsule and its synovial membrane become inflamed. Blood vessels are stretched and hemorrhage into the joint. This inflammation is called synovitis, which is another factor in joint pain and lameness. Injured cartilage secretes an enzyme that changes the character of synovia (joint fluid) from a thick, lubricating liquid to a thinner, less effective product.

Joints may be of the ball and socket type, such as the hip, which allows movement in all directions, or they may be hinge joints like the stifle, which allows movement in only two directions. Some joints, such as those in the spine, allow very restricted movement.

Locomotion joints are mobile structures with significant movement between the bones, and these are frequently involved with big dog lameness. The hip and stifle in the hind leg and the shoulder and elbow in the foreleg are most often affected. Ligaments are fibrous bands that attach the joint bones to one another. Genetic abnormal apposition of one bone to another often causes lameness.

Tendons are fibrous bands that attach muscles to bones, and often these are associated with lameness even though they aren't specifically intra-articular structures.

Big dogs are plagued with hereditary predisposition to joint ailments.

RUPTURED CRUCIATE LIGAMENT

The stifle or knee is a hinge joint that moves in one plane. It is stabilized by certain extra-articular tendons, ligaments on the inside (medial aspect) and outside (lateral aspect), and the cruciate (crossed) ligaments. A common cause of hind leg lameness in canines is rupture of the anterior cruciate ligament of the stifle, which is common in big dogs, particularly immature individuals, and is seen more often in some breeds than others.

Many veterinarians believe that the cruciate ligaments of the stifle are hereditarily weaker in certain large breeds of dogs.

Cruciate ligaments are positioned in the joint to allow movement within a restricted range between the lower end of the femur and upper end of the tibia. One ligament, situated toward the medial side of the joint, is affixed to the front of the tibia and extends to the rear aspect of the opposing femur, and is called the anterior cruciate. It helps prevent these bones from slipping from side to side. The posterior cruciate ligament is positioned laterally in the joint and is affixed to the rear of the tibia, extending to the front of the femur; it is called the posterior cruciate. Rupture or tear of the anterior cruciate ligament is serious in any dog, but because of the weight involved, is more difficult to repair in big dogs.

CAUSES

Unlike cats, dogs must be taught to jump, and if not placed in jumping situations, would rarely if ever find the need to do so. Activities most often incriminated in the rupture of cruciate ligaments are jumping from chairs and stairs, reckless running, turning quickly, and puppies' other playful endeavors. The anterior cruciate acts to constrain the tibia from moving forward on the femur. Thus when the dog is running and makes a sudden right turn on the weight-bearing right leg, the effect is to rotate the stifle and rupture the ligament. Anatomical aberrations such as knock-knees or bowed legs may predispose the dog to anterior cruciate rupture as well.

When the ligament ruptures, the dog usually will limp badly or even carry the affected leg. Sometimes the ligament isn't torn in half, in which case some weight may be borne by the leg. Pain usually is felt immediately, but fades rather promptly unless the stifle is manipulated. It is highly improbable that a ruptured ligament will heal without surgical intervention. If not attended promptly, the meniscus on the affected side may fold on itself, complicating recovery. Although the dog may begin to use the leg after a few months,

> **Jumping is a learned activity, rather than a natural tendency in dogs.**

eventually degenerative joint disease occurs in unoperated joints, and pain will be displayed with every step.

The ligament won't heal by itself, but one of several successful surgical repair techniques may be used. Care must be taken to keep the pup from retearing the ligament. Early diagnosis and therapy is critical to produce a strong, stable joint and during recovery, you must devise schemes to prevent Barney from injurying himself again.

HIP DYSPLASIA (CHD)

One of the most common diseases of active, large breeds is Canine Hip Dysplasia, a complex hereditary joint disease occurring at any time of life. It causes pain and immobility, and eventually may cause a total loss of use in the hind legs. CHD is a developmental disease, one that may not become apparent on X ray until two years of age. Rapid growth, overfeeding, and excessive exercise influence its severity.

In this disease, the pelvic hip joint cup or acetabulum is shallow, and the femoral head or ball is misshapen. The ill-fitting joint results in further deformity and remodeling of bony structures, degenerative arthritis. The pain causes walking to become difficult or impossi-

> **CHD is known as a polygenic hereditary disease because it's produced by a complexity of gene interaction. Only by professional hip evaluation can committed breeders gradually eliminate this serious imperfection.**

ble. As the joint surfaces change shape, cartilage is worn away, synovitis prevails, and eventually the bone-against-bone joint becomes stiff and useless.

CHD is diagnosed by X ray, and every reproducing gene pool member should be screened by a radiologist's X ray evaluation. The Orthopedic Foundation for Animals (OFA) is a national organization that reads and registers X rays sent to them.

PennHIP is another diagnostic technique that is quite beneficial in helping to predict CHD. It's intended to identify the risk factors of puppies at four months of age and gives breeders and owners another tool to clean up the gene pool.

Hip dysplasia treatment is imperfect at best. Conservative therapy is undertaken using anti-inflammatory products. New arthritis drugs, pain relievers, and polysulfated glucosamine plus chondroitin help preserve quality of life. Conditioning and regular low-impact exercise is important. Hip joint replacement has become more available in recent years, and is relatively successful.

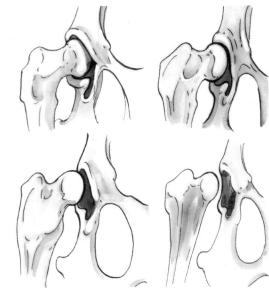

Hip Dysplasia.

OSTEOARTHRITIS OR DEGENERATIVE JOINT DISEASE (DJD)

In some, osteoarthritis follows joint injury, in others it's the result of hereditary joint deformities, and in a few, it is of unknown cause.

Degenerative joint disease is manifested by synovitis, bony spurs or small growths of bone within a joint, cartilage destruction, pain, and stiffness. It may occur in virtually any joint of the body, but is worse in some than others, notably the hips.

> DJD is common in older dogs, especially in larger than normal and obese dogs.

In some instances, surgery may remove spurs and repair some of the degenerative characteristics of osteoarthritis, but often by the time these techniques are begun, the damage to the joint(s) will be too far advanced to be of any great help. Over-the-counter anti-inflammatory drugs may be of value, and other newer nonsteroidal anti-inflammatory products are being developed regularly. After X rays of the joint have been analyzed, some veterinarians prescribe polysulfated glucosaminoglycan (glucosamine), which is sometimes given with chondroitin to encourage regrowth of cartilage.

A recent development using cartilage transplants may renew joint cartilage, but these techniques are of benefit only if the original cause of joint damage can be corrected and the joint stabilized.

ELBOW DYSPLASIA

A number of big breeds are afflicted with elbow dysplasia, an inherited disease causing severe lameness. Akitas, Bernese Mountain Dogs, Bouvier des Flandres, Bloodhounds, Bullmastiffs, Doberman Pinschers, German Shepherds, Golden Retrievers, Leonbergers, Mastiffs, Newfoundlands, and Rottweilers are all named as frequently affected.

Another developmental disease, elbow dysplasia is a degenerative joint disease of the elbow. It is a problem of young dogs wherein the upper tip of the ulna (elbow) bone fails to unite with the lower portion, and remains unattached. It is similar to CHD in that both have multiple inherited causes, may develop later in life, and are manifested by arthritic changes.

Like CHD, elbow dysplasia is diagnosed by X ray, and several surgical treatments are prescribed to relieve the pain of movement. Elbow dysplasia X rays are analyzed, rated, and registered by the OFA.

> Elbow dysplasia often is seen in big dog puppies between five and nine months of age, with signs accompanying exercise.

OSTEOSARCOMA OR BONE CANCER

Extensive and expensive diagnostic testing may be necessary to find the site(s) of osteosarcoma or bone cancer. X ray imaging, ultrasound, blood tests, and occasionally exploratory surgery are used to discover the extent and severity of the disease. Computerized tomography (CT or CAT scans) produce three-dimensional images of internal structures, as does magnetic resonance imaging (MRI), and these techniques are used as well.

After the cancer sites are identified, treatment can be started. To the best of today's knowledge, cancer isn't a single entity. It's a disease complex that invades many different types of body tissues. Cancer destroys normal body cells and replaces them with cancer cells. Cancer is a leading cause of canine deaths that can be difficult to understand, and much more difficult to treat. Whether cancer responds to treatment depends on the cancer cell type, the degree of progression, the tissues invaded, and the dog's general health.

Cancer therapy may consist of different techniques, including surgical removal, cryosurgery, which destroys cancer cells by freezing, killing the cancer cells by chemical means, or destroying cancer with radiation such as X ray. Often a combination of these techniques is necessary. Surgery and radiation (X ray) are most often used for localized or primary cancer, and chemotherapy is frequently used for systemic cancers that have already spread to various body tissues. Therapy isn't necessarily successful in spite of the veterinarian's talent and knowledge and the use of all available methods of treatment.

Large dogs have a higher incidence of bone cancer than their smaller cousins, with the Saint Bernard and Great Dane being most frequently affected. One study of 130 dogs suffering from osteosarcoma found only six that weighed less than thirty pounds. Sometimes cancer seems to follow bone injury, sometimes it accompanies stress or frequent mechanical trauma in the very large dogs, and other times it appears to be independent of any predisposing factors. It's prevalent in the forelegs, and often occurs at the lower extremity of the radius (forearm bone), probably associated with high-impact running. Many opinions have been advanced to account for the prevalence of this disease in large breeds, but to the best of my knowledge, none has been proven, and it's mentioned here for information only.

Sometimes cancer in a companion animal raises a very real question. Costs of specialists and diagnostic testing must be considered. Cost and duration of therapy can be a determining factor. The dog's age and condition of the dog is another consideration, as is the probability of complete recovery, the patient's pain and discomfort, and the expected length and quality of life. Only you, the owner, can decide the course to take.

> When your veterinarian suspects cancer based on physical examination, don't despair; prepare!

MISCELLANEOUS BONE PROBLEMS

A number of other conditions are less prevalent, but one or two should be mentioned because they often involve large breeds.

Osteochondritis Dissecans (OCD)

Predisposition for osteochondritis dissecans occurs sporadically in many breeds, and is often hereditarily prevalent in large dogs. The disease affects joint cartilage, particularly in the shoulder and elbow, and is usually manifested by sudden lameness at about six months of age. It is often medicated, but definitive therapy is surgical. Conservative therapy using glucosamine plus chondroitin has shown mixed success.

Genu Valgum and Genu Varum

Genu means "the knee," and *valgum* refers to the deformity in which the knees are abnormally close together (knocked) and the distance between ankles is increased. *Varum* indicates an abnormal separation of the knees (bowed) with lower extremities bent inward. Thus these scientific terms often seen in medical references simply mean knock-kneed and bow-legged. Either of these conditions can be hereditarily related to growth rate, and they both begin at about three to four months of age. Both are commonly seen in giant breeds and are faults listed in most breed standards.

During bone growth and development, a vascular bed must be provided simultaneously with bone tissue. Causes of both of these conditions are thought to be associated with new bone tissue that is laid down rapidly and before sufficient blood vessels are established within the bone tissue to supply adequate nutrition to this growth.

Retained Cartilage Cores

Retained carilage cores refers to the inadequacy of blood vessels within the bones of the foreleg during the growing phase. In this disease, the forelegs bow forward, and the wrists and feet are rotated outward. The cause is associated with the rapidity of growth of big dog puppies.

Preventive Medicine

Veterinary medicine in the new millenium is loaded with technological advances in preventive, diagnostic, and therapeutic developments. Breaking the surface is a wide range of biological products being marketed, including new vaccines and unique methods of parasite control. Because preventable diseases and parasitism are commonplace in America and are well documented in breed books and canine health books, discussion of them here will be limited to questions often asked with regard to big dogs.

Remember that parasites are often missed because they usually can't be seen with the naked eye. If you travel with Greta and exercise her at highway rest stops on-lead, you will protect her from the usual injuries such as car accidents and dogfights. However, a leash does nothing to prevent exposure to parasites. Even if your home region of the country doesn't harbor a particular parasite, remember that these exercise areas are used by dogs from all parts of the world, and may be seeded with every type of parasite. Greta will sniff around, grateful for the chance to move about, explore, and investigate, and at the same time, may expose herself to various new bugs and worms.

A tick attaches itself, and before you find it, Greta is infected with Lyme disease. She gets a couple of fleas, snaps at them, takes a few

> **Regardless of the cost, preventive measures are cheaper than therapy.**

home, and a few weeks later she has a tapeworm and your yard is infested. She sniffs a pile of dog manure and is instantly exposed to parvo- or corona virus. She sits on a sandy knoll and is exposed to hookworm larva. You camp by a lake and the mosquitoes are loaded with heartworm larva.

Don't leave your big partner at home, but show your route map to your veterinarian before leaving on your trip, and ask about internal and external parasites of the regions you plan to visit. Start her on heartworm preventive if advised. Ask about flea and tick control, even if Greta doesn't encounter them in your backyard. A few weeks after your return, take a stool sample to your veterinarian for intestinal parasite evaluation. If you find Greta scratching or otherwise uncomfortable while on the trip, look her over carefully for external parasites such as fleas, ticks, and lice.

ACTIVE IMMUNITY

Often, owners think their gigantic puppies are invincible; their size alone is so impressive that their immunity is assumed. How can so much puppy be susceptible to a little tiny bug? Let's face it, you're anxious to show off your puppy partner! That attitude may cost your partner's life if you succumb to the enticement of a walk in the park before Greta is well immunized.

She should remain in the safety of her back-yard and forgo the association with other dogs until her immunity to various common diseases is assured. To take her on the streets at a young age is a grave human error and is responsible for many devastating illnesses. A viral exposure theoretically can cause the production of antibodies, but it also may overwhelm the pup and cause death before antibody production reaches a protective level.

Immunity to a disease may be conferred by vaccination or by a natural exposure to and recovery from the disease. In either case, the introduced virus or vaccine antigen stimulates within the dog the production of specialized protein molecules called antibodies. Antibodies are transitory and don't endure forever; therefore their production must be continued for extended periods of time, or production must periodically be renewed by another exposure or booster vaccination.

Antigenicity refers to the potency of a virus or vaccine and its relative capability to stimulate antibody production. When a virus or vaccine causes antibody production, the protection that forms within the animal is called active immunity, which may be high or low, depending on several factors. These conditions include the age and health of the puppy, and the antigenicity of the virus.

In a perfect situation the vaccinated pup is old enough to produce antibodies, in good condition, and in excellent nutritional status. If the antigenicity of the vaccine is high, a great number of antibodies will result from vaccination, and Greta will be immune to the disease.

Similarly, if Greta is quite immature, weakened, stressed, in questionable nutritional status because of parasitism, or otherwise

Don't expose Greta to other dogs and people till she is properly immunized.

Fleas are the secondary hosts for tapeworms.

suffering compromised health, she will be a perfect target for a disease-causing virus! It's true that minor exposure to a virus with low antigenicity may cause a minor disease, and that upon recovery, immunity will be excellent. However, a light exposure in a weakened puppy may kill the pup. Vaccination and immunization

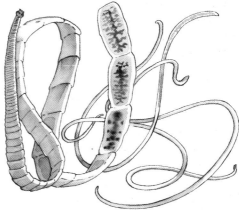

Closeup of the tapeworm.

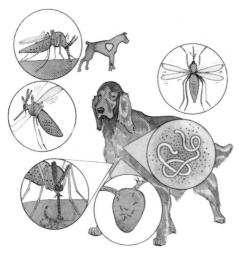

Mosquitoes spread heartworm larvae.

aren't necessarily synonymous. Don't play Russian roulette with your big partner!

VACCINES

Some vaccines are made from live, altered, or modified viruses that reproduce in the vaccinated animal and cause excellent antibody production. Consequently, live virus products tend to produce longer-term immunity than killed-virus vaccines. Other vaccines are made from killed viruses, and others contain only a portion of a virus particle, which also stimulates antibody production. Some vaccines aren't viruses at all, but instead are killed bacterial products called bacterins. All of these agents stimulate the production of antibodies and therefore produce active immunity.

PASSIVE IMMUNITY

As a newborn, Greta has innate protection from diseases for which her dam has immunity. A portion of the dam's antibodies are transferred to her puppies before birth, and more are supplied in her colostrum, or first milk. Because the dam provides her pups with antibody protection,

but doesn't provide the means for producing more antibodies, this temporary protection is termed fleeting or passive immunity.

While very young, Greta's immature immune system is unable to produce antibodies. Within a few weeks those antibodies donated by her mother disappear, and at a certain point Greta's health is at risk. That's the point when human intervention is critical!

Through research, and by laboratory testing, the life of antibodies against each of the dangerous diseases has been calculated, which tells veterinarians when to vaccinate a puppy. This is an inexact determination, an estimation, and is applied in general terms.

Immunity is the state of resistance to a particular disease and is proportionate to the production, quality, and quantity of antibodies.

HOW MUCH?

Big puppies are given the same dose of vaccine as their smaller cousins. A Chihuahua receives a dose of vaccine identical to that injected into a Newfoundland. The number of virus particles in a dose of vaccine exceeds that required to stimulate protective antibody production. Usually, booster vaccinations are scheduled to assure that Greta will produce a safe level of active immunity when her immune system is mature.

Orphan puppies may be born with a deficit of antibody protection if they did not partake of any colostral milk. These pups are at risk at an early age and must be isolated from exposure until they are sufficiently mature to react positively to vaccination.

A few big dogs, notably Alaskan Malamutes, are reported to be particularly difficult to immunize for distemper and possibly other viral diseases. Vaccinations are often repeated at regular intervals during northern dogs' first year of life.

WHEN?

Meaningless idioms cloud the public eye when discussing vaccination schedules. Some literature states that all pups should be vaccinated at six weeks and should have three boosters, given at three-week intervals. The truth is, vaccination schedules differ in every region of the United States, and more importantly, they change according to the veterinarian seen.

Why don't veterinarians agree? The answer is that dogs aren't inanimate cookie cutter creations. They are as individual as we humans are! Maternal antibodies may block vaccination effectiveness in some young pups, puppy health varies, some diseases are prevalent in certain areas but not in others, and natural disease exposure potential is never the same in two situations.

Recently, some veterinarians have reported adverse tissue reactions to various combination vaccines (three-way, four-way, and seven-way)

and they've stopped administering them for that reason. The current discussion regarding *Leptospirosis* is a typical example. Reactions are being reported after injecting the lepto vaccine. What disease risk is involved? Is the species of *Leptospira* included in the vaccine different from the species occurring in your area?

Is cross-immunity a factor? Is lepto prevalent where you live? Ask your veterinarian whether Greta should be vaccinated for lepto, because a consensus among worldwide veterinarians isn't apt to be reached soon.

A vaccination program should fit each individual. One pup has one problem and another has a different condition that might affect immunization. Breed differences may affect immunity. Identical vaccination schedules may serve veterinarians well, but be a mistake for Greta!

If you are vaccinating your partner without consulting a veterinarian, the best advice is to purchase the best and freshest vaccine available, don't buy from mail order catalogs, follow product directions to the letter, begin earlier than you believe necessary, and keep your fingers crossed.

In a British guide dog organization, vaccination was begun at six weeks of age in the 1960s because the pups were raised and socialized in foster homes, and early isolation to minimize exposure wasn't possible. The effectiveness of this early vaccination program was proven in the 1980s when parvovirus was running rampant, and those guide dog puppies suffered much lower mortality rates than other pups.

If you are committed to early vaccination, boosters need to be repeated at regular intervals, and only the highest quality vaccines should be given. The best advice is to rely on your veterinarian's counsel; don't gamble with your big partner's life.

BOOSTERS

Canine diseases are numerous, and vaccine manufacturers often market combination products that are less expensive than the sum of individual vaccines. For instance, combined vaccines against canine distemper, hepatitis, leptospirosis, parainfluenza, parvovirus, and others are available. However, tracheobronchitis (Bordetella), Lyme, and rabies vaccines usually are packaged individually.

It has been proven that some vaccines confer longer immunity than others. For instance, immunizing agents against lepto confer shorter immunity than modified live distemper vaccines. Therefore, when used, lepto vaccination should be given more often than distemper vaccination. However, a dose of lepto vaccine may cost more than the combination of several of the above products. Do you pay the price to administer lepto by itself, or do you ask for a combination vaccine?

Some veterinarians have begun to use blood analysis to determine which vaccine is actually needed, and base their preventive program on these blood tests, which often cost a great deal more than a combination booster.

Regardless of what school of thought your veterinary counselor endorses, vaccinations are heartily recommended for Greta, and boosters are recommended as well.

PREVENTABLE DISEASES

For a thorough discussion of preventable diseases, consult any breed book or dog health book. Here, we'll mention the bare essentials as they pertain to big dogs. Greta probably has the same susceptibility as smaller house pets, but usually she's outside and may be exposed to other dogs.

> Never expose your big dog partner to strange dogs until your veterinarian tells you she is adequately immunized.

Canine Distemper (CD)

Canine distemper is now rare because of vaccine quality. When it is seen, the disease is as devastating now as it was forty years ago! Known in the past as *hard pad* or *dog plague*, it usually causes death, because there is no reliable cure. Usually spread by contact, air borne sneezes and coughs, its signs include cough, lack of appetite, high temperature, ocular discharge, greenish nasal discharge, discolored teeth (in cases of disease recovery), convulsions, nervous twitching, paralysis, and death. Puppies may die suddenly, without displaying any signs.

Canine Hepatitis (CAV-1)

Rare in recent years, the canine hepatitis virus, also known as CAV-1 (canine adenovirus, type 1), also can cause sudden death without symptoms. Hepatitis is often a liver disease, but blood vessels and other organs are affected as well. Its exposure and signs are similar to those seen with CD. One of the telltale signs of this disease is corneal edema, or the *blue eye* syndrome.

Leptospirosis

Leptospirosis, or lepto, as it is often known, is principally a disease of the kidneys and thrives in aquatic regions inhabited by rodents. Muskrats and other water rodents often act as reservoir hosts for lepto and spread the disease in their urine. Signs in the dog are kidney pain, bloody or orange-colored urine, loss of appetite, and fever.

Kennel Cough

Universally, kennel cough is a problematical disease indeed! The croupy cough caused by a number of bacteria and viruses seems to last forever but usually isn't fatal. Exposure is by aerosol, or airborne particles, and usually includes the bacteria known as *Bordetella bronchiseptica*. Some of the viruses that accompany infection are parainfluenza, distemper, CAV-2, and others. Parainfluenza is usually included in canine vaccine combinations.

Parvovirus

Possibly a mutant strain of the feline distemper virus (FPV), canine parvovirus was first recorded in 1978. It's a highly virulent, easily transmitted virus that is often fatal to unimmunized pups. It causes watery diarrhea, vomiting, dehydration, high temperature, and heart disease. In puppies, the virus can cause sudden heart failure without other signs. It is easily spread by stepping in or sniffing affected dogs' stools, even those that are several months old. This hardy virus is highly resistant to common disinfectants, and is one of the major reasons for not taking Greta out of her yard until she is well immunized. Unfortunately, passive immunity from colostral milk is notably weak and often won't protect puppies. The mortality rate is high without aggressive treatment, and even then is significant, since there is no effective antiviral agent.

Corona Virus

Corona virus is another gastrointestinal virus causing signs similar to parvovirus, and is often mistaken for that disease by dog owners. It can be differentiated by blood testing, but usually it is treated similarly. The prognosis is guarded in every case, and the mortality rate often is about the same as parvo.

Lyme Disease

Named for a small town in Connecticut, Lyme disease is now the most common tick-related disease in America. Tiny deer ticks, also parasites of cattle, horses, elk, moose, dogs, cats, and man, act as vectors (transmitters) of Lyme

disease. *Borrelia burgdorferi* is the causative agent for Lyme disease, which also may be transmitted by black-legged ticks and other biting insects. At first seen only in the East, it is now recognized in nearly every region of the United States. Lyme disease signs are fever, sluggishness, joint pain and associated lameness, lymph node swelling, and loss of appetite. A specific blood test is available that will aid your veterinarian in diagnosing Lyme, and a vaccine is available.

Treatment is possible using a wide range of antibiotics, but early diagnosis is critical to success. Don't forget to minimize exposure by maximizing your tick prevention program!

Rabies

Because many big dogs are also hunting dogs, hounds, and other outdoor varieties, they are more likely to come in contact with outdoor fauna. The American Veterinary Medical Association (AVMA) reported 126 confirmed cases of rabies in dogs in 1997. Rabies reservoirs are virtually all warm-blooded animals, especially coyotes, foxes, raccoons, bats, ferrets, skunks, and wolves. This fatal disease remains continuously present in most of America, including the forty-eight contiguous states, Mexico, and Canada. The Centers for Disease Control (CDC) reported 6,280 cases of animal rabies during the first ten months of 1999.

The rabies virus travels by nerve trunks to the salivary glands, thence to the brain. An infected animal soon dies. One sign of infection is paralysis of the throat, resulting in copious stringy saliva drooling from the mouth. In *dumb* rabies, the dog staggers about until death. In *furious* rabies, the infected dog takes offense at the slightest provocation, attacking and biting anything in its path, whether animate or inanimate.

This is a zoonotic disease (transmittable to humans) for which excellent vaccines are available. Canine vaccination is mandated by local and federal ordinances.

Nosodes

If you are a follower of homeopathy, you will see nosodes advertised. These tissue preparations taken from diseased animals are given instead of vaccinations. Canine immunology experts warn against using this approach because it isn't effective and ***will fail if challenged by virulent disease-causing agents.***

Emergencies

How do you determine if a situation is truly an emergency? The following conditions emphatically describe the emergencies that are discussed in this chapter.

- Shock
- Hemorrhage
- Bloat
- Persistent vomiting or vomiting blood
- Sudden increase in water consumption
- Bloody diarrhea or diarrhea that worsens with time
- Lack of appetite for more than forty-eight hours
- High fever
- Choking and pawing persistently at face
- Sudden lameness or deviation of bones
- Automobile accident
- Unexplained seizures
- Anytime your common sense tells you Barney is definitely sick

Record Barney's normal vital signs on the chart on page 74, copy it, and place it in your first aid kit. Only by knowing his normal vital signs can you recognize abnormalities when they occur. Ask your veterinarian about canine first aid and CPR courses that might be offered, and sign up for one.

> **You can't prevent emergencies, but you can be prepared for them.**

FIRST AID KIT

> *These items should fit into a small nylon pack that can be carried on Barney's collar or on your belt.*

Like all travelers, Barney should carry a first aid kit when traveling away from home. Being a big dog, he can carry the kit himself with no trouble. It should include the following items in addition to your cell phone:

- Your veterinarian's phone number, because 911 won't put you in touch with canine emergency personnel.
- Antibiotic cream, 1 tube
- Bandage roll, 3-inch gauze
- Cotton balls, 1 small package
- Eyewash or a bottle of artificial tears to flush foreign material from his eyes
- Disinfectant, 3 percent hydrogen peroxide solution
- Muzzle, 4-foot length of soft cotton rope
- Pad and pencil
- Scissors, blunt tipped or bandage scissors
- Soap for cleaning skin wounds (liquid organic iodine type)
- Syringe, 12-cc capacity for flushing wounds or administering oral medication
- Styptic stick, for minor torn nail bleeding
- Tape, one roll of 2-inch adhesive
- Thermometer, rectal, electronic, or mercury

Average Normal Vital Signs

Pulse Rate	70 to 90 per minute: Taken by placing your finger inside his thigh, slightly above the stifle. It generally is slower in big dogs.
Pulse Character	Strong and steady: Easily felt with each heartbeat.
Temperature	101.5°F (38.5°C): Rectal temperature when dog is at rest. Barney's normal temperature may be a degree or more below that.
Respiration	10 to 30 per minute: Counted when dog is resting. A big dog's respiration rate may be on the low side of normal.
Respiratory Character	Even and deep: Taken during rest, not when panting.
Mucous Membranes	Color of gums, inside of lips, and tongue should be bright pink, moist.
Capillary Filling Time	2 seconds: Evaluated by pressing finger against gums, then recording time required for white impression to return to normal pink.
Eye Appearance	Bright cornea, clear and moist, without notable blood vessel enlargement or yellowish discoloration of sclera (white).

Barney's Normal Vital Signs

At Rest		Immediately After Exercise
_____	Pulse Rate	_____
_____	Pulse Character	_____
_____	Temperature	_____
_____	Respiratory Rate	_____
_____	Respiratory Character	_____
_____	Mucous Membrane	_____
_____	Capillary Filling Time	_____
_____	Eye Appearance	_____

- Tourniquet, or a foot of latex tubing
- Tweezers, or a pair of inexpensive hemostatic forceps
- Vital signs chart

CARDIOPULMONARY RESUSCITATION (CPR) AND ARTIFICIAL RESPIRATION (AR)

Barney has suffered a horrendous accident. He is lying prostrate before you and shows no evidence of respiration. What do you do?

You should begin artificial respiration first. Open his mouth and quickly clear his throat by wiping away mucus with a pocket handkerchief, necktie, shirttail, or other handy cloth. Straighten his neck to align his respiratory passage. Close his mouth and open yours. Place your lips tightly over his muzzle, and blow into his nostrils until his chest rises. Blow gently, but with sufficient force to inflate his lungs. In young puppies, the amount of air exchanged should be considerably less than for an adult dog. Remove your mouth, allowing Barney to exhale. Repeat this procedure about ten times per minute until he begins to breathe on his own.

Barney's heartbeat will indicate the spot where CPR is performed. The exact location is impossible to determine if the heart has stopped, but is easily found in a normal dog—hence the reason for examining him while he is healthy. Lay him on his right side, and note where his left elbow is positioned. Move the elbow slightly forward, and with your other hand, slowly run your fingers over his rib cage; the beating will be quite apparent. Make a mental note of this spot.

Cardiopulmonary resuscitation (CPR) should be used only if no heartbeat can be felt.

The purpose is to manually compress Barney's heart, which should supply blood to his brain and other vital tissues. The technique is simple. Position Barney on his right side and place the heel of your hand (or your clenched fist) on his rib cage over his heart. Firmly compress the rib cage to about half its thickness, then release suddenly. Repeat this chest compression-massage once every second until a heartbeat is detected.

If help is available, ask a friend to perform the CPR while you continue artificial respiration. Once his respiration and heartbeat have returned, cover him with a coat or blanket, and move him to an emergency veterinary clinic quickly.

Attend a canine first aid course or ask your veterinarian to demonstrate CPR and AR.

SHOCK

Blood pressure falls precipitously in shock, but this symptom is difficult to ascertain in dogs, so Barney's vital signs are used instead. In order to stabilize a shock victim, owners need to be aware of their partner's normal vital signs and act quickly to evaluate abnormalities. Shock is a complex multisymptom condition, one for which you must be on the alert when an emergency arises. Barney may present any or all of the signs described below. He may be unconscious or alert, anxious or depressed, feverish or cold.

Signs of shock include pale or bluish mucous membranes, including

Shock is difficult to define because it occurs in many different situations and involves various predisposing factors.

gums and tongue, prolonged capillary filling time, rapid and shallow respiration, weak and thready pulse, and a rapid heart rate.

Shock may be the result of an incident causing internal or external hemorrhage, or blunt trauma. It may be associated with severe animal bites, chemical poisoning, puncture wounds, or snakebites. Shock also is seen in cases of acute allergic reaction to antibiotics or other drugs. Gastric dilatation, torsion, and volvulus is another condition that results in shock. In shorthaired breeds, anaphylactic shock can be cause by massive bee stings, especially those caused by Africanized bees.

Shock is often progressive, and even when help is obtained immediately, it's a common cause of death. When shock is suspected, control hemorrhaging, try to maintain Barney's body temperature, and transport him to a veterinarian quickly. Anti-shock injections such as steroids, epinephrine, intravenous infusions of whole blood, plasma expanders, coagulants, and electrolytes may be used to combat shock and, hopefully, prevent death.

> **If in doubt, muzzle first, then examine.**

When handling a dog in shock, don't put your own body at risk. Take precautions to protect yourself from being bitten by an animal that is gasping for breath, regardless of how well you know him. You can't help your partner if you are incapacitated. This big dog has tremendous power in his jaws and can break your hand bones if you aren't very careful!

MUZZLE

Gentle dogs may snap or bite viciously when in shock, when frightened, or when in pain. Barney will be confused and disoriented when he is hurt. Approach him slowly, keep your voice calm, and speak in low, soothing tones. Extend your hand, but don't grab at him. Avoid direct eye contact with him, and if he shows any apprehension, apply a muzzle before you proceed. Remember, time is important, and helping your partner means handling him.

Take the piece of rope from your first aid kit, tie a loose single knot in the center of the cord, and slip the loop over his closed jaws. Pull the knot snugly on top of his muzzle immediately forward of the stop. Extend the ends of the cord beneath his lower jaw and tie another single knot, then wrap both ends of the cord behind his ears and tie a slipknot. If you don't have a muzzle-cord in your first aid kit, tear a four-foot strip of gauze from a bandage roll, twist it, and substitute it for the cord. If gauze or a cord isn't available, use a long shoestring, necktie, or other cordlike material.

CAR ACCIDENTS

Big dogs, especially puppies, are clumsy and may have difficulty getting out of the way of traffic. If a car hits Barney, you must act quickly to determine whether your best course is an immediate trip to the veterinarian, or he first should be treated at the accident scene to control hemorrhage.

Prevention is the surest way to protect Barney from car accidents. Keep him on a leash!

Use your cell phone to call Barney's veterinarian, tell him who you are, that your dog has been struck by a car, and that you are en route to the clinic.

Control any visible hemorrhage with pressure bandages, then wrap him up and keep him quiet and warm. Don't try to straighten out broken legs. You will only exacerbate hemorrhage and increase pain. Use a board, jacket, or blanket as a stretcher on which to transport Barney. Time is of the essence!

HEATSTROKE

Dogs' sweat glands are amazingly few and ineffective. Thus canine cooling is primarily accomplished by panting, which is an inefficient process at best. Heavily coated dogs are particularly at risk, as are obese dogs. Ambient temperatures more than 100°F are all dangerous, but the worst danger occurs when dogs are locked in automobiles.

Predisposition to heatstroke is primarily caused by the large dog's increased body mass compared with its limited surface area. When a tiny pebble is heated to a given temperature, it cools more rapidly than a larger stone of the same composition heated to exactly the same temperature. Likewise, a small dog has a greater surface area per ounce of body weight, and will dissipate heat more quickly. Small dogs suffer from heatstroke, but big dogs are at greater risk by virtue of size alone. Heat retention also is somewhat dependent on coat. That is, if you have a Newfoundland with a heavy double coat, he will be at greater risk for heatstroke than a slick-coated Mastiff of the same weight. As implied, this devastating condition relates to brain damage brought about by abnormally high temperatures.

Heatstroke can occur in minutes and is manifested by body temperatures between 105 and 110°F. In addition to high body temperature, signs include production of thick stringy saliva and rapid, open-mouth breathing, accompanied by bright red mucous membranes. Within a few minutes, the dog develops a staggering gait and eventually becomes comatose. Blood pressure falls, membranes become pallid, and death follows if the signs aren't reversed. Heatstroke is an emergency, and no time can be wasted before initiating treatment.

If possible, monitor your partner's body temperature as you begin therapy. Treatment should aim at reducing his body temperature. Application of cool water in copious quantities is best. Run water from a garden hose over Barney's body or immerse him in a tub of water; place a fan at a safe distance from the water and point it at him. Don't use tubs of ice or ice cold water, because extremely cold water will cause superficial blood vessels to constrict, which acts to slow cooling and exacerbates the condition. Make cool, fresh water available to the dog and encourage him to drink, but don't pour it down his throat. Stop the cooling process

In the summer, a closed car, even on a cloudy day, will often reach a temperature of more than 150 degrees!

when his temperature reaches about 104 or 103°F, because cooling will continue once the process is started, and the target temperature is about 100°F.

PREVENTION

- Provide shade in Barney's yard.
- Supply Barney with a child's swimming pool filled with fresh water daily.
- Make fresh drinking water available to him at all times.
- Don't tie Barney. The chain may tangle, leaving him in the sun.
- If Barney's coat is long, consider shaving him in the summer.
- Consider leaving Barney inside your air-conditioned house or install a dog door.

POISONING

A presumptive diagnosis of poisoning might be considered if Barney begins vomiting from no obvious cause, becomes suddenly weak, shows evidence of shock, or begins convulsing. Smell his breath. Try to find the source of the poison. Look in the garage and garden shed for open containers. If you find it, check the label for an antidote or treatment. If the likely poison is unknown, check Barney's vital signs, then hasten him to the veterinary clinic.

Record the poison control phone number on Barney's first aid kit.

If the poison is identified and its product label instructs you to induce vomiting, you can accomplish that by placing about a teaspoonful of salt on the back of Barney's tongue. A tablespoonful of hydrogen peroxide may be given orally to produce vomiting. Syrup of ipecac may be administered, but it frequently is slow to work.

Poisoning treatment generally is a task for an emergency veterinary clinic. Be sure you know where the nearest clinic is and the fastest way to get there.

POISONOUS PLANTS

- Azalea causes nausea and vomiting.
- Bird of paradise causes nausea and vomiting.
- Bulbs generally are poisonous.
- Castor bean causes vomiting and diarrhea.
- Dieffenbachia causes oral irritation and salivation.
- Delphinium causes nausea and slowed heartbeat.
- Elephant ear causes oral irritation and salivation.
- Hydrangea causes cyanide poisoning.
- Jasmine causes vomiting and diarrhea.
- Laurel causes nausea and vomiting.
- Lily of the valley causes heart problems.
- Mescal bean causes nausea and vomiting.
- Poisonous mushrooms cause acute digestive, liver, and kidney damage.

Outdoor plant eating isn't just a destructive hobby of your big partner; it can cause far worse trouble. Check your yard for these poisonous plants, and fence Barney away from them.

- Nightshade causes oral irritation and salivation.
- Poinsettia causes oral irritation.
- Prunus causes cyanide poisoning.
- Yellow jasmine causes convulsions.
- Yews (taxus species) causes stomach and heart problems.

CHOCOLATE POISONING

Big dogs often consume everything that appears edible, regardless of where it is found. If you bake or make candy, keep Barney out of the kitchen. As you know, your big partner has a tremendous capacity, and is tall enough to reach the goodies. Like all intelligent creatures, he undoubtedly will have a taste for chocolate. It's extremely unlikely he'll show signs of poisoning when he steals a bonbon of two from the coffee table, but if ingested in sufficient quantity, chocolate is quite toxic to dogs.

Baking chocolate has the highest alkaloid content (400 mg per ounce) and is the most likely form to cause poisoning. Dark chocolate, with an alkaloid content of 150 mg per ounce, and milk chocolate, with 50 mg per ounce, are less toxic but more readily available. For an eighty-pound dog, 40,000 mg of alkaloid, or the amount found in 100 ounces of baking chocolate, usually will cause death. Much less can cause mild signs of poisoning such as nervousness, vomiting, diarrhea, and urinary incontinence. More severe signs include excitement, panting, seizures, and possibly death. If Barney consumes a significant amount of chocolate, call your veterinarian, or induce vomiting as described below.

> If you have containers of chocolate in any form on your table at any time, remember your big dog's appetite and height. Always put away the chocolate when you leave the room.

If you've determined that Barney's made a recent chocolate foray, mix 3 percent hydrogen peroxide with an equal quantity of water, and using a turkey baster, administer about one-half ounce per ten pounds body weight to cause vomiting. If no emesis is seen within ten minutes, repeat the dosage. Don't give a third dose!

Activated charcoal may be given to adsorb the chocolate's toxin. If you'd like to add this excellent remedy to your first aid kit, you can purchase it from health food stores in capsule form. The correct dosage is 1.25 grams per pound of the dog's body weight, orally, mixed in two to four ounces of water. Repeat this dosage every two to four hours.

WOUNDS

If Barney steps on a broken bottle, a sharp tin can, or cuts himself on barbed wire, quickly evaluate the extent of his injuries. If the wound is large or is bleeding profusely, immediately apply a pressure bandage and get him to a veterinarian. If the injury is only a minor scratch or tiny skin tear, clip the hair away from wound edges, clean with an antiseptic soap, apply antibiotic cream, and bandage if possible.

Lacerations involving only the foot pad may not require veterinary care, but should be bandaged to prevent further injury, contamination, and pain. After cleaning and application

> Always take your first aid kit when leaving your yard with your big dog. It can save his life.

of antibiotic cream, place a snug but nonrestrictive bandage on the wounded foot and tape it in place. If you carry protective boots for Barney, this is the time to use them.

SEVERE HEMORRHAGE

Occasionally a big dog may suffer a severe laceration from machinery or a hidden glass shard, or suffer some other similar accident. Profuse bleeding is best handled by locating the source of the spurting blood and applying a snug bandage (pressure bandage) directly over the source to quell the hemorrhage. Tie or tape the bandage securely in place and keep Barney quiet. Use your jacket or blanket as a stretcher, and handle him minimally to prevent further damage.

> **Don't hesitate to grasp and pinch the cut end of a bleeding artery if it is visible and that is the most expedient way to stop bleeding.**

Using your fingers to stop hemorrhage is okay if the arterial bleeder can be found. The contamination you introduce with your bare hand is significantly easier to treat than the blood loss Barney may suffer before you can obtain professional help.

TOURNIQUET

Tourniquet application is rarely necessary and should be considered only when there is no other way to stop bleeding. Use the rubber tube from your first aid kit or fashion a tourniquet from a strip of gauze, a shoelace, a necktie, or a belt. When properly placed, a tourniquet slows the flow of arterial blood from the heart to the injured body part, but allows some venous blood to return to the

> **When a tourniquet is used, tighten it only enough to stop the severe hemorrhage and release it for a few seconds every fifteen minutes.**

heart from the leg. If hemorrhage from Barney's foot wound can't be stopped with a pressure bandage, place a tourniquet just above his ankle. If the wound is on the trunk of the body, the head, or upper leg, a tourniquet can't be employed, and a pressure bandage or finger pressure should be used to stop the hemorrhage.

DEEP PUNCTURES

When running in the woods, Barney may impale himself on a sharp stick or rusty nail. If the cause of the puncture isn't visible, watch for bleeding, and apply a pressure bandage if needed. When possible, determine the cause of the puncture. If it was caused by a stick that might have broken off and remains in his flesh; leave it alone. Make no attempt to remove the wood shard. If you attempt to remove the stick, you might cause increased hemorrhage or leave a piece of the stick lodged deep in the tissues where it is difficult to find.

> **Treat stab wounds with extreme caution, because the extent of damage is unknown.**

Devise a stretcher and carry Barney to your car; keep him quiet and transport him to a veterinarian immediately. Even if you're certain the wound was caused by a nail that has been removed, a visit to Barney's veterinarian is indicated. All deep puncture wounds should be professionally examined to determine whether or not the wound has foreign material trapped within it. Always ask your veterinarian about the need for tetanus antitoxin; the tetanus bacteria likes puncture environments.

NOSEBLEEDS

In the case of a nosebleed, first analyze the reason for the bleeding. If caused by a bump or blunt trauma to Barney's snout, the hemorrhagic crisis usually is self-limiting, and will be alleviated by keeping him quiet for half an hour. If more copious bleeding is seen, apply cold packs to his muzzle for several minutes and keep him quiet for half an hour after the bleeding stops.

> **Bloody noses are common, and usually aren't dangerous.**

If you don't know what caused the bleeding, keep him quiet and call your veterinarian. Such cases may be associated with foreign objects such as foxtails or cheat-grass seeds that have lodged in his nasal cavity. Several specific bleeding disorders may be associated with bloody noses, and if the condition is repeated, take Barney to your veterinarian for diagnosis.

SNAKEBITE

Snakebite is uncommon in urban and suburban locales, but if Barney invades the countryside, beware of rattlesnakes and other poisonous vipers. At least one of the fifteen different species of rattlers is found in most states, especially in dry and farming areas. Rattlers usually are nocturnal, but may be found during the day

> **Rattlers usually warn dogs with their tail to stay away from their other end.**

sleeping on rocks, in hollow logs, on rocky ground, and in burrows made by other animals. Although their rattle is a warning that will usually cause you to stop and look quickly, the same isn't true of a nosey big dog.

Snake venom can cause a multitude of signs, but breathing difficulty and shock are quite common. Buy a book that identifies poisonous snakes, and be aware of the poisonous snake population of the area in which you are hiking. Snakebite wounds are small paired wounds on a lip, muzzle, ear, leg, or cheek. Sometimes you won't see the snake that inflicted the wound, in which case you must quickly evaluate the situation and act accordingly.

The most important snakebite first aid is to keep your canine partner quiet. Don't let him run back to the car. Ask a friend to bring the car to where Barney is, or fashion a stretcher from a jacket or blanket and carry him. Call your veterinarian and advise her of the situation, then hasten to the clinic. Usually antivenin is injected, shock therapy is instituted, and Barney's vital signs are closely monitored. Sometimes a large area of skin sloughs away from the fang marks, but this will heal in time.

PORCUPINE QUILLS

I've seen porky quills in every conceivable part of canine anatomy! Porcupines are quite common in western Colorado and many other wooded areas of the United States.

> **Don't wait till morning to call your veterinarian for quill removal. Some are driven into the flesh so deeply they can't be found the next day!**

These lumbering creatures live on green bark and new tree growth and are especially fond of fruit trees, so they often invade backyards near woodlands. They have no natural predators (except armed humans), and porky populations often increase as humans build homes in pristine country. Porkies are a terrible nuisance, and under some circumstances can cause the death of a dog that is minding his own business in his own backyard.

I'm personally aware of a number of dog deaths associated with porcupine quills. Some dogs apparently rubbed their faces and broke off quills that were lodged in the proximity of the eyes. The quills apparently migrated into the skull, penetrating the brain behind the eye, causing encephalitis and death.

Bizarre signs often accompanied infections carried by quills migrating into livers, lungs, and spleens. On one occasion, a single one-inch-long quill (2.5 cm) had apparently struck a dog's scrotum, penetrated a testicle, migrated into the spermatic cord, and was found by exploratory surgery. The quill wasn't visible on X ray and if not removed might have migrated into the kidney or other internal organ. That dog lived in a fenced backyard, the owners never saw a porcupine, the dog wasn't known to have been quilled, and that single quill seemed to have been the only one spared by the porky. It proved to be quite enough!

Quills may cause a multitude of health problems as they migrate through vital tissues, causing mysterious and challenging clinical signs and strange laboratory results. If a dog has a documented porcupine encounter, and covert signs are observed in ensuing days and weeks, thought should be given to migrating quills.

Contrary to some opinions, a porky can't throw its quills, but typically will spin around with tail swinging, swatting everything within reach. If the tail comes in contact with a dog,

it will bury hundreds of quills in the dog's flesh. If Barney attempts to bite Mrs. Porcupine, he will genuinely regret the encounter and may find his mouth filled with quills stuck deep into his gums, lips, tongue, palate, and quite a few in his face. Mrs. Porcupine lumbers off, chuckling to herself.

The black quill tip that is buried in the flesh has a hard sharp point, and quills may be driven deeply into soft tissue. Tiny barbs encircle the quill tip (much like the teeth of a wood rasp), causing pain when removed. Old wives' tales notwithstanding, cutting off the white end of a quill doesn't decrease pressure within the quill to collapse the barbs, and removal isn't a bit easier. Cutting off the end of a quill makes it shorter, more difficult to grasp, and results in less quill on which to apply traction.

Quills are an emergency! A quilled dog isn't on par with a car accident, but it's very important to get the quills out as soon as possible. If not removed before they migrate into deep tissues, they often abscess, and through their migration cause infections and possibly death.

SKUNKS

Big dogs are often curious to a fault! Any animal smaller than they are seems to deserve their attention and investigation. Instead of standing back a safe distance and barking furiously, Barney may stroll up to the striped kitty and put his best nose forward.

Members of the species *Mephitis mephitis,* the common striped skunks have beautiful black and white patterns, fluffy tails, and curious twitchy noses. Those are about all the good things I can say about those pesky little varmints. They love to sneak around outbuildings in the evening hours and often forage in dog dishes, sometimes challenging Barney for his late dinner. Generally, they retreat before human presence, but if hungry, they've been known to stand their ground. They aren't terribly fast on their feet, but why should they be? No sane person would chase a skunk! Big dogs often display their bravery by doing just that. Skunk smell may not be a true emergency, but it's close!

The oily scent from the glands on either side of the anus can be sighted and triggered on a moment's notice, and the disgusting liquid will travel more than six feet, usually hitting the target squarely. The scent is highly disagreeable, both to the olfactory sense and to all mucous membranes reached. If Barney's eyes are open, he may rub and paw at them, but the scent won't cause permanent blindness; natural tear secretion will wash away the offensive scent, and any corneal damage that is done is probably caused by his pawing.

When a skunk looks his antagonist in the eye and stamps his little black feet up and down, take heed and leave before the chemical warfare begins. If Barney hasn't learned his lesson, and is rewarded for his daring with a squirt of this kitty's odoriferous scent, here are a few treatments you can try. In case of bad weather conditions, you might repair to the garage, basement, or porch. It won't be a pleasant task no matter where you tackle this situation. If Barney is to be allowed in human society sometime later this week, it's

Skunks by any other name still smell as nasty!

essential to deodorize him quickly and as well as possible.

The old standby remedy for skunk odor on a dog's fur is to bathe him with a mixture of water, vinegar, and canned tomato juice. Work it in well, let it set for several minutes, then rinse and repeat. After these tomato juice treatments, rinse and dry him off. In cold climes it's necessary to keep him inside until he is dry.

Another home remedy suggested is to mix one quart of 3 percent hydrogen peroxide with one-fourth cup of baking soda and one teaspoon of liquid soap. Immediately massage this mixture into the coat, using a sponge to soak the facial hair. The author of this mixture, a chemist, advises that the mixture may bleach the hair, which will grow back normally in time.

Other skunk odor removers are readily available in pet supply stores or on the Internet. If skunks are normal inhabitants in your region of the country, it might pay to keep a quart or two of these deodorizers on hand for emergencies.

If you encounter an aggressive skunk, remember that they have frequently been known to be infected with the rabies virus, and that if rabid, the skunk may not react normally. If you encounter a strange-acting skunk, take Barney in the house and call your animal control officer.

Gastronomic Tribulations

"I have Barney and he's a very large dog; therefore I have no need for a garbage disposal."

Wrong, wrong, wrong! A common misconception among new owners of big dogs is that their canine partners can digest anything. Sometimes these animals are fed everything that slightly resembles food, from lasagna scraps and lettuce leaves to potato peels and peanut shells. Because of their stomach capacity, they have gigantic appetites that sometimes are difficult to satisfy, but their digestive organs and gastrointestinal tracts are no different from those of other domestic canines, and not much different from our own!

Digestive problems can reach disastrous proportions in a large dog like Barney. The diarrhea of a tiny terrier presents a cleanup problem, but it's nothing compared with a giant breed's fecal explosion. For that reason alone, it's always advisable to stay on a sound feeding program and keep a watchful eye on Barney's stool and his diet, including both quantity and quality.

> **Big capacities predispose to big problems.**

There are many causes for chronic soft stools; this problem is quite common in large breeds and warrants immediate attention. Among other causes, a sudden change of diet may precipitate cow-pie stools or diarrhea.

When Barney continually has soft stools, it means that he isn't absorbing all the nutrition supplied in his food; he's being cheated at his dish and you're being cheated at the cash register.

QUANTITY

If Barney is perpetually hungry, that's a signal to investigate his diet to be sure his nutrition and eating habits are sound. If you believe Barney's diet is sound, but his stool is always soft or runny, adjust the quantity fed in each meal.

Divide his daily ration into four equal meals a day instead of one or two larger feedings. Often, this adjustment alone will control the diarrhea problem as well as reduce the probability of bloat, another more dangerous side effect of large meals to be discussed in the following paragraphs.

> **Too much of a good food can be as bad as too little food.**

QUALITY

You've invested in an expensive big dog, so don't skimp on the quality of his food. Cheap dog food of questionable quality is a major cause of chronic loose stools. Skimping on Barney's diet by feeding a diet of table scraps, organ meats, bones, and other garbage may result in chronic gastrointestinal upsets. Ice cream, candy, pizza, potato chips, and other human junk foods are difficult for him to digest and should be avoided.

Intestinal parasites or pica (depraved appetite and craving for foreign, indigestible material) may be other causes of your partner's mushy stool. However, often Barney's great size and stomach capacity are to blame. Your son Tim gives him a bite, just a piece of leftover liver, as a treat.

> **Poor quality food produces poor performance dogs.**

Surely that can't cause diarrhea! Because Barney's so big, the bite is naturally proportional to his weight.

Tiny Kathy feels sorry for Barney and secretly slips him another bite or two of the same leftover liver. Bill helps you with the dishes and sees a perfectly good piece of liver going to waste and tosses it to Barney. The next morning, Barney's stool looks like a gigantic cow plop.

Ask every family member to note everything they feed him, no matter how small the quantity. They should write down exactly what they feed, how much of it, and how often. This includes training treats as well as Barney's meals. Likewise, each should write down the times Barney is seen eating sticks, leaves, dirt, and so forth (pica). It's possible you'll be able to correct his soft stools after considering the amounts of extraneous and indigestible food he eats daily.

If more assistance is needed, record the amounts of the particular foods being fed. Be truthful and list all tidbits in his diet. Measure the amount of water that is poured into his bowl, and record the amount he typically drinks in a day. Take this history to your veterinarian, together with a sample of his stool to check for parasites. If the clinician feels a physical examination is needed, go for it!

HICCUPS

Hiccuping is observed more in big dogs than in their smaller cousins. Big puppies have big appetites and eat with gusto, and the rapidly filling stomach may be a major cause of hiccups. The condition is seen most often in young dogs, usually those less than four or five months old.

Though occasional hiccuping is normal, it may cause consternation. If Barney begins hiccuping shortly after most meals, try any of the following remedies:

- Slow down his eating. The easiest way to accomplish this is to put a softball-sized rock in his bowl with the food. He will need to push it about to get his food, and this process will slow down his eating. If you use this remedy, be sure to use a smooth stone, and run it in the dishwasher at least every day to remove all food particles and bacteria. Don't use any stone that he is capable of swallowing!

- If feeding dry food, buy a feeding cube at your pet supply store, fill it with kernels of dry food, and give him room. He will bat the cube about and eventually retrieve every morsel of food.

> **Big puppies' stomachs usually are empty long before their next meal, and this is thought to cause hiccuping.**

- Antacid liquid given in child's dosage will usually relieve hiccuping within a few minutes. Check with your veterinarian before using any human product for this purpose. Most over-the-counter antacid formulas are harmless, but a few have excessive calcium and other minerals that may cause problems in big puppies.

- Rub Barney's tummy gently while he is standing. This is similar to burping an infant, and will usually relieve the hiccuping within a few minutes.

● If hiccups last more than an hour or two, contact your veterinarian.

"GARBAGITIS" AND PANCREATITIS

Guessing that hunger was sufficient cause for Barney tipping over the garbage can and consuming its contents, you might overlook his indiscretion and forgive him as you clean up the trash bags, tin cans, foil wrappers, and other remnants of his clandestine meal. When you discover he's vomited in the yard, you entertain thoughts such as "serves him right!" You might feel sorry for him when he lacks appetitie for the next couple of days, drinks gallons of water, and is depressed and lethargic. You logically associate these signs with his midnight bingeing, thinking he will be better in a day or two. Serious mistake!

The pancreas is a dual-function organ. In its endocrine (hormonal) role, it produces insulin, which is carried by the bloodstream to regulate glucose absorption by body tissues. The pancreas also is a digestive organ, producing enzymes that are released into ducts that empty into the small intestine and there initiate digestion.

Pancreatitis is an inflammation of this organ, and scientists have reported that most pancreatitis is caused by the obstruction of enzyme excretory ducts. Specific causes of pancreatic inflammation are not well described but usually are associated with abnormal diet and the ingestion of rich, fatty, and sometimes highly seasoned foods. Pancreatitis may cause the organ to release digestive enzymes into the bloodstream instead of into the pancreatic ducts. The effect of these powerful enzymes can be the digestion of the pancreas itself. Untreated or repetitions of pancreatitis may cause death.

This disease occasionally is a side effect of steroid administration or associated with pancreatic tumors, but many cases of pancreatitis are related to garbage eating. It's a disease of middle-aged to older, often obese dogs, especially those who normally eat rich, high-fat diets—in other words, those who indulge in table scraps, bones, trimmings, or leftovers (garbage).

> **Pancreatitis may only cause a bellyache for a day, manifested by periodic vomiting and obvious abdominal pain, or it can lead to death.**

Remember Barney's capacity: he can eat enormous quantities of scraps at a single sitting. With the first sign of vomiting, take his temperature, withhold food, limit his drinking water, and keep him confined and under close observation. If he isn't recovering within twenty-four hours of his surreptitious garbage can plundering, call your veterinarian for advice. Watch for signs of pancreatitis that include high fever, abdominal pain, vomiting,

anorexia (lack of appetite), rapid weight loss, diarrhea, and listlessness. If any of these signs appear, take him to his doctor immediately! Pancreatic tissue destruction also may result in diabetes, chronic indigestion, and inability to properly process nutrients.

Treating pancreatitis may require laboratory diagnostic aids, X rays, and hospitalization where intravenous fluids and antibiotics may be administered. In advanced cases, peritonitis, a very serious inflammation of the abdominal cavity, may follow a pancreatitis episode and require surgical drainage. The intense pain of this disease must be managed as well.

> **Barney chews up bones and swallows them. His habit can be very dangerous to his health.**

IMPACTION

Chicken or chop bones, steak bones, ribs, and some roast bones may splinter when your big dog crunches them. His big teeth can grind some bones into small pieces, but sharp bone shards may catch between his upper molars, or penetrate the membranes of his mouth or throat. They may be swallowed and can cause intestinal penetration, gut irritation, or diarrhea. Another problem that bones cause is colonic impaction. Because of Barney's physical size, impaction or constipation is a definite possibility.

Tiny swallowed bone chips travel without being digested through his small intestine. When this aggregate reaches Barney's large bowel, water is absorbed from the mixture, leaving a dry mass of small bone chips packed into the rectum. The rectum is the final section of the large intestine that normally stores feces between bowel movements and further absorbs water. When the chips reach this organ, the concretelike mass is too dry and hard to move and Barney stubbornly refuses to pass it. He may first display some straining, then he stops eating, and finally he begins to vomit.

Impaction therapy usually consists of colonic lavage (enemas), and sometimes forceps are used to physically break down the impaction. The treatment usually is performed with Barney under sedation, and sometimes a general anesthetic is required. Unfortunately, the rectum may be injured by repeated impactions, and eventually colonic nerves may be damaged and result in chronic enlargement (megacolon) and loss of bowel control.

Your response to Barney's bone eating must be to stop it immediately and allow him no access to bones in the future!

GASTRIC DILATION AND VOLVULUS (GDV)

A recent Purdue University study reports that the number of gastric dilation and volvulus (GDV) cases in veterinary teaching hospitals increased 1,500 percent in the thirty years between 1964 and 1994. Perhaps some of this increase reflects better diagnostic criteria and better recognition among owners. Also, big dog owners are increasingly on the alert for this devastating disease, and lay plans to rush their affected dogs to hospitals for treatment. Ownership of big dogs also has increased remarkably in the past few decades, and this can't be overlooked.

GDV (also known as gastric torsion and bloat) is an often-fatal condition most commonly seen in big dogs that have deep, large chests. The disease involves a complexity of factors, but predisposition for GDV may be hereditary. The size and anatomy of the dog, amount fed, rapidity of eating, height of his

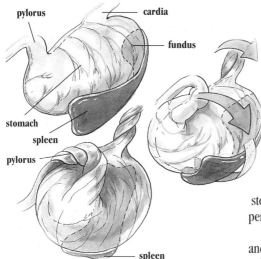

pylorus — cardia

fundus

stomach

spleen

pylorus

spleen

stomach by way of the esophagus. In the stomach, digestive juices, including stomach acid, are mixed with the food, which becomes a semi-liquid mass called *ingesta*. The muscular stomach contracts and slowly empties, pushing the ingesta into the small intestine, where digestion is continued.

Now picture the dog's anatomy. The stomach lies more or less in a horizontal plane. In big dogs, the wide rib space in the forward abdomen allows the stomach to swing from side to side, like a pendulum.

Big dogs often gulp their food and water, and air swallowing is a common side effect of gulping. Barney's voracious appetite results in the saclike stomach becoming rapidly loaded. Add the often-desired water that he drinks immediately after his big meal.

food and water dishes, activity before and after meals, and total water consumption at mealtimes are all involved. Other predisposing factors include feeding a single meal daily and fearful temperament. In fact, a happy temperament is named by the Purdue study as a decisive factor in reducing GDV occurrence.

> **GDV is a big threat to big dogs!**

When the stomach is filled with food, air, and water, Barney's activity comes into the picture. If he bounces about, his pendulant stomach may flip over, which forms a twist in the terminal esophagus and the small intestine. The flipped stomach, together with the tight twisting at each end, is called gastric torsion or volvulus, and that's deadly! The food's normal passage is effectively sealed off by the twist in the small intestine. Vomiting is impossible because of the twist in the esophagus. These twisted organs quickly lose blood circulation and cause excruciating pain, which exacerbates the condition.

Spotting an afflicted dog is easy. He will appear uncomfortable first, standing and turning in circles. Then he becomes depressed. Behind his ribs on his left side, a notable abdominal bulge begins to appear and soon grows to a generalized distention of both sides of his abdomen behind his rib cage. His mucous membrane color becomes dark as his breathing is impaired. Attempts to vomit bring up only stringy, foamy esophageal mucus.

How Torsion Occurs

Think of the stomach as a pouch situated between two tubes, the esophagus and the small intestine. Normally, food mixed with saliva leaves Barney's mouth and arrives in the

> **A life-threatening gas attack.**

Within a few hours, fermentation of the ingesta causes gas production, and these toxic gases soon are absorbed into Barney's bloodstream. As the quantity of gas increases, balloonlike pressure builds and stretches the stomach, and the pain increases. Barney attempts to belch and vomit, but all he can bring up is a small quantity of thick saliva and mucus from the esophagus. The toxemia, circulation impairment, and pain contribute to shock.

A veterinarian may attempt to pass a tube down the dog's throat to relieve the stomach gas, but due to the esophageal twist, efforts to reach the stomach in this manner often are futile. Immediate but temporary relief from the gaseous bloat sometimes is attained by plunging a large-bore hollow needle or trocar through the abdominal wall and into the stomach. This procedure allows the gas to escape, but is fraught with complications.

Shock progresses rapidly; Barney staggers and becomes glassy eyed as his pain and toxemia advances. Immediate shock therapy is begun; surgical manipulations untwist the stomach, relieve the bloat, and reverse the physical conditions. The stomach is stabilized to prevent recurrence.

Unfortunately by the time an affected dog reaches a veterinary hospital, he may have reached the state of advanced toxemia and irreversible shock and efforts to save him are futile; the extensive damage to his organs proves fatal. GDV causes death of an estimated 30 percent of its victims, and when torsion goes untreated, most dogs die.

Prevention

• Inherent disposition and temperament are important. Start out with a happy pup, do everything feasible to keep him happy, and avoid personality conflicts and stress.

• Halt all physical activity and enforce a period of rest before each meal is fed.

• Divide his well-moistened daily diet into several small meals; don't allow him to overload his stomach!

• Slow down his eating by using the methods mentioned previously.

• Reduce air swallowing by building a feeding bench that is approximately as high as your big dog's chin, and secure his food and water bowls to it.

• Enforce a peaceful rest period for an hour or more after each feeding.

• Supply fresh drinking water at all times, but carefully monitor (restrict) the big dog's water consumption when exercising and before and after meals.

• Be sure his drinking water is not ice cold.

• Never feed human leftover food.

> To reduce the probability of this condition occurring, you can take a number of measures, which also apply to the next subject discussed.

AIR SWALLOWING, BELCHING, AND FLATUS

These conditions are associated with nearly every big dog. In the preceding discussion, air swallowing was mentioned as a factor in GDV. It is likewise an element of belching and flatus. Copious quantities of air and gases are belched or passed through the bowel in most large and giant breeds. Socially unacceptable gas production is minimized by strictly feeding a highly digestible diet and can be further reduced by implementing the measures listed above.

> Barney's social graces are very suspect!

VOMITING

Vomiting is another problem that sometimes is associated with a large appetite. If blood is seen in the vomit, a trip to the veterinarian's office is indicated without delay.

First, as repulsive as it may seem, it's necessary to carefully examine the contents of Barney's vomitus. If it contains birdseed, potato peelings, apple cores, sticks, or rocks, you must put a cover on your trash containers and raise the bird feeder a couple of feet. If he is housed with another dog, it's necessary to feed them separately, and if you see evidence that Barney has stolen your cat's food, feed the cat in a place that is inaccessible to your giant partner.

> **Occasional vomiting episodes may not cause alarm. When vomiting occurs frequently, it may signal serious problems.**

Barney is a voracious eater, and if his stomach is filled too rapidly, he may overload and vomit. When vomiting occurs shortly after meals and isn't accompanied by noticeable signs of illness or lethargy, and the vomitus contains nothing except dog food, it's probably associated with overeating, lack of digestibility (inappropriate diet), eating too rapidly, or too much in a single meal. In these cases, the condition is easily diagnosed and treated by common sense.

Divide his daily diet into smaller portions at intervals throughout the day. Sound familiar? If he is fed a dry dog food kibble, mix it with a small amount of warm water and let it stand for several minutes before feeding. If his kibble is mixed with canned food, stop the canned food for a few days to see if its seasoning or quality is causing the upset.

Eliminate the possibility of dietary allergy; change Barney's food to a bland, different type of food. At one time, a lamb and rice diet was both bland and different, but today, many foods contain these ingredients. Read the ingredient list on the dog food you use. Choose a small bag of another diet containing none or few of these ingredients. If the vomiting episodes decrease after a few days, change to the new diet. If vomiting persists, contact your veterinarian.

OBESITY

Obese older dogs may be lazy. In their laid-back, relaxed states, they store calories they formerly burned. As in most species, when exercise diminishes with age, food intake must be adjusted accordingly. Reevaluate Barney's nutritional needs regularly, especially when there is any change in his activity.

If you decide that a food reduction is indicated, be sure to consider nutritional needs above all else. Reducing the quantity of food won't reduce Barney's appetite, and your partner may develop pica (craving for abnormal and indigestible items). Dietary restriction may also stimulate vices such as snatching food from your dining table.

> **Weight gain or loss should be considered carefully. If it is accompanied by signs of illness, see your veterinarian right away.**

You can maintain meal quantity by reducing the amount of dog food and substituting low-calorie ingredients such as canned green beans, rice cakes, or carrot sticks. Special reduced-calorie diets are available in pet supply markets or from your veterinarian. Always discuss reducing diets with your veterinarian. Less calorie intake should be accompanied by more exercise to burn stored calories.

A sudden weight gain accompanied by a greater than normal appetite is cause for alarm. A number of health problems, including diabetes, may cause weight gain.

> A delicate nutritional balance exists in all big dogs.

Weather extremes also will affect necessary caloric intake.

In a perfect world, Barney will burn practically all the calories his diet furnishes, and store only the amount that is needed for continued caloric expenditure. How do you tell whether he is maintaining good condition?

Run your hand over his ribs. You should easily feel the ribs under a thin layer of fat, but ribs shouldn't be visible. If Barney's ribs become noticeable, especially when their visibility is accompanied by loss of vitality, it's cause for alarm. Even if weight loss is associated with old age, your partner should be examined by a veterinarian to determine the cause.

WEIGHT LOSS

When Barney's activity is increased, such as when he begins obedience training, coursing, agility work, or field trials, you must increase his food intake to meet his caloric needs.

Feeding Your Big Dog

Before domestication, dogs hunted and gorged on their kill. Eating their prey's gastrointestinal tract's contents provided vegetable roughage to supplement a red meat diet. Small bones and rich organ meats provided adequate vitamins and minerals. These prehistoric dogs survived by their wits and did so quite nicely. Since we don't expect Greta to chase and kill her supper and feast on neighborhood antelope, we must provide her meals.

Canine nutrition has been studied extensively, and ongoing research has proven that dogs attaining different sizes have different growth rates and different nutritional requirements during the growth phase. Large breeds take longer to mature than the small breeds; toy breeds may reach their adult weight at six to nine months of age, but larger breeds will still be growing at that age. A Newfoundland or Great Dane puppy may not reach her adult size until she is eighteen months old.

In the previous chapter, we discussed eating diseases and the importance of care in feeding your big partner. Growing puppies' rapid growth rates predispose them to problems in their skeletal development. It is extremely unwise to overfeed big dog pups in an effort to obtain the maximum possible growth.

As a puppy, Greta requires two to four times more energy than an adult dog of her same weight. She also must have more protein than the adult her same weight, and that protein must have all the essential amino acids.

Her need for minerals and vitamins must be balanced to her growth rate, but they must not be overfed. Balance is critically important in big dogs' diets at every stage of growth and development. Keep in mind these important factors as you read the following general discussion about nutritional requirements.

> Although stunting may be related to poor nutrition, ultimate adult size isn't produced by excessive food.

NUTRITIONAL TERMS

Kcal is a nutritional abbreviation for one kilocalorie (large calorie) and describes the amount of energy produced by food when oxidized in the body. By strict definition, one Kcal is the amount of heat energy required to raise 1 kg of water from 15 to 16°C.

Bioavailability refers to the amount of a food ingredient actually digested and absorbed by the dog. When an ingredient is fed in a form that isn't absorbed, it is of no value. When a given amount of a product is consumed and the amount of energy that is excreted in feces is deducted, the result is the *apparent digestible energy*. From this figure, the energy excreted in urine is deducted, and this establishes the *metabolizable energy*. Bioavailability of nutrients contained in a dog food is thus defined.

Amino acids are the building blocks or breakdown products of protein, and are the elements actually absorbed and used by the dog.

Fatty acids likewise are the usable components of fat. Some of the amino and fatty acids are essential and must be furnished by diet, whereas others may be formed by Greta's metabolism.

AAFCO stands for the American Association of Feed Control Officials, which is made up of representatives from each state. This organization regulates dog food label statements such as *Complete and Balanced*, which is the AAFCO designation for a food that lacks no nutrients as proven by feeding trials.

> Understanding these terms will enable you to properly interpret most nutritional information.

DOG FOOD TYPES

Hundreds of different dog foods grace the counters of American markets. There are basically three types of dog food, but palatability varies tremendously. Dogs easily distinguish flavors through their taste buds; dogs are all different and no two dog foods taste the same. Meats, poultry, malt, garlic, fish, and sweetness are among the best-liked flavors. It's not necessary, nor is it a good idea, to vary Greta's diet

> You should decide which type of food to choose and stay with it forever, unless your veterinarian suggests another in special circumstances.

daily or even weekly or monthly. Big dogs appreciate variety in their life, but take care you don't offer them a new food every day or they'll turn up their noses at today's menu, waiting for something better.

CANNED FOODS

Feeding your big partner canned food alone may bruise your bank account and might furnish an inadequate amount of roughage for Greta. Canned food also is incriminated as a cause of urinary frequency, because it is more than 60 percent water and often contains preservatives that may have a diuretic effect. Often, meat packed in canned dog food isn't of the highest quality in spite of what dog food commercials would have you believe.

> Canned foods are expensive, but they store well and are highly palatable.

SEMI-MOIST

Looking like ground beef, these soft morsels sell well because of their appearance. They have a major disadvantage in cost and contain rather large quantities of sugar and chemical preservatives that are not in Greta's best interest.

When feeding semi-moist foods, water consumption seems to rise significantly, making dogs urinate frequently. Semi-moist foods are also occasionally incriminated as the cause of certain allergic reactions.

> Semi-moist dog foods are quite palatable but expensive, and they don't store as well as canned foods.

DRY FOODS

As the saying goes, you get what you pay for! Balanced nutrition is possible for a big dog eating dry food exclusively, but all dry foods are not created equal; they vary greatly in nutritional content and palatability. If Greta is disenchanted with the dry food chosen, add some bouillon or meat flavoring to the water you use to soak the food. However, you shouldn't need to flavor a dry food to get a healthy dog to eat it, and you shouldn't need to add supplements to a dry dog food to make it complete and balanced.

> **Least expensive and reasonably palatable, dry dog foods store well, rendering them favorites among big dog owners.**

WATER

Other nutritional elements may be varied under various circumstances, but a source of clean water is always essential and must be constantly available to Greta. That doesn't mean adding water to a dirty pan. Dogs, like humans, prefer cool, fresh water in a clean pan. Buy several stainless bowls so that one or two can be cleaned in the dishwasher daily.

If Greta seems to be perpetually thirsty, and you fill her water bowl frequently, record the actual amount of water she drinks in twenty-four hours.

> **Use large stainless steel bowls for Greta's food and water. Glass bowls break; ceramic bowls may have firing problems and leach lead into their contents; plastic bowls are porous and capture bacteria.**

Call your veterinarian and ask if the amount is excessive.

FAT

All essential fatty acids are found in both animal fat and vegetable oil. Fat is calorie-dense nutrition, containing 9-Kcal energy per gram, more than twice that of carbohydrate or protein. A diet high in fat can create problems in big dogs, both growing puppies and adults. It may contribute to obesity, too rapid growth, and other nutritional imbalances. It's been proven that dogs will voluntarily eat less of a high-fat diet, which may result in consuming less protein, vitamins, and minerals. This is especially true in young puppies. For these reasons, beware of fat-rich diets.

Adult diets should contain approximately 5 percent fat, which includes 1 percent linoleic fatty acid. A higher concentration of fat may be desirable under certain circumstances to improve coats, but increased fat must be carefully monitored.

> **Dietary fat is essential, but excessive fat is harmful.**

PROTEIN

Amino acids from vegetable sources have lower bioavailability than those derived from animal proteins. Essential amino acids are arginine, histidine, isoleucine, leucine, lysine, methionine, phenylalanine, threonine, tryptophan, and valine. Amino acid deficiencies may result in dull coat, antibody formation reduction, growth suppression, weight loss, musculature wasting, and in extreme deficiency, even death. Adult maintenance diets should contain approximately 18 percent protein, including specific amounts of these ten essential amino acids.

Protein levels must be balanced with dietary energy, and too much protein may be harmful, especially in giant breeds. Nutritionists usually recommend 20 percent protein for immature pups, but sometimes this quantity of protein is contraindicated for the large, fast-growing breeds. Following weaning, the dietary protein requirement is gradually decreased.

Increased protein demands are seen during pregnancy, lactation, and work. Old dogs require lower amounts of protein. If high quantities are fed, the excess protein may aggravate compromised kidneys.

> **Protein levels of both animal and vegetable origin must be monitored as well.**

CARBOHYDRATES

Carbohydrates or starches provide calories derived from plant tissues. It's impractical to produce dog foods without this inexpensive source of calories, although canines have very small carbohydrate requirements. A food combining animal protein with plant carbohydrates and animal or vegetable fats is generally preferred nutrition for a dog.

> **The sources and quality of protein, carbohydrate, and fat are as important as the quantities.**

MINERALS

Specified amounts of twelve different essential minerals are listed in the AAFCO nutrient requirements in specified percentages. The National Research Council (NRC) reports on the role of two of these important minerals. To provide the optimal mineral balance, the diet should contain a ratio of 1.2 parts calcium to 1 part phosphorus, and under some circumstances, up to 1.4 to 1. The sources of these minerals are also significant. For those interested in further information on mineral requirements, *Nutritional Requirements of Dogs* can be purchased from the National Research Council by telephone at 1-800-624-6242. This inexpensive volume is updated regularly and will answer virtually all of your technical questions about canine nutrition.

> **Mineral excesses can cause many problems in big dogs. Consult with your veterinarian before adding any mineral to Greta's diet.**

VITAMINS

The AAFCO advises that eleven vitamins in specified amounts should be included in adult maintenance diets. You'll be interested to learn that vitamin C is not listed. Dogs manufacture sufficient quantities of vitamin C to meet their needs, and require no external source of this vitamin.

Vitamin A is toxic in high doses, and its use should be considered with

> **Vitamins, like other nutrients, must be monitored closely in big dog diets.**

care, although it is often safely prescribed in modest doses for various diseases.

Vitamin D requirements depend on dietary calcium and phosphorus. Additionally, the requirement for vitamin E is related to fatty acid intake.

Rather than discuss each vitamin independently, it is probably best to state that the requirements and results of excessive or insufficient intake are covered in the NRC book mentioned above. For those who wish to try to formulate their own kitchen diets, please obtain and read the NRC book.

SUPPLEMENTS

A food with the AAFCO declaration on its label *Complete and Balanced* diet, such as a premium dry food, needs no vitamin or mineral supplementation. By the same token, it's a mistake to feed a bargain brand dog food and hope to cover its inadequacies with inexpensive vitamin-mineral supplements.

> **Supplements are rarely needed, can be dangerous, and should be discussed with your veterinarian.**

Dietary supplements are sometimes used to improve Greta's coat and make it more glossy. Such coat conditioners usually contain fatty acids and are rarely necessary, have marginal benefits, and can be harmful to fast-growing large breeds. They are, however, usually harmless when added to adult dog food diets and may be prescribed by veterinarians to compensate for stress factors. The best way to attain and maintain a shiny coat with rich colors is through selective breeding and sound nutrition, not a bottle of coat enhancer. Check with your veterinarian before you add any vitamin-mineral supplement to Greta's food.

MEAT

Protein and fat bioavailability in dog foods of yesteryear were sometimes less than desirable. Nutritionists of that era recommended adding bone meal and meat, especially liver or tripe, to dogs' diets. Remembering those recommendations, big dog owners often make the mistake of mixing meat with their partner's otherwise balanced diet. Big mistake! If you add meat to a growing pup's diet, adjustment must be made in other areas. Unless you have facilities to analyze and test the final product being fed, adding meat to an already balanced diet is dangerous!

> **Dogs like meat, but it shouldn't be added to a balanced dog food.**

BONES

If Greta likes to chew, and it's inconceivable that she won't, it's okay to give her a large, raw marrow bone occasionally. Cooked bones, whether baked, boiled, or fried, will splinter and should never be allowed. Don't give her raw or cooked bones from roasts, steaks, chicken, chops, or fish. The best bone by far is a flavored nylon bone that is specially designed to satisfy her chewing need and help maintain strong teeth and gums.

> **Adult dogs enjoy a big, raw knucklebone to chew on occasionally.**

DOG FOOD LABELS

The label on a product may state that the food is complete or complementary. If complementary, it should be fed together with an additional and usually specified food source. If the food is complete, it will provide a balanced diet when fed by itself for a specified stage of a dog's life.

Reading dog food labels is a science.

Labels are legal documents. To know which food to buy, you must learn to read the dog food labels. If you can't understand the label, call or write the manufacturer with your questions. Don't buy a product because of the price tag. You may be very lucky, but probably you'll be very sorry!

Ingredients are always shown on the label and are listed according to quantity. If beef is listed first, that product is in greater quantity than ingredients that follow. If corn flour is listed second, it is present in greater quantity than the next ingredient.

A label stating that a dog food meets the recommendations of the NRC means only one thing. It meets *maintenance* requirements. Such a food should be adequate for maintaining dogs under minimal stress, but isn't necessarily acceptable for other dogs with particular needs. It may not supply the increased energy demands of work, training, growth, pregnancy, or lactation.

Labels often specify the *total* nutrients, not the *bioavailable* nutrients. In such a case, a letter or phone call to the manufacturer should clear up the question. If you receive an inadequate response, shop around for another food.

The ingredient list should list the source of protein in the food. Protein of vegetable origin such as wheat, corn, or soy flour may provide an excellent total protein analysis on the package, but it may be misleading if that protein is not bioavailable.

FEEDING TRIALS

Some foods will include a label declaration stating that the food has passed the AAFCO feeding trials for the entire life cycle of canines. These products should contain the right amount of bioavailable food elements required for puppies, youths, and working adults.

If the AAFCO declaration isn't shown, it doesn't necessarily mean the food hasn't been subjected to feeding trials. Call or write to the manufacturer and ask for reports of feeding trial results, and ask about the sources of protein and fat. Ask whether the formula is kept constant, regardless of the seasonal variation of ingredient costs.

If you are unable to understand the information provided by manufacturers, consult your veterinarian. If he isn't able to help you make an informed decision, borrow a text on the subject. Most veterinary clinics have reference sources for the nutritional requirements of dogs, and more information is available on the Internet. However, without expert credentials, the writer of Internet articles and information may be no better informed than you are. If in doubt, ask your veterinarian. He should be the final source of information regarding

Quality of and balance between fat, protein, carbohydrates, thirteen vitamins, and twenty minerals is critical, especially in an immature large dog.

Greta's diet, and should help you reevaluate her nutrition every few weeks during her fast-growing phase.

SAFE TREATS

Low-calorie biscuits or other tasty dry products are the best treats. Tiny pieces of baked liver or small bits of well-done roast beef are favorite treats among trainers, but in large quantity, these rich tidbits can throw a big dog's nutritional balance out of whack. Remember what was said about treats contributed by the whole family.

NUTRITIONAL INFLUENCES

Internal parasites such as round-worms, tapeworms, hookworms, and protozoan parasites rob nutrition from your dog and may be associated with dietary deficiencies. Often manifested by thinness and a dry, coat, dogs suspected of parasitism should be subjected to routine microscopic fecal exams. This quick test will identify which parasite is present and is extremely valuable when raising a puppy.

External parasites such as fleas, ticks, mites, or lice rob the dog of nutrition by invading the skin and taking blood. Both internal and external parasites are capable of causing stress and other vague physical and mental signs in the dog.

> **Greta's nutrition may be influenced by factors other than what she is fed.**

Pregnancy, whelping, and lactation are significant stressors on a big brood bitch's system, and will always cause the bitch to lose coat and appear ratty for several weeks. These stresses are partly nutritional in origin, and should be addressed individually in each brood bitch.

When Greta passes middle age, her ability to absorb certain nutrients is impaired. All dogs' nutritional needs change with age; if those needs aren't met, she won't live a normal, healthy, long life.

OVERFEEDING

The most important message of this chapter is that regardless of what Greta's diet is, she shouldn't be fed to capacity during her puppy months. Possibly she should never eat her fill. Big dogs are often gluttonous, voracious eaters. They eat everything that is edible and immediately look around for more. The most dangerous habit for an owner to acquire is to give more food after their big partner has just finished a meal. Instead, adopt a policy of grooming, petting, and relaxing with her after meals!

Generally, puppies require twice as much energy per pound of body weight as mature adults. Racing Grey-

> **Every dog deserves a tidbit now and then, especially during training.**

> **Most big dogs are never quite filled up.**

hounds require up to 20 percent more energy when they are in training, and Malamutes working under polar conditions require 50 to 100 percent more energy than backyard dogs. Select a good quality name brand food, and feed Greta a quantity that produces a thrifty body condition. This means weighing her regularly, running your hands over her ribs, and using a discerning eye. If you can feel her ribs through a thin fat cover, her coat is glossy, her eyes are bright, and she is curious and active, her diet is probably okay. If you have any doubt, consult with your veterinarian.

HOMEMADE DIETS

Your kitchen can be used to concoct Greta's food. No question about that! She'll eat your leftovers, chew on steak and chicken bones; she'll probably even swallow some of your vitamins. She's your dog, but believe me, she deserves better!

No one can deny that scrap meat, cheeses, milk, bread, and other foods contain many normal ingredients of a dog's diet. However, if you intend to formulate Greta's diet from scratch, please buy a gram scale, read a book written by people with correct, current knowledge of big dog nutrition, and proceed with caution. Homemade diets require a thorough understanding of the specific nutritional needs of the big dog, of the nutritive value of different ingredients, and of nutritional interactions. Methods of preparation and storage also may affect the availability of individual nutrients.

> Many owners think they know more than dog food manufacturers about their dog's needs.

Breeding Your Big Dog

Greta is now two years old; she was x-rayed, and the OFA report was excellent. Likewise, her eye examination was performed and she's CERF certified. You've had her faulted by a breeder; she was credited with more good than bad features, and she's won a couple of fun matches. She's easily trained, a delightful companion, and finished her obedience training at the head of her class. You really aren't interested in showing and competitive obedience, but you're naturally proud of your big dog partner. You've spent hundreds of dollars achieving these goals, and now you want to recoup some of your expenditures.

Indeed, why not?

The following questions remain to be answered before embarking on a Greta-breeding project. Conscientious dog breeding isn't about making money. It's about producing puppies that are at least as good as their parents, preferably better. If you've had no experience raising big dog puppies, please take the time to talk to several breeders. Ask questions such as:

- I paid a lot for Greta; I didn't buy her as a brood bitch, but won't she have great pups?
- She's smart and a wonderful companion, but is she breeding quality?
- She's never been in heat, but I'm impatient.

Before even considering raising puppies, examine your motives, review your facilities, your time, and your financial situation.

- When should I breed her?
- Where can I find a good stud dog?
- What is the average stud fee? Will his owners take "pick of the litter"?
- If she doesn't conceive, how do I arrange remating, and does that cost extra?
- Where do I board her if I must leave town while she's pregnant?
- Will Greta require special attention during pregnancy, and will she receive it in a kennel?
- How much of my time is required with whelping, and will I need help?
- Is there much mess involved with whelping? I'm not good at that kind of stuff.
- How much time is required to feed and clean up after the pups?
- Do puppies need much attention before weaning? How important is socialization?
- How much time will I spend on paperwork? Does the AKC charge for puppy registration?
- How many puppies will Greta produce?
- Are risks involved for my big partner? Are cesarean sections ever required?
- Am I responsible for puppy vaccinations?
- What are the odds of having sick puppies?
- When should the pups be examined, and is it necessary to have them checked for worms?

- How much room and what special facilities does a litter of big puppies require?
- Is puppy food expensive? Will I need much?
- Does a ready market prevail for big dog pups?
- How can I find good homes for Greta's babies? Do I need to guarantee the pups?
- What do I do with puppies I can't place? What if a puppy isn't normal?
- How much profit is realized in each litter? Why so little profit in such a big project?

Probably when all those questions are honestly answered, your next question will be asked of your veterinarian: "When can you spay Greta?"

This is a good spot for a commitment check. Whatever you do, don't contribute to the dog over-population problem facing the United States. More than five million good dogs are euthanized every year because they don't fit into their owners' life schemes. Don't become part of that statistic by breeding your dog for the wrong reasons!

Dog breeding requires a resolution possessed by a very few dedicated individuals. It's true that some backyard breeders give it a shot, but the results usually are discouraging, and sometimes disastrous! Unless Greta is a show-winning champion with personality and trainability attributes to match, her pups won't be highly sought after. If she was purchased as a probable show prospect and has proven herself in the ring, you might consider breeding. If not, forget it! You can't hope to come out financially ahead.

Conscientious breeders dedicate their lives to improving the breed, not producing litters for profit. If this fact alone hasn't discouraged you from your intention to recoup some of your expenditures, further information is presented for your edification.

DOG PSYCHOLOGY

Do you really know enough about dogs to begin this venture? Does your knowledge and level of experience qualify you to embark on this path? Can you predictably produce healthy pups? How will you handle situations such as death of the dam before she weans pups? What about cannibalism? Why does it occur, and what can be done to avoid it? How will you handle congenitally deformed pups? What will you do with runts in big litters?

BIG DOG IDIOSYNCRASIES

Everything biological is relative. Many breeds discussed hereafter aren't giants but are slightly smaller sporting dogs, hounds, and working dogs. Their breeding problems are fewer, and raising pups may be more appropriate from some standpoints. However, the same remarks apply relative to out of pocket costs, commitment, time, facilities, puppy placement, and litter value.

> Read all you can find about dog breeding, including nutrition, breed idiosyncrasies, whelping, dystocias, puppy deformities, and complications.

> Don't depend on puppy sales for retirement income!

DELAYED ESTRUS

Giant breed females may not begin estrous cycles until past two years of age, and heat cycles often are erratic and difficult to evaluate

> **Financial commitment to good breeding practices is essential.**

for exact breeding time. Sometimes costly blood tests must be used to ascertain when females are fertile. Add delayed estrus to irregular cycles and you have another reason to forgo breeding.

DELAYED MALE MATURATION

If you own a male and wish to breed, your situation is even more problematic. No conscientious breeder will use an unproven male. Many beautiful males are available to sire litters, but only those that are proven winners in shows or field trials are in demand. This means more money must be spent on traveling, entry fees, trial equipment, training fees, and other miscellaneous expenses before your male is ready to reproduce.

> **Great males are rare among giant breeds.**

The same examinations are needed to prove your male's eyes, hips, elbows, and so forth. He must possess an impeccable personality with few if any faults. Hereditary conditions of all his relatives will adversely affect his breeding value; his pedigree will be carefully scrutinized. Even if all these items are covered and he's earned a clean bill of health, his breeding career might be jeopardized by such irrelevancies as the wrong coat length or color!

Probably the least of your worries is his sexual maturation. Normally, larger dogs, especially giant breeds, mature much later than their smaller counterparts. Your male may not reach breeding age until two years, possibly even three. By this time, if his desirability is strong among breeders, you will have had him examined and certified for important hereditary faults.

SHORT BREEDING LIFE

Most breeds discussed here have an abbreviated breeding career. Greta may produce her first litter by three or four years, and end her brood life at six. Males naturally enjoy a lengthier sexual performance period. If bitches aren't removed from the gene pool by six or seven, they usually produce smaller litters and weaker puppies, and are more inclined to suffer dystocias (difficult births) and other older brood-dog diseases.

Mastitis (breast infection), mammary neoplasia (breast cancer), pyometra (uterine infection), and stillborn pups are more common in older brood bitches. If spayed before her first season, Greta will likely never face mammary tumors, but breast cancer becomes more likely every year that a female goes unspayed. Surgical removal of the tumors is the practical therapy and usually is accompanied by ovariohysterectomy (spaying).

Pyometra (uterine infection) is a deadly disease because when the bitch's uterus becomes infected, the cervix remains closed and pus is trapped within. Sometimes the condition goes unnoticed for several days or a week because of the big dog's trunk size. Most veterinarians agree the condition is not easily treated!

In advanced pyometra cases, the bitch often is toxic, and anesthesia poses a serious risk. Sometimes conservative therapy is attempted. Often, the doctor elects to perform an ovariohysterectomy in spite of the surgical risks, is successful, and Greta lives. Your

> **Greta's puppy-raising career is over too soon. I haven't met my expenses yet!**

veterinary bill will reflect the seriousness of pyometra and difficulty of treatment.

UTERINE INERTIA OR FATIGUE

Medical problems at whelping time must be foreseen. Be sure you will have medical and if needed, surgical support, and that house calls can be made in case of difficult birth (dystocia).

Uterine inertia or fatigue is one of the major causes of dystocia. An older dog has less muscular strength than a young, vital bitch. She may deliver a few puppies normally, then simply stop labor and seem to rest. Unfortunately, she may not resume labor, and cesarean surgery will be required to deliver the remainder of the litter. In a healthy bitch, cesarean presents little surgical risk, but if fatigue and reduced physical condition is factored in, risks are considerable. Anesthesia can also be risky to both puppies and dam, but experienced veterinarians usually can meet these risks.

PSEUDOCYESIS (FALSE PREGNANCY)

False pregnancy refers to the condition in which the bitch has all the signs of pregnancy except the fetuses. It occurs during the time of normal gestation, whether expected or unexpected. In other words, a couple of weeks after Greta is in heat, she has some personality changes. In another couple of weeks, she begins to show signs of nipple enlargement, and later begins to make her nest under your bed or in a closet. Her appetite increases, and you may see some clear discharge stringing from her genitalia. She may adopt a stuffed animal, put it in her nest, and try to nurse it. Her mammary glands often fill; occasionally milk drips copiously from her nipples.

Before breeding Greta, discuss every phase of this important project with your veterinarian.

If breeding was attempted during her heat, you may expect to see a normal litter, but whelping time comes and goes with no puppy appearance.

If she was not purposefully bred, you kick yourself because you think she somehow managed to mate with the neighbor's mutt, and you're trying to decide whether to sue.

In either case, consult with your veterinarian before you assume the pregnancy to be false. Don't lose sight of the fact that she could be pregnant with only one or two large puppies, and that such a situation might result in dystocia. If you wait to see what happens, Greta could be in a world of trouble. Other possibilities exist to relieve your anxiety over false pregnancy. Why not ask your veterinarian to palpate her abdomen for pups? The problem with this idea is that big dogs' abdomens are difficult to palpate, and a high margin of error exists if the correct time for palpation is missed. If she wasn't bred intentionally, you aren't apt to think of this technique during the appropriate window of opportunity. If puppies are found by palpation, your only question relates to the date of whelping. If no puppies are found, your veterinarian may be unsure without further tests.

Why not have X-ray or ultrasound imaging performed sometime during (false) pregnancy? Images made by either technique generally are safe but must be cautiously employed. Imaging is an excellent idea, but don't bet the farm on total accuracy. Timing is critical in order to get an absolutely positive diagnostic ultrasound or X ray. The big dog's massive abdomen holds many organs that can appear suspicious and lead to false assumptions. Puppy skeletons are usually visible near pregnancy's end, but by then you often can diagnose pregnancy from across the room.

No therapy is required for pseudocyesis unless it is psychological. Sometimes you can help by taking her adopted toys from her and giving her more exercise, attention, and love.

WHY NOT NEUTER?

Neutered dogs make great companions. There are a few drawbacks to neutering, but none that adversely affects Greta's health and longevity.

Spayed or castrated dogs aren't allowed to compete in AKC conformation shows or formal field trials, because these events were designed to improve breeding stock. Neutered dogs can participate in practically all other endeavors such as obedience trials, agility and fly-ball events, tracking, search and rescue programs, and so forth. Unless you are totally committed to breaking into the dog breeding business, it's best not to begin.

> **Spaying Greta before her first heat should be considered.**

WHEN AND WHY TO NEUTER

Early castration and spaying is now being performed across the country with good results. Neutering either sex at an early age appears to have no ill effects on growth or personality. It apparently doesn't affect growth rate, obesity of adults, or trainability. It may prevent aggressiveness in young adults, and is a surefire way of preventing pregnancy and probably breast cancer. It should be less risky than similar surgery performed on mature big dogs because anesthesia time is shortened, smaller bodies are more easily handled, and fewer fat deposits interfere with recovery. Because this technique

is relatively new, results may be skewed by first reports, but it appears to be quite promising. Ask your veterinarian about early spaying and neutering.

Many veterinarians prefer to spay females before their first heat to preclude mammary tumors later in life. Pyometra prevention has been mentioned as well, but the principal reason for spaying Greta will be to stop her heat cycles and prevent any possibility of inadvertent pregnancy. A study reported in British veterinary literature indicates that spayed females lived longer than males or intact females.

Castration will permanently prevent your big male partner from producing puppies. It will give him one less thing to think about, and may enhance his devotion to his owner. If done early enough, it may help correct certain behavioral problems. Castration should be scheduled as soon as you're sure your male isn't destined to be a show or field trial dog. The best time is either very early in his life, or before one year of age.

> **Neutering your big dog will provide peace of mind for you as well as the dog!**

RAISING PUPPIES

As you can see, this short chapter is devoted to investigating reasons why you shouldn't breed Greta. This is because there are few reasons why average owners should breed their dogs.

If you are serious about breeding Greta, and have jumped through the hurdles imposed earlier in this chapter, go for it! Dog breeding is the sole subject of several books, and those interested in reading on this subject can try *The Complete Book of Dog Breeding* by Rice, published by Barron's.

Short Lives of Tall Dogs

The bigger the dog, the shorter its life. That's a rule of thumb that usually works but may not always be correct. Life expectancy of your big dog partner is influenced by many factors that have been discussed in detail throughout this tome. If Barney isn't quite as big as a giant and has avoided diseases that lead to an early demise, and you have committed yourself to providing the best nutrition and preventive health care, you can expect to have your partner with you for more than 11 years.

A recent survey study in the United Kingdom reports that life expectancy of all breeds averages 11 years and one month. The life expectancy for dogs dying of old age without other influencing factors was 12 years and eight months. Similar studies in the United States haven't been reported to the best of the author's knowledge, but because British dog care and ownership is similar to ours, their report should be significant.

Although Miniature Poodles were at the top of the life expectancy list at 14.8 years, a fairly large dog breed, the Collie, enjoys an average life span of 13 years. The German Shepherd, another relatively large breed, averages 10.3 years. Great Danes, however, enjoy only an 8.4 year average life span.

We must realize that the British figures are mean age averages for all breeds and all causes of death. Diseases such as cancer caused nearly 16 percent of all deaths, and heart disease caused half as many deaths. The survey indicates that only 8 percent of dogs reported lived more than 15 years, and disease or euthanasia caused 64 percent of all deaths. Mutts usually lived longer than purebreds, although Whippets, Miniature Poodles, and Jack Russell Terriers outlived mixed breeds.

> **Big dogs usually display age related diseases by nine years old.**

According to Professor Michell, president of the Royal College of Veterinary Surgeons, dog owners should forget the idea that six or seven years of human life is equal to one year of a dog's life. No such man-made formula works when all factors affecting longevity are considered.

One calculation for life expectancy states that the first year of a dog's life is equal to 21 years of human life, and each year following the first is equal to four human years. By this theory, an 8-year old dog would be 21 plus 28 (4 times 7) or equal to a 49 year old human. This formula may be nearer to correct than the time-honored one to seven calculation, but it may err as well when extraneous factors are thrown into the formula, such as exercise, nutrition, and dogs' size.

SHORT TEMPERS OF OLD DOGS

• A formerly tolerant, gentle dog may begin to be grouchy with small children as he reaches old age, not because he dislikes toddlers, but to defend his arthritic joints.

- He may lose his appetite, but if you check his breath, you'll see why. Loose teeth and infected gums have caused him to lose his desire to chew.

- Deafness leaves Barney at risk from people's feet. They sneak up and startle him, catching him unaware.

- Nuclear sclerosis, resembling cataracts, often impairs old dog vision, and actual cataracts are common to aged dogs as well.

- Cognitive dysfunction may cause emotional changes in old dogs; some will display loss of appetite, urinating and defecating in the house, pacing, or barking for no reason.

These signals may be early forerunners to Barney's demise; they should be noted and seriously considered. He's beginning to warn you of the day when it will be time to give him up.

The life span for big dogs is relatively short, but it can be maximized by good care throughout his life. Think about this fact while he is yet young and act accordingly. At a certain time in his life, time will catch up with him; you'll need to face up to his old age and the eventuality of giving him up. How can you do that? When and why should you consider euthanasia?

ALL THE WRONG REASONS

There are dozens of inappropriate reasons or excuses for putting a dog to sleep. Veterinarians have heard them all; here are a choice few.

- He's just too big to handle. I can't cope with torn clothes and muddy footprints, among his other bad habits!

Truth: It's not Barney's fault if you didn't take the time to train him and teach him good manners when he wasn't so big. That isn't a legitimate excuse for euthanasia. He's not too old to learn, but are you young enough to teach? If not, find him another home with a patient, experienced family.

- I'm sorry, but I can't endure his frequent feeding schedule. My little kids are afraid of him now that he's nearly 150 pounds. His size and care have become more trouble than he's worth.

Truth: Those probabilities should have been thought of before you acquired him.

Cop outs!

These excuses are human problems for you to deal with, not dog problems or an excuse for ending a companion's life. Look to rescue organizations for help in finding him a new home.

- I can't afford him. I budgeted enough for his care, but now that he's ill, I can't afford the massive medical bills.

Truth: You have options. Have you explored every avenue available to you for financial help? Rescue organizations, no-kill animal aid institutions, veterinary colleges, and others may provide low cost veterinary care.

- We're moving away and will be living in an apartment that doesn't allow pets.

Truth: Rescue organizations and foster homes save many big dogs. Contact your local pound, shelter, or breed club for advice. Ask the AKC for help finding the nearest rescue organization. Veterinarians often can put you in touch with no-kill shelters. Barney deserves another chance!

ONE LEGITIMATE REASON: OLD AGE

He's been eating a geriatric food for a long time, but his joints creak, his hearing is gone, eyesight is dimming, and finally, he's an old dog. He sleeps most of the time, and his coat is bedraggled. You hear him going out several times a night, bumping into objects that he would have seen a year ago. It's been months since he asked to play catch. Old joints hurt; getting up is an obvious chore, and he moves slowly and deliberately.

Although he's been house-trained since puppyhood, lately he's been leaving damp spots on his rug where he lies. He's always been a superclean partner, but recently he has fecal accidents, then acts bewildered and ashamed.

You know Barney isn't comfortable; it's time to give him up, but he's been such a wonderful companion you can't bear the thought of taking him to your veterinarian for the last time. Maybe he'll die in his sleep. Wouldn't it be nice if Barney went to sleep one night and didn't wake up? Unfortunately, that's not likely.

Pleading eyes dimly look to you for comfort, and how you wish you could give him relief from his pain. You reach for the ibuprofen bottle and a bite of cheese to wrap his nightly pill in, and you know that's the best you can do.

Then one day Barney can't get to his feet. With help from your family, you carry him outside, but his rubbery legs won't support him and he falls, lying in a dejected heap. Suddenly you know it's past time to provide the relief he's begged for in the last few weeks.

Euthanasia is the final act of love and kindness you can give your well-loved partner. Barney will suffer no fear or apprehension when a trusted veterinarian administers the lethal injection. You will stay with your old friend, and being at his side will tell him of your love and assure him that you haven't abandoned your faithful partner.

> No dances left on Barney's card? Don't extend his suffering for your self-gratification!

EUTHANASIA

The decision has been made for you. Your big old partner deserves a painless departure from the cares of his tiresome world that has become a painful, confusing burden. Call Barney's veterinarian and request to take him to the hospital before regular office hours, so there will be no wait. Better yet, ask the veterinarian to come to your house to perform this humanitarian procedure.

Only your kindness and love should be apparent on Barney's last day. Administration of the lethal injection should always be accomplished unhurriedly and without anxiety. His veterinarian will handle him gently and calmly, speaking to Barney in comforting tones. The injection will be prepared in advance, so the syringe being filled in his presence won't alarm him. An assistant may steady your old partner as the clinician makes a quick venipuncture. The lethal fluid is rapidly injected, and death follows instantly and painlessly.

GRIEF SUPPORT

Ask your veterinarian for information. Books and Web sites are available as well. For many dog owners, grief over lost canine companions is devastating, second only to the anguish of losing spouses, friends, and relatives.

> It's time to give up your old buddy.

Attend group support meetings to aid in finding comfort. If none is available nearby, start a group; sharing your loss with others makes the process much easier. You've just lost a friend, a big dog partner. Don't be afraid to shed some tears. Go through the natural grieving period, but keep your mind open to another big buddy somewhere down the trail at some time when you are sure the time is right for you.

WHAT DOG NEXT?

Remember the joy Barney brought to your family. Remember his puppyhood years and the happiness you derived from his antics, but don't waste your life with perpetual grieving and despair. Don't build a shrine in your memory that blocks out all other dogs.

> **Support groups will help you through the loss of your big partner.**

Get another dog when you're ready, but don't seek another Barney. Try a similar breed. If you must get another dog of the same breed, try to find one with significant differences. Perhaps his breeder can furnish a female pup, or one of a different color.

> **Barney's gone but not forgotten.**

Obtaining Barney's spitting image will always remind you of him, and will result in comparing the new dog with him at every turn. Your tendency will be to pressure him into being what he is not. He will suffer from comparison in your mind, and will end up being frustrated and less than both of you deserve.

Purebred Big Dogs

Researching the following breed information has made one thing abundantly clear to the writer. Big dogs are malleable and they change roles frequently, yet they have significant similarities in their backgrounds. They are interrelated in many ways; often big dogs share progenitors, and this has made separation into various groups nearly impossible.

For instance, a differentiation must be made between herding dogs and those developed to protect or guard herds of sheep or cattle. Though rarely defined elsewhere, a herding dog is used to assist herdsmen and to obey their commands. The herding dog's duty is to move a flock, keep it together, and to a lesser degree, protect the herd. A herding dog is a quick thinker that is taught many intricate maneuvers. It will perform instantly and without question when a whistle, voice, or hand signal is given. Focus on its handler is deeply ingrained in the herding dog's behavior, so much so that it seems instinctive. This focus means it's easily trained to participate in action sports and obedience, as well as herding trials.

Generally, a herding sheepdog living in a human companion role for many generations retains its herding instincts and is quite content to live with its family and assist in raising the children. To a lesser degree, it will protect the home against intruders of the two- and four-legged varieties. A herding dog often has the propensity to gently drive or usher a gaggle of children or family pets into a herd and keep watch over it.

A flock-guard or protection dog was developed to act independently from the herdsman's commands. Over the centuries, this activity also has become instinctive. This dog was specifically designed as a big, powerful, occasionally aggressive dog that worked in a self-reliant or autonomous role. Flock guarding meant living with the sheep, meeting and associating with herdsmen only at mealtime, and taking few or no commands from its benefactors. Under some circumstances, these dogs instinctively separated themselves into groups that worked twenty-four hours a day, in a sort of rotation. The guard dog's job was to keep the flock safe at all times, and if necessary, to forfeit its life in this endeavor.

A guard dog, schutzhund, or attack dog belongs to a slightly different type. Usually a naturally aggressive dog, it is specifically trained to defend its handler, to attack on command, to stop attacking when commanded, and to hold its handler's prisoners. Although quite intelligent, this dog is trained to neither fear nor respect its opponent, which is most often another person. A guard dog is extremely obedient to its handler, a powerful dog that acts only on command and never on its own initiative. Unfortunately, this factor sometimes is neglected in guard dog training; the attack dog makes its own decisions, and its role becomes one of maliciousness and viciousness.

In the following discussion, breeds aren't separated by group, but are instead arranged alphabetically because they may have been developed for one purpose but are serving in another role and are included in another group. Many of these purebred dogs aren't AKC recognized, and a few are rarely seen in America. Size is the sole common factor of the fifty-one breeds discussed.

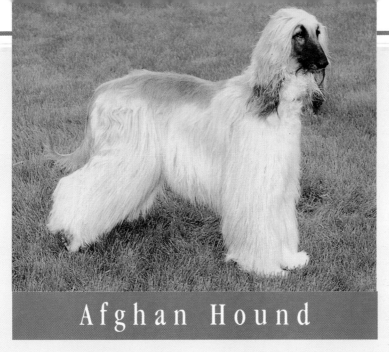

Afghan Hound

This hound is sometimes referred to as Noah's Dog, or the Dog of Noah's Ark, which infers that it is one of the oldest if not the oldest breed in existence. According to some writers, the breed sprang from the small peninsula between the Gulf of Suez and the Gulf of Akaba, where the Mountain of Moses is located. Ancient Egypt claimed this area during the period between 3,000 and 4,000 B.C., and the Afghan Hound is said to be mentioned on papyrus dating from that time. This claim is scarcely provable, but it lends mystique and antiquity to the breed and harms no one. One of a number of large sight hounds found along the India border, it has sometimes been called the Eastern Greyhound, Persian Greyhound, Barakazai, and the Kurram Valley Hound.

Regardless of historical fantasy or fiction, the Afghan's long, silky coat is the product of at least half a century of selective breeding, and requires constant attention, combing, brushing, untangling, and smoothing. A pet Afghan's coat can be sheared off, but breeders don't usually recommend radical clipping, which may further separate show dogs from companion roles.

An Afghan requires lots of exercise and thrives on activity in spite of its prominent role as show dog and pet. Lure coursing, obedience, and other canine activities can be used to burn this hound's energy and keep it content.

CURRENT FUNCTION

Afghans of America today are mostly show dogs, companion dogs, and backyard pets. Some compete in coursing trials, but they are infrequently observed there. The Afghan is a calm, reserved, independent dog that exhibits its noble ancestry as it trots the backyard perimeter.

ATTITUDE

Reserved, aloof, and self-reliant, the Afghan is rarely timid and is somewhat dominant with other dogs, but gets along with children if not pestered. This bold and courageous dog insists on its own territory, and is often best placed with families with older children. Not known as particularly affectionate pets, Afghans chase every moving animal, and this trait may get them into trouble with other house pets. Not a natural watchdog, the Afghan often will shun all humans except its family.

APTITUDE

Coursing trials were invented for the Afghan and other sight hounds. In that sport, very little handling is necessary. Seeming to thrive on the glamorous show dog life, this dog takes more training than some other breeds. Its independent nature seems to run counter to what the trainer has in mind, often resulting in problems. It's said that scolding is the best way to

Origin

This resident of Afghanistan was probably developed from a blend of dogs found in various regions of its native country. Its specific history is controversial because of the diversity of cultures within that country. In the mountainous northern region, heavily coated, dark-colored hounds with a compact structure are seen. In the southern and western warm, arid, desert regions, light-colored, sparsely coated, rangier hounds prevail. No doubt these factors, among others, influenced the current Afghan common to America.

Original Design

The Afghan's original purposes are clouded by antiquity. In some areas of Afghanistan, it may have been utilized primarily as a guard dog and herding specialist. In other regions, it might have been developed and used as a sight hound, hunting before the horses of kings and noblemen. Sometimes, we read, they hunted in braces of two, in packs, or singly, both with and without human hunter guidance. They may have been used in combination with falcons as well. These uses probably influence the breed's independence that endures today. Quarry for this hunting dog was deer, hare, and various wild predators that might be a threat to the Afghanistan herds. Its agility and ability to turn at high speeds made it valuable in such coursing, but in the bargain, the Afghan was used to flush game birds and animals. It first made its way to England, came to America late in the 1800s, and was admitted to the AKC Stud Book in 1926.

instill resentment for your handling, and an Afghan will perform only when treated with kindness and a soft hand. For this reason, the Afghan isn't often entered in performance games or trials.

APPEARANCE

The Afghan Hound stands 27 or 28 inches tall (68.5 to 71 cm), although 29-inch (74-cm) dogs aren't unknown. Its powerful speed and catlike agility are its paramount features, but these are somewhat masked in the show ring by its magnificent, long, and glamorous coat. The Afghan's aristocratic carriage and practiced gait make it an eye-catching spectacle. Never plain or coarse, this dog fairly oozes its Eastern origin. Its long, silky coat can be of any color, with combinations of colors being desirable.

Akita

Images of the Akita or a dog much like it adorns the tombs of Japanese rulers and noblemen in various districts of Japan. Known as Matagi-inu, esteemed hunter, Akita ownership was once limited to people of noble birth, and a special vocabulary was used to address this aristocratic dog. Purity of bloodlines is closely guarded in its native country, and the dog was declared a Japanese national monument in 1931.

The Akita coat requires little regular combing and brushing, except during spring and fall, when heavy shedding occurs.

This big dog's need for exercise is relative to its size, and must be provided daily to keep it content. This sometimes presents a problem, since the Akita can be aggressive toward other smaller pets, and should always be exercised on-leash.

CURRENT FUNCTION

This strong, bright, flashy, clean-appearing working dog is in significant demand as a companion, playmate for children, guard dog, and in some cases, police dog. Sledding and skijoring are among the Akita's other talents. It seems strange that it is used only rarely in its original role as hunter, although it retains its keen nose. Bench showing attracts this colorful dog, and its natural stance is often hard to beat.

ATTITUDE

Bold and courageous might best describe the Akita. When this dog's heritage is considered, its aggressiveness toward other big dogs can be understood. It isn't the dog for everyone, but should be considered if you need an independent dog with great intelligence and strength. Suspicious of strangers, it's known to have great devotion and loyalty to its family, and will guard its children by the hour.

APTITUDE

Training the Akita should be undertaken by an experienced person who can communicate with the dog in a quiet but firm manner. This dog is quite intelligent, and understands commands when given with consistency and logic. An Akita requires no special training to protect its family and can easily be spoiled if it is instructed in guarding duties. The Akita is typically stubborn but responsive, and obedience training usually progresses well if nagging and nit-picking don't accompany each lesson.

APPEARANCE

This big dog usually stands at the upper end of the standard, 28 inches (71 cm). Its colors include any and all, including pure white, black, pinto, and various brindles. Masks and clear outlined spots of the pinto are striking when well balanced. Coat is double, with the outer coat standing off the body, giving the dog a plush appearance. Its tail is curled and waggy, and the curve of the tail dips below the level of its back. Muscular and sturdy, the Akita has an alert, happy expression.

Original Design

This dog was originally designed to function as a hunting dog with deer, bear, and wild boar as its quarry. In such a role, selective breeding leaned toward strength, tenacity, and fierceness. The design was mindful of the bitter winters of the mountainous country; thus came the dog's thick, protective coat. At various times in history, it has doubled as a fighting dog, sled dog, and draft dog, and in hard times, its meat and skin provided sustenance and warmth to the Japanese people as well.

Origin

The Akita was developed during the seventeenth century in the Akita Prefecture of northern Japan. Since that time, it has gained popularity both in its native country and elsewhere around the world. It was developed by selective breeding of the Matagi-inu or hunting dogs of Honshu Island, and its appearance is much the same as other northern Spitz-like breeds. The Akita came to America in 1937, and a heavier influx followed World War II when American soldiers returned from Japan with the noble dog. It was admitted to AKC registry in 1972, and its popularity continues to grow.

Alaskan Malamute

At the top of the world, near the Arctic Circle, is a snowy land originally called Alyeska (vast country). In this icy land populated primarily by Eskimos and musk ox, live the Innuits (people) called Mahlemuts or Malamutes. Centuries ago these nomadic people discovered the advantages of moving from place to place by dog power. They developed a big, tough, weatherproof freighting dog that bears their name, the Alaskan Malamute. These people are so interconnected with their dogs that visitors rarely mention them without also speaking of the beautiful working dogs.

The Malamute's thick, double coat is best left alone between shedding seasons except in older Malamute pets when regular brushing will aid in prevention of mats. In hot climates, this dog's coat may require more attention as well.

Extensive exercise of the adult Malamute is critical if it is to be kept content. For good health and happiness, it must have both mental and physical exercise daily from maturity onward. In snowy environs it is easily exercised by sled pulling, weight-pulling contests, and skijoring. The Malamute will carry its food in backpacks on summertime weekend excursions. Sled training is often continued by putting wheels on the sled during warmer weather.

CURRENT FUNCTION

Today, Alaskan Malamutes are bred in areas south of the arctic lands. They are bred as companion dogs, pets, and for exhibition. Some are used in weight-pulling contests, and skijoring, and yes, some still pull sleds carrying people who pay a bundle of money to experience the thrill of riding in a sled behind fifteen or more big Malamutes. As the team zips around snowy curves, up and down mountain valleys, the air is filled with the dogs' happy talking.

ATTITUDE

Affectionate, intelligent, friendly, and noble, this dog, either male or female, often is dominant when not in harness. The Malamute is wonderfully tolerant with children, but doesn't see the point of fetching a ball and couldn't care less about swimming or tracking. This good-natured pet doesn't recognize strangers and is not first choice if you're seeking a watchdog. A Malamute will wander away when not with its family, and may take extensive excursions if unconfined. Rarely grouchy, it should be socialized with small pets while still a puppy, although even when properly socialized, it has little respect for cats. It minds its own business and rarely bothers other dogs when out and about, but if a silly dog challenges, it will fight at the drop of a hat. Comical and playful, the Malamute is a poor choice for those who want total obedience from their companion.

Origin

The Malamute was developed in Alaska long before that region became a state, so the Malamute is an American dog by default or annexation. The time of development and the specific progenitors of this breed were never recorded, but speculation supposes them to be similar to other northern breeds that are collectively referred to as wolf-Spitz types. When Russian explorers discovered the land, they told of the nomadic Mahlemut people who drove big dog teams pulling sledges loaded with skins and food. This dog is still used in much the same manner today, although in continental America, it has progressed to fill other roles as well.

APTITUDE

The Malamute learns quickly and easily grasps obedience commands, but rarely obeys them slavishly. Training should be undertaken by those with tremendous understanding of the breed, patience, and a good sense of humor. A Malamute likes working with a handler, but has a whimsical attitude and takes the lessons lightly. Rough handling and discipline are a waste of time and may be counterproductive. This dog can be used in agility trials but only if it has proven itself trustworthy with other dogs and dedicated to its handler; such a Malamute will lose to a Border Collie anyway. A Malamute's idea of fun is to pull something. Anything. It will pull you on skis or in a wagon. Be sure you have a pulling harness fitted properly before you begin, and when the game is over, your Malamute will tell you.

APPEARANCE

The Alaskan Malamute ranges in size, and no minimum or maximum height is given in the breed standard. Generally, it's shown at a height of more than 25 inches (63.5 cm), which is the freighting size, but many are 27 or more inches (68.5 cm) tall. Balance between mass and height is critical, and if a dog's weight, height, bone structure, and musculature are in balance, its height is less important.

Original Design

In its beginning, the Malamute probably was selectively bred as a freighting dog, one that would work in large teams without undue quarreling. The original requirement was tremendous strength and stamina, willingness to work, and sufficient toughness to pull enormous loads over the snow packed terrain without regard to climatic conditions. No luxury or sports model was needed. The Malamute was the tractor, the workhorse of the North. Its color was irrelevant; its selection was based on a single function—working.

This big dog has an arctic look, and is supposed by some to closely resemble a wolf. Upon closer inspection, the Malamute's expression and attitude gives it away. Its coat is thick and coarse, with a soft, oily undercoat. It ranges in color from black to white, with most being gray with shadings of black, with white on the underbelly and a darker cap or mask. Its tail is carried over the back and is never tightly curled.

Anatolian Shepherd Dog

The Anatolian Shepherd Dog is named for Anatolia, the western plateau of Turkey in Asia. Safety of the flock was a major concern in ancient herding cultures, and this dog was developed to protect both the flock and herdsmen whose responsibility it was to feed and care for the dog.

In American society, the giant Anatolian's grooming needs are few. Weekly combing and brushing will suffice except during seasonal shedding, when more attention is needed.

Exercise requirements are considerable. Freedom to run within the confines of a large yard is mandatory. Daily excursions in other environments will suit this dog well. Keep in mind that a bored dog is a liability. It may develop nuisance habits, become melancholy, suffer significant depression, and at the very least be an unhappy dog that brings no pleasure to its family.

CURRENT FUNCTION

Sheep and cattle herds may still roam Turkish plains, but in America, most livestock are confined within fences. Yet livestock herds are a fact of life, and when the herds are on open range, the Anatolian Shepherd Dog still is in demand. The Anatolian isn't the dog for everyone, especially beginners. It is well suited to a companion-protection role in society and adapts to practically all environments with proper socialization.

ATTITUDE

Whether guarding herd or home, the Anatolian is a beautifully equipped, powerful flock protector that warns intruders first with a low growl. If the intruder doesn't retreat, the Anatolian's response escalates. As a puppy, this dog should be carefully socialized with children as well as small household pets, neighborhood youngsters, and friends. It's reserved toward strangers and dominant toward other dogs and needs early socialization training in a puppy kindergarten–type environment. It's an extremely brave and vigilant dog that takes its work seriously. This characteristic

The constant search for livestock grazing land motivated ancient Turkish nomads to develop this giant flock-guarding dog. Livestock herds were moved daily and were constantly exposed to predators. Safety of owners and their herds was highly problematical in the ever-changing environments that included packs of wolves, mountain lions, bears, and human thieves and assassins. Devising a security system to keep up with herd movement would have been impossible without dedicated protection dogs, trained to defend flocks and families with their lives if necessary. A trustworthy dog was needed that would act independently of the herdsmen, one that would respond quickly and definitively toward intruders but was easily socialized. Thus, this breed's progenitors are virtually unknown. Belonging to a nomadic culture, it could have roots in any of the countries in which they traveled, and probably is a composite of many herd-protecting breeds. Neither is it known when the Anatolian breed became uniform in size, colors, and character, since its selection was always for function, with little regard to form.

The guarding dog population swelled because herdsmen fed their dogs well. Ever increasing dog numbers promoted selective breeding based on performance and provided these wise dog husbandmen a vast gene pool from which to choose the most talented protectors. Less capable dogs were culled and disposed of; to allow them to live would be counterproductive. These carefully selected dogs worked in teams, some during the day, others at night. This partially learned behavior was practiced, perfected, and over many generations became instinctive to the Anatolian breed. Without being told, some Anatolian Shepherds stayed in camp, looking after their people and smaller animals. Others went in twos and threes, guarding each group of animals.

sometimes may appear to be stubbornness or independence.

APTITUDE

The Anatolian's role as a protection dog differs from that of a guard dog in that its reaction is based on instinct and cleverness, rather than attacking on command. In fact it often refuses to accept many human commands, and may resist training based on these commands. Characteristically, it will live with a family, learn the routine activities of its environment, and respond to the protection needs of its human flock. The Anatolian's instinct is to protect its flock, and it will do this without training. As you might guess, this breed doesn't adapt well to routine obedience work, but with calm and patient leadership, its intelligence may see it through some lessons. As with other big dogs, best training results are achieved when consistency, love, and determination are practiced by its owner, the alpha pack leader. Don't forget, its socialization and training must begin as a puppy and continue throughout life.

APPEARANCE

Anatolian Shepherd Dogs measure up to 32 inches (81 cm) at the shoulder. This is

an athletic, agile, and powerful dog, well muscled and with bone structure that isn't bulky
but is matched to its strength. Most are fawn
or chamois, with black masks, but all other
colors are permitted, including pinto, white,
and brindle. The coat ranges from short to
medium, and is smooth or rough, depending
on region of origin. Its tail is long and finishes
with a curl.

Original Design

Anatolian Shepherd Dogs had a useful
design, one that no doubt was under con-
tinual evaluation and change, and it's fair
to assume that protection dog secrets
were shared among the wandering families. This dog was big and strong enough
to fight off wolves, clever enough to cir-
cumvent two-legged thieves, and sound
enough for long hours in the field. It
made do with sporadic water sources and
lived the life of its herd. It was a tough
protector that operated independently of
human commands.

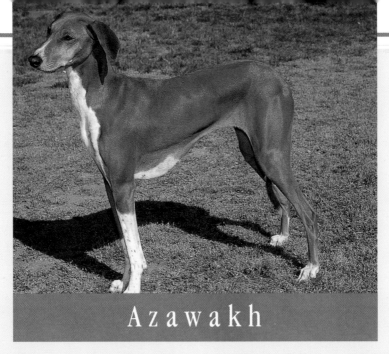

Azawakh

The Tuareg peoples are traditionally among the most independent and feudal societies extant. Many of these nomads continue to roam the Sahara with their herds of camels, zebu cattle, and goats. Contrary to most Moslem customs, the Tuareg women don't wear veils and they do occupy an important place in society. Male warriors wear long robes and head and facial covers characteristic of this interesting people who call themselves Imochagh, meaning "free," "pure," or "independent."

The Azawakh is an ancient breed developed by this mysteriously masked and robed nomadic Tuareg people of Mali, on the continent of Africa. The Azawakh dogs are called Oskas or Idi-Idi by the Tuareg nobles and also are known as the Tuareg Sloughi in the West. This sight hound is seen in limited numbers in America, and is slightly more popular in Europe. The Azawakh Club of America was founded in December 1998 to promote the breed and to encourage adopting the standard of the French Federation Cynologique Internationale (FCI). The breed is also recognized by

the United Kennel Club in England and has recently been recognized by the AKC Foundation Stock Service (FSS).

Coat care is relatively simple, with weekly brushing sufficient except during heavy shedding seasons. Wiping with a chamois or rubber slicker brush will remove shedding and dead hair.

If this hound is kept in the backyard, its exercise needs often present problems. Rarely content with leashed walks, the Azawakh needs much more and should be taken for a free run daily. In many locales this is impossible or illegal since sight hounds are prohibited off-lead because of their propensity to chase and catch other animals.

CURRENT FUNCTION

This dog, described by some as being almost feral, still guards and adorns Tuareg camps and hunts as it has for thousands of years in its native land. Gaining popularity recently in Western countries, it is being bred and kept as a coursing hound, pet, and show dog.

ATTITUDE

Fiercely loyal, this slender, powerful runner is intelligent, but according to some it retains an instinctive aboriginal character. The Azawakh is quite independent but loving and playful with its master while suspicious of strangers. Somewhat temperamental, this lively dog shows its affectionate and gentle nature to those it loves, and being a guard dog, is quite defensive of its home.

APTITUDE

Well equipped for a limited role in society, this trim sight hound is best suited for coursing and hunting game. Training may be a problem, and extreme patience is required by soft-spoken handlers. It blends well with other similar dogs, and is said to be quiet and reserved with children. Able to reach speeds of 40 mph (64 kph), this powerful dog has stamina to match its speed. This and other chasers and hunters shouldn't be trusted with small house pets, and unless the owner's insurance is paid up, the Azawakh shouldn't be exercised off-lead.

APPEARANCE

The Azawakh stands about 27 inches (68.5 cm) in height, although considerable range is seen, with some measuring 29 inches (73.5 cm). *Streamlined* is the word for this dog's

Origin

This breed's time of origin is unknown but believed to be several thousand years ago. Azawakh's native soil is found in the sub-Saharan Sahel, the district found within Mali, Niger, and Burkina Faso.

appearance. The Azawakh is exceptionally thin and athletic with absolutely no excess baggage to encumber its running ability. Its coat is short, soft, and ranges from sable to sandy to red, or roan. A white blaze on the chest is allowed, and white feet are required by the standard.

Original Design

As far as is known, the Azawakh has always adorned and guarded the Tuareg camps. Sometime in the past, this hound was undoubtedly bred from other hound stock and probably was originally developed to catch and dispatch the fleet footed gazelle and small game of the desert areas.

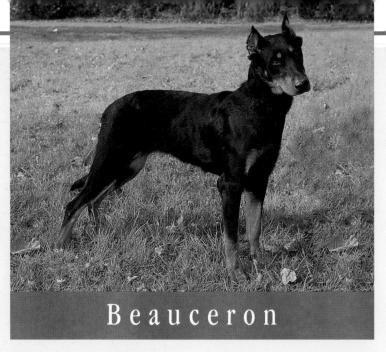

Beauceron

The Beauceron, also known as Bas Rouge (red stockings) and Berger de la Beauce, is relatively rare in America but is well established in Europe and especially in its native France, where it claims its place among other popular sheepdogs.

Its slick, short coat requires little attention except during seasonal shedding.

Not compatible with sedentary life, this herding dog wants significant exercise, including regular extended walks, and like other herding breeds, prefers to run off-lead when possible. A large yard and lots of personal attention are important for this big dog.

CURRENT FUNCTION

Although still a relatively rare breed in America, the Beauceron serves here in the role of companion dog and energetic pet with active families. Lacking the tasks for which it was bred, this dog has adapted well to modern society. A Beauceron is a devoted pet that takes its family-guarding role to heart. When possible, it will spend endless hours with its owner and bonds tightly with family, making it an attractive companion.

ATTITUDE

Clever and courageous, intelligent and active, this dog characteristically is devoted to its family and is very watchful and vigilant. It needs early and continued socialization with other pets and children to become the best companion but generally is quite trustworthy. The Beauceron is said to have a stubborn streak that must be dealt with gently, and it will require of its handlers great patience coupled with appreciation, rewards, consistency, and understanding. It responds best to owners who will spend a great deal of time bonding. Continued handling and playing with the Beauceron pup will assure its temperament and prevent aggressiveness.

APTITUDE

Quite trainable, the Beauceron serves in France as a police dog, herd protection dog, and companion. It trains easily if the owner devotes sufficient time and patience to this endeavor and gives distinct, meaningful commands. The Beauceron frequently exhibits a great nose, and was used as a mine detection and hospital dog during World War II. In this regard, it might be trained for search and rescue or tracking. Training might be directed toward agility trials, fly-ball contests, and other canine games, although the deck is stacked against winning, and your Beauceron may finish second to smaller, lighter dogs.

APPEARANCE

Standing up to 28 inches (70 cm), this breed looks like a cross between a German Shepherd and a Doberman, proving that looks are deceiving. Its ears are often cropped, and French registration requires double dewclaws on its hind legs. Its coat is short and smooth with a dense undercoat. Typically black with tan markings, it is also seen in blue or harlequin colors that are also marked with tan or red on its head, throat, and feet.

Origin

Developed in France during the Middle Ages, this dog sometimes is called Berger de la Beauce because of its place of origin of La Beauce, which is in the plains region around Paris. It is a multipurpose, guard-herding-working-hunting dog that probably descends from other similar French farm dogs. The Beauceron shares heritage with the Briard, although their looks aren't similar. In 1809, a priest penned the differences between these dogs, describing the Beauceron as a shorthaired Mastiff type. In 1900, the Beauceron was exhibited at a show, and breeding became more specific to form than function.

Original Design

The Beauceron served extensively as hunters of wild boar and as livestock protectors, and during the World Wars, they were extensively employed in military duties, especially as sentry and messenger dogs. Its early civilian duties centered around guarding flocks of sheep and herds of cattle, protecting them from predators. It also is a talented herding dog, assisting herdsmen in moving their charges from place to place.

Bernese Mountain Dog

Possibly the best known of the four varieties of similarly colored Swiss Mountain Dogs, this dog also is known as Berner Sennenhund and Durrbachler. As is the case with many working dogs, this big dog filled many roles in its native Switzerland.

The Bernese Mountain Dog is the only Swissie with long, silky hair that needs frequent attention. The coat should be combed as often as necessary to prevent tangles and mats, especially in spring and fall.

The breed is an ambitious one that as an adult enjoys daily exercise, but its needs are not as great as some other breeds. More likely to remain with its handler on walks, it tends to be more trustworthy off-lead than some other big working dogs. Supply this dog with a cart to pull, backpacks to carry, or long walks in the park.

CURRENT FUNCTION

This intelligent dog is a devoted companion to its family, especially a family with small children. Though rarely used for pulling carts today, this dog seems to delight when placed in a harness and allowed to pull small children in a dogcart. This calm and biddable companion takes dog show competition in stride.

ATTITUDE

Loyal and vigilant, the intelligent Bernese rarely barks, but is attentive to visitors and observes them closely. Friendly and possessing a calm demeanor, this dog is usually a wonderful baby sitter and child's pet that will protect his children from harm. It is usually good with small pets providing they are properly introduced. Notably calm, the unassertive Bernese will guard your property in a low profile manner and introduce unannounced strangers with a short full-throated bark, then stand ready for your command.

APTITUDE

A very loyal and biddable dog that thrives on consistent and kind teaching, the Bernese is a

Origin

Home for the Bernese Mountain Dog is the farm country, notably the canton (state) of Berne in the middle of Switzerland, where it functions as a companion and watchdog. Other Swiss Mountain Dogs are the Appenzeller, a shorthaired, curly-tailed dog, the Entlebucher, a shorthaired, naturally bobtailed, smaller dog, and the Greater or Large Swiss Mountain Dog, a shorthaired dog that is larger than any of the others. Ancestors of these dogs are lost to antiquity, but are thought to have been Mastiff-type dogs that were brought to Switzerland by the Romans two thousand years ago. These big dogs were probably crossed with native herd dogs and selectively bred for present purposes, sizes, and colors. The Bernese Mountain Dog lost popularity in the 1840s, and for forty years it diminished in numbers to a point of near extinction. It was reborn late in the nineteenth century and fanciers organized a breed club in 1907. The breed has thrived since; it was brought to America in 1926 and entered in the AKC records in 1937.

APPEARANCE

This tricolored big dog stands up to 27½ inches (70 cm) and has a thick, moderately long wavy or straight coat that is never curly. It is colored jet black with rust and white symmetrical markings. White chest markings usually form a cross, and white facial and feet markings are prominent. These dogs have a definitively masculine or feminine appearance, with the males having a sturdier, heavier appearance, larger head, and more muscle development.

Original Design

The Bernese was originally designed as a draft dog, guard dog, and companion. In those roles, it pulled carts that delivered milk and produce, and protected its master's purse on market day. It was equally at home in harness and in the family parlor.

quick study and an eager student. It is responsive to voice commands and rarely requires corporal punishment or correction. This intelligent friend will accept guidance and training in practically any endeavor.

Black and Tan Coonhound

Raccoons are small game, not the cute, harmless, and fuzzy little critters often depicted in kids' coloring books. Reaching three feet in length and weighing up to thirty pounds, these highly intelligent, short-tempered, sharp-toothed characters are wild animals in every sense of the word. The Black and Tan Coonhound was developed with the nose to locate and the stamina to follow this nocturnal quarry, and the temperament to face the raccoon in its home waters. This big trail hound will follow any scent it is put upon but was developed specifically to trail raccoons and possums, primarily at night. A tenacious and fearless hunter, it's commonly used to trail mountain lion, bear, and other large game.

Its relatively short coat is easy to care for. Occasional combing and brushing to remove dead and shedding hair should suffice.

Exercise needs are considerable, and this often exempts the Black and Tan from companion dog status where only a small yard is available. Join a tracking club, involve your Black and Tan in search and rescue, or com-

mit yourself to frequent exercise chores. Bored hounds are usually vocal dogs that develop numerous nuisance vices.

CURRENT FUNCTION

Although possessing a mellow and restrained disposition, the Black and Tan is more often than not found in hunting or trailing situations. Generally, it's a clean, gentle, easy dog to love, but its instinctive behavior leads it into various difficulties. It's a show dog but not one that cares to serve primarily in that capacity. Its love for the outdoors, woods, waters, and game scents usually prevail.

ATTITUDE

Strong and stubborn, the Black and Tan has a friendly, peaceful demeanor in family environments. It's easy to get along with, but not characteristically a children's dog. Even-tempered and gentle, its disposition is agreeable, but in the absence of trails to follow, it often becomes fidgety and jumps at every opportunity to escape and follow its nose. Frequent association with other hunting hounds have made the Black and Tan compatible with other dogs, but early socialization and great care should be taken when introducing small family pets.

APTITUDE

The intelligent Black and Tan is easily trained, but not particularly adept in some canine games. Successful obedience training comes with more difficulty in the Black and Tan than in less independent breeds, but the dog is well suited for trail and tracking competitions. Like other hounds generally, easy training means fine-tuning the Black and Tan's instinctive actions.

APPEARANCE

The Black and Tan stands up to 27 inches (68.5 cm), but an oversized dog isn't penalized and many are taller. It has considerable bone, and is sturdy, deep chested, and well muscled. Its coat is dense and short. As the name implies, this dog is nearly solid black, with tan markings above its eyes, on the sides of its muzzle, and on its chest, legs, and breeching. White is undesirable and may be reason for disqualification. Its moderately long tail is carried free.

Original Design

This dog has remained much the same since it was conceived. It was and is primarily a hunting dog, one that is most content in a hunting environment. It is a persistent trailing dog, but one that takes its own time with nose to the ground, instinctively following trails totally by the quarry's scent.

Origin

Black and Tans presumably were bred from Bloodhound and American Foxhound progenitors, with influence from the Talbot hound that has been in England since the eleventh century. Developed in America, the Black and Tan's home ground is in the Southeastern regions of the United States, where it has been known for more than two hundred years. The AKC admitted the Black and Tan to its registry in 1945 after years of resistance by independent Black and Tan hunters and breeders.

Bloodhound

The ability of any dog to follow a scent trail more than 200 hours old and for more than 130 miles (220 km) is phenomenal but possible if the dog in question is a Bloodhound. Controversy surrounds the Bloodhound name. Perhaps it is a shortened version of blooded hound, meaning a purebred aristocrat. Or maybe it relates to this dog's ability to track lost or stolen game by the scent of their blood. In either case, the dog's nose is the key to its existence, and the breed is the most famous scent hound in the world. It's also the largest scent hound, and its woebegone countenance is probably one of the most photographed.

The Bloodhound's coat requires very limited attention except during shedding seasons, when more brushing and combing becomes necessary.

Exercise is sometimes a problem in backyard Bloodhounds. Like the Black and Tan, this dog needs a tremendous amount of daily walking to become and remain a good pet, and without exercise or working, it will develop bad habits. Without question, the best exercise for a Bloodhound is allowing it to pursue woodland trails on its own. If that is impossible, join a tracking club. Your Bloodhound will love you for the chance to prove its instinctive gift.

CURRENT FUNCTION

Not terribly popular as a companion dog or pet, the Bloodhound is often kept in show homes, by tracking enthusiasts, or by hunters who breed it to another breed to improve the offspring's scenting ability. In demand by regulators for identifying drugs and contraband, and for trailing convicts, this dog's reputation is well known by police, and its talents are appreciated in courts as well. The Bloodhound continues to find its place among the best search and rescue dogs of today.

ATTITUDE

Boisterous as a puppy, the Bloodhound is a gentle, amiable creature, easy to know and love. Affection exudes from this heavyweight,

Origin

Very likely dating back to ancient Greece and Rome in the pre-Christian era, the Bloodhound spent much of its history in European monasteries, where it was maintained and bred for search and rescue work. Saint Hubert monastery in the Belgian highlands was named for the priest who resided there. In that monastery, a nearly solid black hound known as the Saint Hubert Hound is generally accepted to be the principal progenitor of today's Bloodhound. The twelfth century is often stated to be the period when the Bloodhound was developed, and European clergy are credited with breeding and maintaining this noble beast's purebred status. This European hound was imported to America in the mid-1800s, where its talents were improved by selective breeding.

and sensitivity is one of its principal characteristics. It is a friend to nearly everyone it meets, but when on a track, it's all business. Concentration and tenacity are other natural attributes of the Bloodhound; it's nearly impossible to distract when on a trail. A Bloodhound puppy is easily socialized with its human family and other pets, and herein lies a problem. Without proper supervision, its large size and mellow disposition allow children to unintentionally abuse it.

APTITUDE

For tracking, the Bloodhound is instinctively knowledgeable and wants only fine-tuning of the rules of the game. Other training requires endless patience and tact to succeed. Consistency and being certain that your Bloodhound understands the lessons are equally important. Soulful eyes and pathetic glances can't be taken seriously or failure will follow. Obedience training runs counter to the independence of this breed. One of the Bloodhound's most impressive characteristics is its power and stamina; it will outwalk most humans, and do it easily, all day long. Once on a trail, they will follow it to fruition, regardless of weather or hardships.

APPEARANCE

A Bloodhound stands up to 27 inches (68.5 cm) tall, but larger hounds are preferred,

soulful appearance. Said to have a noble mien or look of wisdom imprinted on its face, the somewhat comical and pathetic expression of a Bloodhound is enchanting. Its smooth-haired coat is black and tan, red and tan, and tawny, with small amounts of white permissible on feet and chest. Its extensive rudder is carried high and is used to tell its handler details of the invisible trail being followed.

Original Design

Ironically, humanitarian uses in the monasteries gradually developed instincts that led to slave tracking in early America. Slaves were hunted by many mongrel scent hounds as well, and purebred Bloodhounds probably weren't popular with slave control, because once a slave was found, the docile Bloodhound wouldn't attack or even hold the miscreant at bay.

providing their quality and dispositions are sound. This is a heavy-boned working hound, one that is bred for strenuous labor in all kinds of weather. Perhaps the most outstanding physical feature of a Bloodhound isn't its great strength, but its skin, which hangs in folds and flews, seeming to be two sizes too large for its frame. Loose skin wrinkles drape its head in copious quantities, adding to its

Borzoi

Known as the Russian Wolfhound until 1936, this patient and wise hunter is not only fast on its feet, it's courageous and tough in the bargain. It was admired and kept by ladies of the Russian czar's court, prized by aristocrats, and a favorite of the famous author Leo Tolstoy. Although primarily a coursing hound, it has the carriage, personality, and rugged beauty to match its regal heritage.

The Borzoi coat is silky and requires regular attention. Combing and brushing can't be avoided in order to keep this great hound well groomed. If a dog isn't being shown, its longest hair can be sheared to prevent tangles and mats.

The Borzoi requires extensive exercise, without which boredom and nuisance behavior may alter its temperament. In many parts of the country, this and other sight hounds are banned from off-lead exercise because of their propensity to identify any moving animal as quarry, and give chase.

CURRENT FUNCTION

Lure-coursing events, companion duties, and dog shows share the modern vocations of the Borzoi. This sensitive and gentle dog is quite at home in a big backyard with a family of children and adults. Popular among dog show enthusiasts, the Borzoi combines a rich coat with flashy colors and clean lines.

ATTITUDE

Sound temperament has been bred into Borzoi for centuries. Because ladies of the court favored this statuesque canine, it's easy to see how a good-natured quality was preferred and carefully selected. Said to be more distant and aloof than other companions, Borzoi are nevertheless loyal to family and suspicious of strangers. Not typically rough-and-tumble playmates, they often prefer dogs and children who honor a calm environment. Generally they are quite peaceful and clean indoors, and aren't given to slavishly following their master about.

Origin

According to some writers, this totally Russian sight hound was developed by crossing the extinct Lapp sled dog with the Collie. Believed to date from the time of Mongol invader Genghis Khan in the thirteenth century, the Borzoi is related to the Russian Owtchar and possibly other sight hounds. The first breed standard was written in 1650, at which time the sport of coursing reached its zenith among Russian royalty. The Borzoi claims the distinction of having more money and manpower dedicated to its breeding, care, and training than any other breed during its heyday in the years prior to the 1917 Russian revolution. Sometimes more than a hundred hounds were teamed in trios to entertain grand dukes and lesser royalty who followed the fleet Borzoi on horseback. The usual game was the wolf but the quarry wasn't always killed; preferably it was muzzled and bound by huntsmen, who set it free when that dubious task was completed. The first Borzoi was brought to America from England in 1889, and today's standard varies little from the original.

APTITUDE

As is the case with other hounds, obedience isn't the Borzoi's best game. Training must be undertaken with great patience, based on mutual respect between teacher and pupil, and miracles shouldn't be expected. Its aptitude today is much the same as it always was, as a calm, patient pet and an enthusiastic gazehound. It's occasionally used to course coyotes, rabbits, and other small game, and is an excellent lure-coursing dog.

APPEARANCE

Borzoi stand no less than 28 inches (71 cm), with many being shown above this height providing other qualities are not compromised. Although never curly, its coat is long and silky, and often quite wavy. Colors are many and

Original Design

Borzoi is derived from borzii, meaning "swift" in Russian. Fleet, sleek, and streamlined, the original Borzoi was designed, without other motives, specifically to outrun, overpower, and pin the rapid running wolf. Borzoi sometimes ran in braces and trios, and occasionally as singles. Borzoi types became muddled and mixed during the late nineteenth century in England and America, when significant outcrossing was practiced, but the Russian kennel of Grand Duke Nicholas provided the solution to this dilemma, and the true Borzoi types were reinstated.

various, with none being unacceptable, and some being quite startling and beautiful. Its springy gait is distinctive and beautiful, giving the true impression of tremendous speed. Often somewhat Roman-nosed, the expression on their streamlined head reflects their calm demeanor. A deep, narrow chest gives the dog plenty of heart and lung capacity for great endurance.

Bouvier des Flandres

Flanders is a historical region in northern Europe along the borders of Belgium, the Netherlands, and France. Politically, the boundaries of this region have changed frequently. Once it was a vassal of the Holy Roman Empire and was ruled by the French until 1815, when it came under the Kingdom of the Netherlands. In 1830, Belgium won its independence and retained both East and West Flanders. The Bouvier des Flandres is also known by various descriptive terms such as Belgian Cattle Dog, Vulibard (dirty beard), Koehond (cow dog), Toucheur de Boeuf (cattle driver), and Chien de Vacher (cow herd's dog).

The Bouvier's coat is double and tousled, perfect for an outdoor working dog. Regular weekly grooming is required for pets, but is more demanding in show dogs.

Exercising this dog's mind and body requires attention, but its needs aren't excessive. A big yard, children to play with, and a walk or two each day to stimulate and satisfy its other interests will suffice.

CURRENT FUNCTION

A herding dog tends its flock, whatever that may be. Generally, a herding dog makes a fine family companion since it can spend its time herding and caring for children. The Bouvier is no exception, and in America, it has grasped that role well.

ATTITUDE

Steady, determined, devoted, and fearless, the Bouvier des Flandres is wonderful with children, whom it watches intently and herds around the yard when possible. This dog is affectionate but not doting; it's an intelligent dog that acts appropriately on its own under many circumstances. It relies on daily contact with its family members, bonds tightly, and interacts with them. Lacking this inclusion into the family circle, it likely will become bored, and noisy, and develop various vices.

APTITUDE

This Dog of Flanders's instinctive protective

attitude is quite well established, but training a highly intelligent dog is easily accomplished as well. The Bouvier's wartime uses demonstrated this dog's dedication to its handlers and to training and commands. It carried messages from unit to unit under fire and at great risk. It located wounded soldiers on the battlefield and signaled medical corpsmen to their aid. Sometimes insufficient challenge creates a problem in inactive or older families. Training the Bouvier then becomes a necessity. Successful training depends on rewarding accomplishments consistently and being sure the Bouvier always knows what is being asked. If the dog is becoming bored, join an agility, fly-ball, or obedience club. Use this dog's intelligence to keep it busy!

APPEARANCE

A height of 27½ inches (70 cm) is the upper limit of this statuesque dog. The Bouvier was originally of various sizes and appearances, but gained uniformity in 1912 when a breed standard was adopted. Its coat is double, with the outer coat being harsh and rough, and the undercoat is soft and dense. Colors range from fawn to salt and pepper, gray, brindle, and black. In America its ears are often clipped, but either way, this dog has the appearance of alertness. Its bushy eyebrows and beard give it a certain distinction and add to its personality.

Original Design

Cattle driving was the primary reason for development of this beautiful breed, but it has also served in the military with great distinction, sometimes is used as a guide dog for the blind, and occasionally is chosen for police work.

Origin

Flanders embraced a farming culture when the Bouvier was developed. Spanish Crusaders probably brought the Bouvier or its predecessors to Flanders. A herding dog chosen specifically to tend and drive cattle, it wasn't necessarily uniform in conformation or color. Early in World War I, the breed nearly became extinct because of the destruction of its homeland, but a few dedicated Belgians managed to retain their brood stock. The dog spread to most European countries, and was regularly imported to America after World War I. The AKC recognized the Bouvier des Flandres in 1931, and it gains popularity annually.

Briard

Known as Chien Berger de Brie (the Shepherd Dog of Brie), this French sheepdog has also been known as Dog of the Grasslands. This herd guarding dog was a perfectionist in his original duties and is much the same in his adopted role in human society.

The six-inch coat of the Briard needs biweekly grooming and care to keep it clean, neat, and free from tangles and mats. This attention must be doubled during shedding seasons.

Exercise requirements are somewhat less stringent, and reasonably long walks in the park or countryside in addition to a big backyard will suffice to keep the Briard in good mental and physical condition.

CURRENT FUNCTION

Lacking wolves and other predators to threaten American suburban sheep, in recent years this distinctive dog in recent years has laid claim to the title companion dog, and serves in this quieter and less dangerous role quite nicely.

ATTITUDE

The Briard is an intelligent, tough, spirited, and independent dog, an excellent companion pet with the right family. It's fearless and prepared for anything, be it a romp with the children or a nap at your feet, but it's not timid or shy. Sometimes it's a bit impatient, and it doesn't appreciate pestering. When socialized properly, it happily lives with other pets, but may be aggressive or dominant toward strange dogs. This dog is family oriented and does poorly when ignored or separated from its owners and children. The Briard is naturally suspicious of strangers, but when introduced properly will accept almost anyone as a friend.

APTITUDE

Training this dog is best accomplished with a loving touch and ample rewards. Consistency and gentleness will win this dog's attention, but it has a long memory and never forgets unjust treatment or force. This big dog is easily trained by an experienced, understanding

Origin

In twelfth-century France, Charlemagne bred Briards under the name of Chien Berger de Brie, indicating that the dog hailed from the old Province of Brie. In truth, many long-haired herd dogs are known to have been developed all over Europe for untold centuries. Similar in conformation to the Bearded Collie, Komondor, Kuvasz, Puli, and Old English Sheepdog, the Briard probably shares progenitors with these and other cattle- and sheepherding dogs. Briards found greater conformation uniformity by 1897, when the breed standard was written, and in 1907, a French Briard club was founded. The dog was imported to America, where the Briard Club of America adopted a similar standard in 1928. Briards were registered by the AKC in 1922.

Original Design

The Briard was a herd-protecting dog in its native France, and perhaps to some extent in its early days in America. It was originally designed to protect herds from wolves and other predators and poachers. Its strong herd-guarding instincts live on and are equally important to American owners.

handler who first encourages focus and a desire to please its master.

APPEARANCE

The handsome Briard stands up to 27 inches tall (68.5 cm) and is a powerful dog without coarseness or extra bulk. This full-coated herd-protection dog turned family pet is unique in appearance and personality. Its thick, coarse, hard coat lies flat or is slightly wavy and covers its eyes, flowing into a handsome beard. Any uniform color except white is permissible. It usually appears black, gray, or tawny, and the deeper colors are preferred.

Bullmastiff

Sturdy and *powerful* are the words that come to mind when watching a Bullmastiff in the show ring. It moves with silent athletic authority and shows no evidence of puppy clumsiness or indecision. Also known by the descriptive name of Gamekeeper's Night-Dog, this big dog is nevertheless a wonderful companion if trained properly.

Coat care is minimal; regular grooming with a slicker brush usually will suffice to keep the coat in excellent condition. Extra grooming during shedding is important.

This is a dog that requires little strenuous exercise, and daily walks on lead and romps in the yard will usually suffice to keep your companion in good mental and physical condition.

CURRENT FUNCTION

Few estates of today rely on dogs for security, but if they did, the Bullmastiff would be first choice. Instead, this dog serves its family as a companion, watchdog, and show dog. It may be seen in obedience competition, and may be

sufficiently quick and clever to try its paws at agility competition, although such contests usually go to smaller herding-type dogs.

ATTITUDE

The Bullmastiff is a docile companion but an excellent watchdog. It's quite tolerant toward children but is often dominant among dogs. It needs early socialization with both humans and canines to develop into its potential as a great pet. It's reliable, intelligent, faithful, and devoted to its family. The Bullmastiff doesn't kennel well, and confining it away from its family is a mistake.

APTITUDE

This breed typically is sensitive to vocal tone changes and trains well if fairness and consistency are employed. Intolerant of abuse and rough handling, the dog is usually quite obedient and is a quick learner as long as it understands what is expected of it. Usually the Bullmastiff has an excellent nose, and this feature can be used to invent scent games to play.

APPEARANCE

The Mastiff stands up to 27 inches (68.5 cm) tall and is a sturdy, muscular, big dog. Bred for use and not beauty, it is nevertheless a beautiful companion. Its athletic build, relatively short muzzle, wrinkled face, and sad eyes set in a black mask are among its many attractions. This dog moves freely and smoothly, with great power in each stride. Originally, the dark brindle dogs were preferred for nighttime sentries, but red and fawn are more popular in America today.

Origin

In nineteenth-century England this breed sprouted from the need to protect large estates from game poachers. The strength, tenacity, and ferocity of the Bulldog was mixed with the greater size and trainability of the Mastiff, and the result was the big, silent, tough, and quick Bullmastiff. The Bullmastiff was brought to America, gained popularity, and was entered in AKC registry in 1933.

Original Design

The Bullmastiff was developed to defend the property of men from other men. Other features were secondary to this original concept. It moved silently around buildings and in woods and attacked interlopers only on command. Feared primarily because of this silent vigilance that could be disastrous to stumble upon, it proved itself invaluable to gamekeepers and groundsmen. The Bullmastiff was capable of knocking a man to the ground and holding him there for the keeper, and would do this while wearing a muzzle if required.

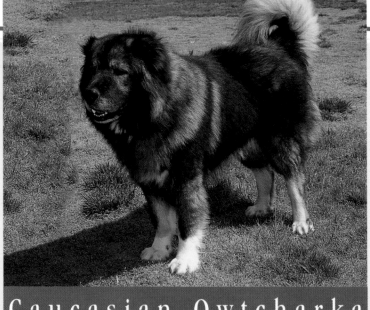

Caucasian Owtcharka

This dog is rarely seen in America, but is common in Russia and surrounding countries. The Owtcharka or Ovtcharka is also known as the Caucasian Sheepdog.

It's seen in three different coat types, all of which require minimal grooming except during shedding season.

Best situated with a family with a big yard, this big dog's life doesn't revolve around exercise but it will do best when plenty of time is given to leashed walks and play.

CURRENT FUNCTION

Flock-protection dogs are in low demand in America. In this country, this Russian breed is best known as a companion and guardian of families. It's reported to be easily trained and adaptable to new roles, which might assure its future in this country.

ATTITUDE

Naturally protective, this calm and collected dog is even-tempered, and with plenty of socializing while young, is trustworthy with other pets. It's strong willed, independent, and stubborn, like other flock-guarding breeds. Though it's a family companion, the Owtcharka sometimes forgets its size and overwhelms small children and may become bossy with them. It needs thorough socialization and must completely understand its place in the family pack order. Males often are dominant toward other dogs, particularly other males, and have been known to show aggressiveness toward both humans and other dogs. Beware of timid, aggressive, or shy parents when you are shopping for an Owtcharka pup.

APTITUDE

No guard training should be initiated; the Owtcharka's instincts will take care of that. This breed is said to be more inclined to try to please its handler than some other flock-protection dogs. Training shouldn't be attempted by those unfamiliar with this type of dog. Begin consistent training slowly and at a young age.

Origin

The Caucasian region of the world includes Georgia, Armenia, Azerbaijan, Iran, and Turkey. The Caucasus Mountains and the steppes of Russia were the origin of this breed that was developed as a flock-guarding sheepdog. The Owtcharka is said by some to have descended from Mastiff breeds, but most authorities suggest its progenitors came from Mesopotamia, where it was a working sheepdog. Tribes of nomads brought dogs with them into the Caucasus Mountains as they searched for better grazing land for their flocks. The Owtcharka remained there, remote and isolated from the world for many years. It was first seen in German dog shows in the 1930s. The breed underwent several conformational controversies, and today the Georgian type resembles a bear and has heavier bone and coat. In recent years, it's been seen throughout Europe, but its acceptance is limited. America is home to a modest number of Caucasian Owtcharkas.

Kindergarten exposure is essential. Dominance training should help if begun early and continued for life. If obedience lessons are anticipated, make the exercises short and keep them fun with lots of rewards and vocal appreciation.

APPEARANCE

No maximum stature is noted, but 25½ to 30 inches (64 to 76 cm) is suggested as a minimum for this big dog. This dog is well balanced, muscular, and powerful. It is seen in all colors except solid black or brown. The Caucasian Owtcharka usually appears in gold, gray, brindle, and combinations of black and brown.

Original Design

Although Ovtcharka or Owtcharka means "shepherd" or "sheepdog," this dog is a herd-protection breed, as differentiated from a herding dog. It was developed to bond with its herd, virtually living with its livestock, to guard them from predators and thieves. It wasn't given commands that must be obeyed, but gradually became instinctively associated with the sheep rather than the shepherds.

Chesapeake Bay Retriever

A truly American dog, the Chessie is first and foremost a big, robust hunting dog. It's said that the Chesapeake Bay is superior to any other breed in the ability to withstand inclement weather.

Ruggedly beautiful, this athlete's coat is easily cared for and should be left alone except during shedding seasons. Too much brushing and combing will harm the rough texture of its all-weather coat.

Exercise requirements are significant, and must not be overlooked. Not a dog to be kenneled all the time, the Chesapeake is an energetic hunter that may develop intolerable vices if bored. Retrieving games, swimming, leashed walks, and a big backyard will usually be sufficient.

CURRENT FUNCTION

If lucky, today's Chessie still is serving in its original field sport role with slight modifications. Rarely finding a hunting day that produces more than a few ducks, this brave dog lives for the next retrieve. It's a never-tiring, energetic dog in retrieving games, but will adapt to other games willingly if led to do so. Slowly being recognized in the show ring, the Chessie is a good family companion and often serves as a watchdog as well. It has been trained as a guide dog, and willingly accepts assistance work, tracking, obedience trials, and agility contests.

ATTITUDE

The Chesapeake is loving but boisterous, obedient but has a mind of its own. It's friendly and energetic, often plays roughly, and sometimes doesn't know when to quit. Often considered a one-person companion, it accepts other members of the family in secondary roles. A dedicated swimmer, the Chessie can't pass up a lake or river without taking a dip. It lives to retrieve and will wear out most children in this game. This dog wants to be included in family events, and if refused may become moody.

According to most accounts, the Chessie evolved from progeny of two native Newfoundland pups that were shipwrecked off the coast of Maryland in 1807. Other accounts question whether the Newfoundland originated in that country or in England. Some give accounts of other breeds that were woven into the Chesapeake fabric. Regardless of origin or specific breeds that might have influenced it, Chesapeake Bay waterfowl hunters developed this retriever during a time when their activities were critical to the residents of that region. Records of the Chessie's exploits indicate that it often faced rough water, ice and snow, rapid currents, and wind to retrieve 100 to 200 ducks in a single day. When meat hunting was replaced by other sources of table fowl, American sportsmen adopted the Chessie to retrieve ducks and geese from lakes, bays, and rivers across this nation.

APTITUDE

Training this dog isn't recommended for beginners and is best suited to confident, strong trainers that will use consistency, patience, and gentleness. The dog is so tough that some consider it hardheaded. Not so! The Chesapeake is sensitive but must understand exactly what you want from it. Hardheaded training with a heavy hand is wasted on this dog, which bonds strongly with its handler and is loving, obedient, and intelligent. Vigilant and uneasy with strangers, this dog is instinctively a good family security system that needs early socialization with other pets and children.

APPEARANCE

The Chessie is a big-hearted dog with a big attitude in spite of its slightly smaller stature.

The Chesapeake Bay was designed as a soft-mouthed water retriever. It instinctively loves water, swimming, retrieving game birds, and other strenuous activity. Tenacious and an expert swimmer, the Chesapeake will dive again and again to pick up a wounded duck without regard to freezing water, strong currents, or bone-chilling weather.

The breed standard's upper limit is 26 inches (66 cm), although I suspect a really fine specimen may sneak in at 27 inches (68.5 cm). This dog is a well-balanced athlete with a muscular body. A Chesapeake's coat is thick, fairly short, wavy or straight, accompanied by a fine, dense, wooly undercoat. Its outer coat is usually oily, the better to shed icy water. Colors vary from deep brown to deadgrass (a light tan), with no markings permitted except a tiny white patch on the chest or abdomen. Solid colors are always preferred.

Curly-Coated Retriever

Appearing totally natural and tidy, whether appearing in a show ring or a hunting soirée, this robust dog enjoys immense popularity with those who know and use it. It's an outstanding water retriever with graceful beauty and rugged conformation, and is one of the oldest retriever breeds. Agile and active, this trim, biddable, and intelligent dog is possibly most popular in Australia and New Zealand, where it is used on quail as well as waterfowl. Its eagerness to hit the water, regardless of temperature, and its stamina, swimming prowess, and diving propensity put it in tight competition with the best of the retrievers. Said never to give up on wounded waterfowl, it's been known to dive endlessly until the wounded bird is captured. Some authorities have claimed this dog is too slow for field trials, all the while admitting its competency. Early in Curly-Coat history is found a hard-mouth claim that seems to be unfounded in recent years.

The ease in caring for the Curly's coat further lends this beautiful hunting dog credibility as a pet, and weekly light brushing will usually suffice, with more attention due during shedding. Its tightly curled coat retains hair, making it a good house dog that doesn't leave mats of coat on the furniture and rugs.

The Curly-Coat, like other retrievers, is an active dog with significant exercise needs. It is best to get it into a hunt club, initiate retriever games, find a safe swimming lake, or arrange for regular long walks. Regular exercise and personal interaction is necessary to keep it happy and amiable.

CURRENT FUNCTION

Field trials and gundog duties are still at the head of the list of the contemporary Curly-Coats, but the breed fills the bill as an excellent choice for the weekend suburban hunter who wants a good companion for the family and an intelligent, faithful guard dog. Nonhunting families who appreciate its trim lines and enduring strength often own this dog. When given sufficient exercise to prevent nuisance

Progenitors of this breed are not well documented. The Curly-Coat may be descended from French Poodle, Irish Water Spaniel, English Water Spaniel, and the smaller St. John's Newfoundland or Labrador Retriever. There can be no doubt that its ancestors were hunting dogs that also may have included setter and spaniel. Perhaps first alluded to in 1803 in the English *Sportsmen's Cabinet,* the breed was developed in England and was first recognized and shown in 1860 at Birmingham. The Curly-Coated

Retriever Club of England was formed in 1896. This dog was introduced very early into New Zealand and Australia, where it has remained quite popular among companion dog owners and the duck- and quail-hunting public. By 1907 the Curly-Coat was found in America, and the first AKC registration was in 1924. Its popularity was limited when first introduced, but it competes well in the field with the Chesapeake, Labrador, and Irish Water Spaniel, and its popularity has increased since the 1930s.

habits such as barking, pacing, and moodiness, the Curly-Coat makes an excellent pet.

ATTITUDE

Its calm, sweet disposition make the Curly-Coat a gentle family companion. It's an affectionate and faithful pet that enjoys the companionship of people and one that may become easily bored and moody if ignored for long periods.

Original Design

The Curly-Coated Retriever was developed primarily for retrieving waterfowl. It has proven itself on upland game birds as well, and now is relatively popular in field trials. Its time-honored role has been in the field, but it has now established itself in the show ring and in many of the other exhibitions and contests such as agility trials, fly-ball and Frisbee contests, and obedience trials.

A natural guard dog, it is mildly suspicious of strangers.

APTITUDE

Said to be easy to train, this retriever was bred for the water, and instruction may be limited to teaching simple commands. An excellent memory accompanies its marking ability. On land, the Curly-Coat is quite adept at locating runners that might otherwise be lost to the hunter. Retrieving games are easily taught, and its athletic build gives it an advantage at agility contests and obedience work.

APPEARANCE

Males stand up to 27 inches (68.5 cm) at the withers. This is a big dog, strong, muscular, and athletic with a deep chest and relatively short body. Its head is long and well proportioned, with small, close lying ears. Its coat is tightly curled and black or dark liver in color, and eyes are black or deep brown. The Curly tail is fairly short and tapering, covered with tight curls and carried straight.

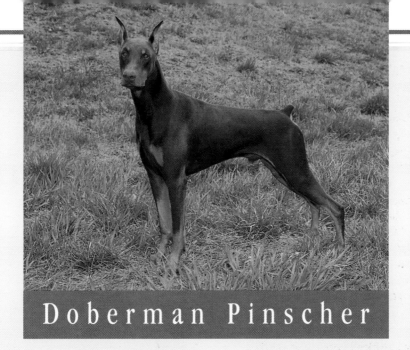

Doberman Pinscher

What dog comes to mind when you think of regal stature with clean lines, and immediately gives you the impression of boldness, alertness, and intelligent cleverness? What is the consummate powerful guard dog that when met assesses you with one quick Wyatt Earp glance? The dog possessing all these qualities and more is popular in American homes. The Doberman Pinscher needs lots of attention, training, exercise, and complete understanding. The Doberman probably is more misunderstood than any of the popular dogs in America. People often fear this dog without knowing why. Its very image sends shivers up spines, and if two Dobies are standing in a yard, that's the one place you wish to avoid!

This dog's physical care is minimal. Its sleek coat wants brushing now and then to keep it shiny, but other than that, its needs are few.

Exercise is usually afforded by a big backyard to patrol, family members to watch, and some high-quality time walking regally alongside its master every day.

CURRENT FUNCTION

The well-trained Dobie is right at home caring for and guarding its human family. It protects the children, dwelling, vehicle, and other possessions with pride and efficiency. In the bargain, Doberman owners find they have their lifestyles changed by this beautiful dog. A Doberman owner must give it a fair share of personal time for exercise, training, and companionship. This dog is certainly no shrinking violet. Its presence is immediately known and appreciated by one and all. It has added dog shows, obedience trials, police work, tracking, agility trials, and assistance performance to its other skills.

ATTITUDE

Active and cunning, this big dog bonds tightly with its owner, proving its loyalty at every step. Its intelligence is never questioned, but sometimes this powerful dog is so devoted to one person, other members of the family are accepted with reservation. Socialization with every person in the family is extremely important from puppyhood to old age. Usually a Doberman is quiet, although frequently a pup is boisterous and rowdy and tends to play a bit roughly with its children. As an adult, its self-assured pride puts spectators and interlopers at an immediate disadvantage.

APTITUDE

One look from an adult Doberman stops a stranger in his tracks, and this dog needs perpetual training to soften rather than enforce that characteristic. This highly intelligent dog grasps lessons quickly, but take care never to move too quickly with lessons. Don't raise your voice, nag, or abuse the Doberman in any way and be sure one task is fully understood before teaching the next. Failure of proper

Origin

The region of Apoida, Thuerigen, Germany is the place the Doberman Pinscher was developed, the time was about 1890, and the dogs used were the Rottweiler, German Shepherd, German Pinscher, and English Black and Tan Terrier. Louis Dobermann was the principal human involved, and his intent was to breed a security dog to protect his life and position as tax collector. He needed something more than an alarm—he wanted an alarm with teeth, and the results of this crossbreeding provided the necessary deterrent to thieves and muggers.

Original Design

Originally and traditionally, the Doberman has served its master well in the duties requested. It was and is devoted to its role as protector, companion, and assistant to people in all walks of life.

training will produce shy, snappy, or untrustworthy dogs. Training should be consistent and on-going, and should be undertaken only by experienced, patient people. Guarding qualities are instinctive with the Dobie, and additional guard training should be commenced only in particular situations by specially trained trainers.

APPEARANCE

The ideal Doberman stands about 27½ inches (70 cm) or slightly taller. Its sleek, streamlined, and squarely balanced body is muscular and powerful, with great endurance exuding from every pore. Its proud in-command carriage is one of its greatly appreciated characteristics; it always seems to know exactly what is happening. Its smooth, short, thick coat lies flat and is allowed by the standard to be of several colors including black, red, blue, and fawn (Isabella). Markings are rust colored and are allowed on the face, throat, legs, chest, and under the tail. Ears are usually cropped in America, but European Dobies are often seen with natural ears. Blue Dobermans often come with a variety of undesirable defects. These problems should be discussed with your veterinarian and the breeder.

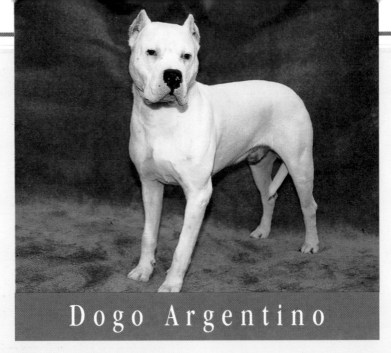

Dogo Argentino

Otherwise known as Argentinean Mastiff and Dogo Argentinof, this dog was bred from a Spanish fighting dog, diluted or improved by crossing with half a dozen other breeds. With its reputation always preceding it, the dog seems to have a lot to live down or prove.

Its short white coat is easily cared for with a rubber grooming mitt or brush.

Its exercise requirements are significant and must be addressed even when a large yard is furnished. Regular long walks are needed, and because of the Dogo's reputation, it must be closely controlled on-lead when off your property. This dog may respond well to a head collar.

CURRENT FUNCTION

This brave and temperamental dog is reputed to be loyal to its handler but dominant toward other dogs. It's well suited for its original purposes, and has considerable stamina, nose, and hunting speed. Since it's every inch a hunter, other house pets may be considered prey and always are at risk. After making its appearance in South America the Dogo was banned in Great Britain because of temperament concerns. Today's Dogo Argentino is reputed by fanciers to be an excellent family companion and totally trustworthy around people. Even after its historical temperament adjustment by the introduction of blood from other, more gentle breeds, it remains a questionable pet or companion for the average family.

ATTITUDE

Reported by breeders to be a fine outgoing companion that is friendly with people and appreciates human affection, the strongly developed hunting instincts influence much of the Dogo's attitude. It possesses strong concentration, determination, and courage. Although it is said to tolerate the family's children quite well, the Dogo may be untrustworthy with neighborhood children. It needs daily human contact, work, exercise, and interaction to remain happy. A bored, neglected Dogo can become a terrific nuisance.

APTITUDE

Training should be undertaken by experienced, patient trainers who will proceed with consistency and gentleness. Definitely not a dog for the beginning handler, the Dogo Argentino requires a great deal of knowledge of the breed and its idiosyncrasies. It needs early and continued supervised training and socialization with humans and other pets to moderate its strong hunting, guarding, and fighting instincts. No guard training is necessary to elicit protective reflexes; the Dogo instead needs special training in judgment.

APPEARANCE

Standing about 27 inches (68.5 cm), this Mastiff always is seen as a white dog, rarely having any markings. Its powerful, clean lines and athletic musculature combined with its relatively small eyes and clipped ears give it a unique, foreboding appearance. Its straight, long tapered tail gives it a streamlined look that finishes this sleek dog to perfection.

Original Design

Designed to pursue and confront wild cats and boars, this dog's aggressiveness was originally an important part of its makeup. Tough and ready to go, the Dogo Argentino was and is designed to be a hunter. It's also occasionally trained for schutzhund, military work, police assistance, and search and rescue.

Origin

The Dogo Argentino's principal progenitor was the Fighting Dog of Cordoba, Spain, which was bred expressly for pit fighting. This pit dog is reported to have possessed blood of the Bull Terrier, English Bulldog, Mastiff, and Boxer. In the early 1920s, the aggressive, domineering, and fearless Fighting Dog of Cordoba was used to create the Dogo Argentino by crossing it with the Great Dane, Great Pyrenees, English Bulldog, Bull Terrier, and the Dogue de Bordeaux. Further crosses were accomplished with the Pointer, Irish Wolfhound, and Boxer. The resulting canine was developed in Argentina to hunt wild boar, puma, and jaguar. In that endeavor, it excelled, and it is said to be temperamentally stable, tough, and quite intelligent.

Dogue de Bordeaux

The Dogue de Bordeaux is a Mastiff-type breed of great power that possesses possibly the most massive canine head in the world. Also known as Bouledogue Français, and occasionally called French Mastiff, this is a tough, strong, imposing dog.

Its sleek, shiny coat is easily groomed with a chamois cloth or rubber slicker brush, and such grooming usually elicits positive bonding responses from this big dog.

It's much like other Mastiffs of the world in that it grows rapidly and should not be exercised heavily as a pup, and as an adult, this somewhat sedentary breed requires only average exercise such as a few daily walks and an occasional romp in the park. A big backyard is essential.

CURRENT FUNCTION

Today this big dog is employed as a guard dog, companion, and pet. Although it is rarely seen in America, its popularity seems to be increasing. Like most other Mastiffs, it requires a lot of its owner's time, but is a remarkable companion for the patient and loving family. It's not yet registered with the AKC for that organization's shows and other activities.

ATTITUDE

Described as having a gifted guard-dog temperament, this breed is not notably aggressive, although often the male Dogue de Bordeaux is domineering toward other dogs. Guarding is instinctive and accompanied by the expected vigilance and courage. Forming a strong bond with its owner, this dog is affectionate and an excellent companion. Its demeanor is calm, quiet, and balanced, and typically it has a high stimulus threshold. The Dogue de Bordeaux's stocky, athletic, and imposing size lends it a dissuasive appearance that tells interlopers to beware. Timidity and aggressiveness are major personality faults of some Dogues de Bordeaux, and to prevent these characteristics, careful selection from known nonaggressive parent stock is critical. Socialization and training should be begun while it is a puppy and maintained for the life of the dog. With plenty of experience and interaction with other small animals as a puppy, this dog is equable and its behavior usually can be trusted around other pets. Suspicious of strangers, it usually will adopt its master's attitude and accept friends and introduced visitors.

APTITUDE

Perhaps best suited as a family companion and guard for the children, home, and property, this dog's training is critically important. Obedience and other training needs to be kept calm, fair, and above all, consistent. A heavy hand and nagging or dissuasive actions should never be used when training a Bordeaux. Often this dog becomes quite attached to the trainer and will perform to please this person, who must never forget to offer affection, approval, and treats when lessons are performed correctly.

APPEARANCE

Standing about 27½ inches (70 cm) the first and most dominant feature to catch your eye is its huge head. The Dogue de Bordeaux's head volume and shape are quite distinctive with a

Original Design

Originally designed for hunting boars, pit fighting, and guarding homes and property, this dog once was used as a butcher's dog, presumably pulling a cart and guarding its owner's money and property. Its great strength and tenacity served it well in all these endeavors.

Origin

An ancient French breed, finding its heritage in the Aquitaine region of France, this dog has evolved in three types, the Toulouse, Paris, and the Bordeaux type, which is today's Dogue de Bordeaux. This dog was quite popular in its native land and was shown in the first French dog show in 1863 under its present name. This breed, like many others, was reduced in numbers during World War II, but regained its footing in the 1960s.

deeply furrowed face. Its heavily muscled body and legs move with suppleness, freedom, and great strength. The coat is short and sleek, without white markings. Colors seen include mahogany red or red-brown with a black or red face.

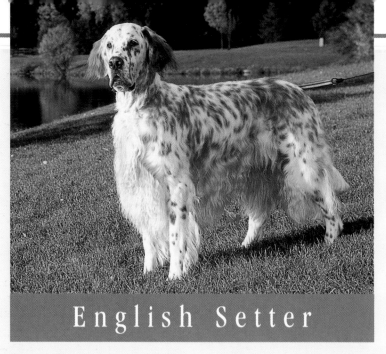

English Setter

The flowing grace of this dog's smooth, effortless, ground-covering gait, accented by its magnificent coat, is truly beauty in motion. This elegant dog's ability as a bird hunter has been surpassed by its status as show dog and companion.

The English Setter's coat requires hours of attention, including daily combing and brushing.

An extremely athletic dog, the English Setter is a typical sporting breed that needs plenty of regular exercise and thrives in active families. Daily walks, retrieving games, long walks, and runs are critical to prevent boredom.

CURRENT FUNCTION

A strong, intelligent, and useful dog, the English Setter has remained popular for many talents besides its hunting ability. It's a colorful, eye-catching dog in the show ring, and its alertness and beauty has made it very popular as a companion. The blue and orange coloring is hard to resist in spite of its need for daily grooming. Responsive in either a field or home setting, this dog excels in pointer field trials and in backyards, playing with children.

ATTITUDE

Friendly and lovable are words frequently used to describe an English Setter's personality. It's a good natured and sensitive dog that bonds closely with family and socializes well with other pets. Cautious in the presence of strangers, this dog is a trustworthy and faithful companion that's large enough to cause an interloper to think twice, although most Setters consider everyone a friend.

APTITUDE

Though easily trained, the English Setter has a mind of its own and responds best to consistent and patient handling. This dog learns its lessons well if not forced or hurried and is often considered a one-man dog in the field. It is sensitive, but that doesn't mean the English Setter is timid by nature. It simply

Origin

Said to be the oldest gun dog in America, the English Setter is one of the earliest British hunting breeds and probably dates to the sixteenth century. It is undoubtedly related to the Spanish land spaniels of the period, although pictures in books of 1582 show this setter to have a substantially different appearance from the spaniels of that day. The progenitors of the breed may include Spanish Pointers, Water Spaniels, and Springers. The contemporary type was developed from established English Setters bred by Laverack in about 1825. These dogs were first shown at Newcastle-on-Tyne in 1859. Shortly thereafter, Llewellin imported to America and Canada some of his setters, which were of the Laverack blood crossed with other successful field trial English Setters from northern England. This Llewellin strain became immensely popular among field trial proponents, almost to the exclusion of other English Setters. Laverack setters continued to perform well in other fields, as well as in the show ring. This separation of strains did a great deal of harm and no good for the breed as a whole, because more attention was paid to the pedigree than to the dogs' field ability. The Llewellin strain wasn't confined to distinctive colors, although many novice dog watchers assign that term to lightly marked, blue-ticked dogs.

well-balanced, lean, and muscular body covered by a luxurious long, silky coat of several startling colors. It gaits smoothly and covers ground with scant effort. This breed's overall harmony of parts makes it difficult to fault. Coats have white ground color with varying degrees of flecked markings and roan shadings of orange, yellow, black, and tan. These are called tricolor, blue belton, lemon belton, liver belton, and orange belton. The term belton got its name from the town of Belton, England, where Laverack developed the breed. Belton now refers to the roan or flecked color characteristic of the English Setter. Its chest, legs, and ears are moderately feathered, as is its tail, which is held high when on point.

Original Design

Setters's duties were designed and developed prior to the advent of shotguns. Their duty was to locate upland game birds, and by steady crouching and staring, cause the birds to set or huddle together until the hunter threw a net over them. When shotguns were perfected, the English Setter was modified to first point the game, and then after the gunner arrived, to retrieve the birds that were shot. Hard running is an attribute of this dog, whose stamina and athletic ability ranks among the best sporting breeds.

reacts more positively to kindness than roughness. It's an industrious hunter that thrives on its owner's attention and affection. Its elegant carriage and classy appearance have earned it the title of hunting dog aristocrat.

APPEARANCE

This big dog often stands about 25 inches, but some references list its height as 27 inches (68.5 cm). A moderately long, silky, flat coat of mottled color contributes to English Setter appearance. Pages of prose have been written about the form and grace of a winning English Setter. Suffice it to say that this dog displays a

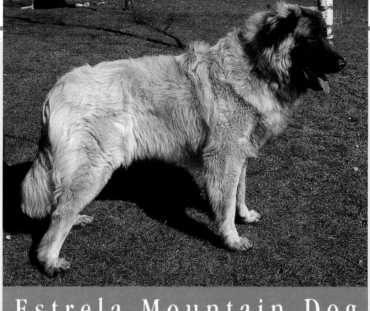

Estrela Mountain Dog

This sturdy, well-built Mastiff-type dog is a large Portuguese flock-guarding dog that has found its modern niche as a family watchdog or guard. It's also known as Cão da Serra da Estrela in its native land.

The shorthaired Estrela is simply groomed with a slicker brush, and the longhaired variety also is relatively easily groomed by weekly combing since the longer hair resists tangling. The coat needs more attention during seasonal shedding.

The Estrela's exercise requirements are quite significant, much the same as other herding and guarding breeds. This dog needs plenty of space in which to run, and doesn't accept close housing well. Invent games to increase owner-dog contact and hone the mental interest of your companion, or at least give the Estrela a long daily walk on-leash.

CURRENT FUNCTION

The Estrela has proven its worth as a working guard dog, family pet, and children's companion. It has an inherited barking characteristic that is used as a warning to its family as well as intruders.

ATTITUDE

Said to be undemonstrative, this dog is nevertheless an alert, powerful dog whose guarding instincts are well developed. Its friendliness and affection is largely the product of intensive puppyhood socialization and training. Characteristically sober, but eager to learn and anxious to please, it lives to work and usually makes an excellent obedience dog. A loyal and intelligent dog, it's inclined to be stubborn at times, usually when bored with too few or too often repeated lessons. Its intense bonding with its handler may interfere with re-homing later in life.

APTITUDE

Thorough training must be initiated while young; this dog needs canine and human socialization from an early age onward.

Origin

Central Portugal's mountainous region was the Estrela's place of development, where it was used to guard flocks and farms from predators and thieves alike. The period of its development and its progenitors aren't easily calculated because specific information of the breed is nearly nonexistent.

Original Design

Originally, this dog was developed by farmers to guard herds and protect the family household. The Estrela served well in those capacities, but when flocks diminished in number and fences took its place in protecting the flocks, this breed launched into other professions.

The Estrela has a very long memory and is said to never forget a bad experience. Its training should therefore be undertaken gently and consistently, with affection and rewards when lessons are learned and performed correctly. As with other Mastiff-types, nagging or force is counterproductive and unnecessary.

APPEARANCE

Standing up to 28½ inches (72 cm), the Estrela's strength, vigor, and great power are easily seen. Two types of coat are seen, one longhaired, the other short. Both are colored brindle, reddish-brown, fawn, wolf-gray, and yellow, with white markings.

Fila Brasileiro

This shorthaired Brazilian dog is also called a Brazilian Molosser or Brazilian Mastiff. He is a guard and tracking dog of the finest quality. This breed is banned in Great Britain, and elsewhere should be kept in suburban and rural environments.

Its coat is short and easily groomed with a slicker brush or chamois cloth. Routine grooming increases bonding, and frequency is advised.

The Fila Brasileiro is best kept penned behind a strong fence when not on duty. There it can attend to its exercise needs, which aren't terribly significant. If the dog is obedient to commands, its mental acuity is improved with daily walks outside its back-yard. A head halter may be the key to the best possible control of this big dog, but it should be introduced with loving care, and never with demands.

CURRENT FUNCTION

Little information is available to enlighten us about this breed, but it apparently is still used to guard homes and hunt big cats such as the jaguar in its native land. In the United States and elsewhere, it usually is kept as a guard dog and loyal companion.

ATTITUDE

Aggression was carefully bred into the Fila, and it continues to be suspicious of strangers. It is often termed a natural guard dog, pre-sumably meaning that it needs no special training to do its job guarding factories, farms, ranches, and estates.

Occasionally used as a police dog, this Mastiff is said to be affectionate and obedient to its handler, its family, and frequent visitors. Generally, it accepts children of its family, but not necessarily their playmates.

The Fila's acute sense of smell makes it difficult to surprise, and it's known to act independently when sneaked up on. It has strong territorial instincts and isn't likely to accept or be friendly to new pets in the family.

training should be calmly carried out with understanding of this characteristic. Patience and gentle, light-handed training is preferable to abrupt, nagging or dissuasive handling. It's said to accept correction willingly, and to be sensitive to voice intonation, but abuse and negative reinforcement is counterproductive. Obedient to handlers, the dog reacts quickly to strange situations.

APPEARANCE

Standing about 28 inches (71 cm), this short-coated brindle dog is massive and loose skinned. It has pendent, large ears, a thick, powerful neck, and a strong, massive body. Often weighing well over one hundred pounds, the Fila moves with strength and agile drive. Colors usually are brindle, and nearly every shade is seen from tan to mahogany to black.

APTITUDE

The Fila is best trained by a confident, strong, and consistent person. Its personality and character are often difficult to fathom, and

Origin

This bulky breed originated in Brazil sometime after the discovery and colonization of that country in 1500. It originated from crosses between Bulldogs, Mastiffs, Bloodhounds, and other breeds, while attempting to claim all the outstanding characteristics of these breeds. *Fila* means "to hold," referring to its former duties related to tracking and holding runaway slaves. It was officially registered by the Brazilian Confederation Kennel Club in 1946 and has steadily grown in popularity, with about 8,000 being registered annually. In the United States, it is registered with the Continental Kennel Club in its Mastiff group.

Original Design

The Brasileiro was developed to guard estates, track and bring down large wild cats, control cattle, and track slaves who escaped from the early Brazilian plantations. This breed fell heir to the powerful musculature of ancient Bulldogs, used primarily for pit fighting and baiting bulls. It inherited its basic conformation from the Mastiff, and its excellent scenting ability, voice, and loose skin from the Bloodhound. Somewhere in that mixture, or perhaps from Portuguese herding breeds that may have sneaked into its gene pool unannounced, it derived cattle-driving abilities that appear in the breed today.

German Shepherd Dog

Probably the most versatile dog of all time, the German Shepherd can do it all! Its history is one of the most interesting ones in the annals of dogdom, and its adaptability and many talents are outstanding.

Grooming this dog is relatively simple and consists of weekly combing and brushing, with more attention required during shedding season.

Often, its exercise demands are greater than owners realize. Mental challenges and physical exercise should be balanced to prevent boredom and stagnation. Analyze your Shepherd's interests, then join a tracking, obedience, or agility club. If your Shepherd is allowed to sit around the house every day, you will never realize its potential, and it won't be happy and contented.

CURRENT FUNCTIONS

Capable and willing, this dog is now, or has recently been, an acclaimed movie star, war hero, police dog, and one-dog home security system. It's also a talented schutzhund, guide dog for the blind, tracking competitor, and famous search and rescue dog. It's routinely used as an assistance dog, agility competitor, obedience trial performer, and show dog. Its keen nose equips it as a discriminating scenting dog in search and rescue, customs work, immigration inspection, narcotic and firearms inspection, and agricultural detection. Besides those talents, it makes a fine pet and family companion.

ATTITUDE

Intelligence is apparent, indeed almost plainly visible in the face of this clever and crafty dog. The German Shepherd Dog is eager to learn, and even more eager to please its master. Capable of solving complex problems associated with guide dog duties, it's quite biddable and ready to try any game for which rules have been established, and will sometimes devise its own games. It's a devoted dog that will lay down its life for its family, yet is sensitive and quiet. With a tendency to be a bit independent and temperamental, it's self-assured and seems to know its talents and appreciate their use and development. The Shepherd is a loving, loyal companion. What more can be said?

APTITUDE

Training is easily accomplished, but the trainer must realize before starting that inept training can mask or hide the German Shepherd's talents. It quickly understands commands, and often performs exercises the first time they are demonstrated, or at least much sooner than expected. This big dog may reverse the trainer-student roles, and without warning begin performing an exercise to its own standard. The German Shepherd must be led along at its own pace, which is often faster than that of its trainer. It's a mistake to use nagging, force, or negativity when training a Shepherd. A winning trainer is patient, consistent, presents lessons simply and distinctly, and doesn't repeat lessons endlessly. A winning Shepherd has a winning trainer.

Origin

According to at least one of its biographers, this German herding and guarding dog's ancestry can be traced to prehistoric times and certainly from the Roman era. Perhaps it was the original flock-herding dog that stepped into this role from wolf progenitors. Whether or not we accept that as undeniable truth, we must concede that the German Shepherd is an old breed, traceable to probable ancestors in the 1800s, when the breed was in general use by European farmers as a sheep driving and guarding dog. In 1899 its first breed club was formed, and within the next fifteen years, it was seen in nearly every European country and in America. From that known beginning, through endless selective breeding, the German Shepherd Dog has evolved to its present state.

APPEARANCE

The German Shepherd Dog's breed standard lists its *desired* height range as 24 to 26 inches (61 to 66 cm), but when meeting a well-muscled, alert Shepherd on the street, you would swear it stands well over our arbitrary 27 inches (68.5 cm). This dog has a big attitude that carries it well into this book. Its body is deep and well muscled, and its coat is wavy, dense, double, and medium in length. Colors are many and varied, with only white being specifically excluded. Its large, erect ears and noble, sculpted head are well balanced. In keeping with its sheep-tending heritage, the Shepherd gait is a ground-covering trot that can be maintained for endless hours.

The White German Shepherd Dog Club International is a widespread, well-organized society that is presently sponsoring shows, obedience trials, and other events. Their apparent intent is to build WGSD recognition and encourage local and national German Shepherd breed clubs to recognize and accept the White Shepherd as a color variation of the German Shepherd Dog. It will be interesting to see how this dichotomy of interests, apparently based on color alone, will finally be resolved.

Original Design

In the German Shepherd's beginning, it was a farm flock-herding dog, but one that was closely associated with its master and family. In that capacity, it moved flocks and herds from one place to another, stayed with its charges to protect them from predators, and during its coffee breaks, kept track of the children and did about everything a dog can do. Its superior intelligence and trainability were quickly recognized by one and all, and the rather limited herding function was expanded to numerous other endeavors.

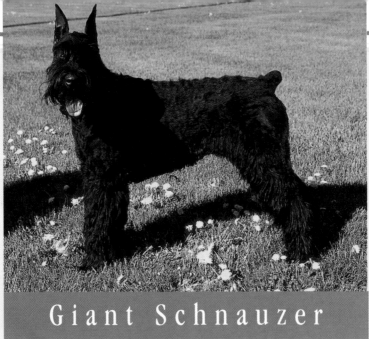

Giant Schnauzer

At various times this big, stylish dog has been known as the Russian Bear Schnauzer, Munich Schnauzer, Riesenschnauzer, and Münchener, and is the largest of three separate and distinct breeds of Schnauzers.

The Giant Schnauzer is an active, energetic dog with significant needs for exercise and play if it is to live happily and peacefully. Usually not noisy, it may become loud when ignored.

This dog is also quite intelligent. It therefore needs games designed to appeal to this intelligence.

CURRENT FUNCTION

Properly socialized and trained, the Giant Schnauzer is a wonderful companion and pet. Its intelligence earns it a place in various competitions such as obedience trials and agility, and its athletic build, toughness, and hereditary guarding instincts qualify it for schutzhund exhibitions. Recently, the Giant Schnauzer has taken its place as a police dog in its native Germany, and possibly in other countries.

ATTITUDE

Bold and protective of its family, this dog often is quite boisterous as a pup and requires a good deal of handling and socialization when young. It typically is reserved or suspicious of strangers and may be aggressive toward strange dogs. Alert and vigilant, the intelligent Giant Schnauzer is loyal and trustworthy with its family's children and has great stamina and energy. Shyness is occasionally seen, but not when a pup is carefully selected and well socialized. Timidity or viciousness is considered a major fault in this breed.

APTITUDE

Generally, the Giant Schnauzer is eager to learn and to please if a variety of lessons are taught with great consistency. The dog has a mind of its own and shouldn't be expected to jump to the trainer's whistle every time it's blown. Patience and gentle training is best, especially when training sessions are kept short with frequent changes from one exercise to another.

Origin

Sharing its origin with other Schnauzers, the Giant Schnauzer hails from the regions of Wurttemberg and Bavaria in southern Germany, where it probably was bred from Standard Schnauzers and Thuringian Shepherds. Its ancestors also may include the Bouvier des Flandres, a drover's dog, and at some time Great Dane crosses may have occurred, as well as crosses with one or more of the rough-coated German sheepdogs. The Giant Schnauzer's early history dates back to 1492 paintings, and it also is depicted in a statue erected in Stuttgart, Wurttemberg, in 1620. First exhibited in the Munich dog show in 1909, a few Giant Schnauzers were brought to America before World War I, but it wasn't until much later that the breed became popular in this country.

Coat care always will be needed; begin when it is a puppy, and train it to stand patiently for clipping, stripping, and grooming since this will continue for its lifetime. The Giant's coat may be professionally hand-stripped for showing, but this duty really belongs to the owner because it is an excellent bonding tool requiring discipline for both dog and owner.

Exercising a Giant Schnauzer is not a duty but a pleasure. A well-trained Giant will accompany you everywhere, whether it be a long walk, a romp in the park, or playing its favorite game in the backyard. Remember this dog's heritage, and teach games that appeal to its quickness and intelligence. Agility and obedience training may supplement exercise requirements.

APPEARANCE

Standing up to 27½ inches (70 cm), this big dog has a classic, sculptured appearance when trimmed, especially when its ears are cropped, although in America it may be shown either cropped or uncropped. Muscular and athletic, the Giant Schnauzer is a powerful dog with a crisp, long stride and decisive action. Its coat is hard, wiry, and quite dense. Its colors range from black to salt and pepper, and no white markings are allowed.

Original Design

First developed to assist farmers and dairymen in moving cattle, this dog found other niches as a guard dog in breweries, a cattle drover in slaughterhouses, and a cart dog and guardian of butcher shops.

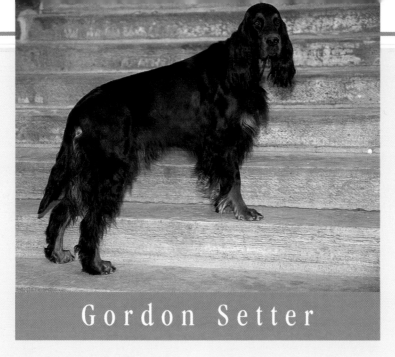

Gordon Setter

This beautiful setter is a typical athletic sporting dog, bred to hunt upland birds in all types of cover, in all kinds of weather. Known at various times in history as the Black and Tan Setter, this largest of the setter breed's elegant appearance and sturdy stability has made it a natural choice of discriminating hunters for hundreds of years. It's true that the intelligent Gordon isn't the fastest dog in the field, but its nose is one of the best! By comparison with lighter-boned sporting breeds, the Gordon may seem to be a slow or deliberate hunter, but one who isn't given to false points. In past years, it's had unjust criticism laid at its feet, but it has answered with continued performance in rough cover when a thorough, close-quartering, and methodical hunter is needed.

A fair amount of coat care is required for the Gordon. Daily combing is necessary, with more attention given during seasonal shedding.

Exercise requirements are considerable, and like all sporting breeds, the Gordon thrives on regular exercise, regardless of function. Without adequate attention to exercise, it often becomes moody, nervous, and disobedient.

CURRENT FUNCTION

The Gordon Setter is seen in two general types: a smaller, quicker, more responsive hunting dog, and a sturdier, bulkier show dog. The breed standard allows considerable range of size to accommodate owners who prefer one type over another. Any size is the right size for companion duties, and as such, this setter has many endearing pet qualities.

ATTITUDE

Never shy, timid, or short-tempered, and with a kind, loving disposition, the Gordon is a choice family dog. It socializes well, is good-natured, and displays gentle protectiveness with children. This quiet dog makes a cheerful, active pet, always ready for a romp or walk. Sometimes reserving its adoring devotion for one family member, it accepts other members

Origin

The Black and Tan setter has been known for more than 400 years, and the Gordon name is more than 300 years old. The only setter developed in Scotland, this dog's progenitors haven't been well recorded but probably include the Bloodhound and the Collie. Bred and kept by the fourth Duke of Gordon in his Banffshire, Scotland, castle, this large setter was developed in rough Scottish terrain for its endurance and superior sense of smell. The breed has been in America since 1842, where it has gained popularity as a gundog but often suffered in field trials against smaller, lighter-boned, faster setters. The AKC accepted the Gordon in 1892, and since that time it has enjoyed a rather low profile among field trial enthusiasts.

willingly and shows affection to everyone at the table. Somewhat suspicious of strangers, the Gordon often is a fine, easily controlled but fearless guard dog with a fantastic memory for friends and relatives.

APTITUDE

Still primarily a gundog, this breed is a dependable hunter that can serve as weekend companion for an amateur field sportsman. Little bird training is necessary if the handler blends consistency and patience in training techniques. Since the Gordon is slightly on the suspicious side, it's important to emphasize canine socialization in a Gordon puppy. Natural evolution of the breed has placed the Gordon in backyards because of its personality and regal elegance. If a sporting dog personality is preferred, a Gordon pet is one of the best to be found. Although not regularly seen in agility trials, Frisbee, or fly-ball contests, the Gordon's trainability makes it a candidate for these sports or obedience trials.

APPEARANCE

The Gordon stands up to 27 inches (68.5 cm) and has the same basic build as other setters. Slightly bulkier and well muscled, it doesn't appear coarse, but rather gives the impression that it can stay in the field all day. Its distinctive black and tan coat is soft and straight to wavy and has moderate feathering of legs, ears, and tail. The distribution of tan markings is emphatically listed in the breed standard, and any deviation in these patterns is penalized in shows.

Original Design

The Gordon was initially bred to locate game with its expert nose, to quarter close to the hunter, and to endure long hunting days. It set the covey of birds, patiently waiting the netting of its quarry. The advent of shotgun hunting slightly altered its use, and it was further developed to point birds for the sportsman and to retrieve game. It was purposefully designed as a larger, tougher bird dog, capable of meat-hunting or sporting activities. It's often a one-man dog and is criticized for being overly affectionate toward its handler.

Great Dane

The Great Dane has been known by many other names, including Dogue Allemand, German Mastiff or Deutsche Dogge, and Alaunt, or boar hound. The Dane isn't Danish, has never been Danish, and the source of that title is problematical.

Coat care requires nothing more than frequent massage with a rubber brush or chamois. If grooming can be scheduled daily, from the time of puppyhood onward, both owner and Dane will benefit from the bonding contact.

Its exercise requirement is not as great as its size might indicate, and this dog does well in a large yard, with daily walks and occasional romps in the woods. The Dane is often found in urban settings, gracing the apartment floor and thoroughly enjoying life on a leash. This dog is quite people oriented and does poorly if kept in a kennel or tied up for any length of time.

CURRENT FUNCTION

Because boars and wolves are rather scarce in American suburbs, today the Great Dane is kept as a good natured companion, family guardian, and well-loved pet. It often is seen in obedience classes or walking on-lead in parks, and one of its favorite places is with the family's children in a station wagon or van, headed to the grocery store.

ATTITUDE

The original Great Dane was so ferocious that the breed was barred from New York dog shows for a time because of its attitude. All that has changed through selective breeding by conscientious breeders. Today this dog is a gentle, lovable giant. Affectionate and loyal, intelligent and devoted to its family, a typical Great Dane is calm, quiet, and sensible. The Dane is trustworthy around family pets that have been properly introduced, but should be watched around strange dogs. This dog is always spirited and friendly, but never timid or aggressive, and if either of these faults are observed in a pup's parents, try to find another litter to choose from.

Some authors claim the Great Dane is a descendant of the Roman Molossian dog, and others say its ancestor was the ancient tiger dog of Egypt that lived in about 2200 B.C. Italian paintings of the 1580s depict dogs with Dane-like appearances, and 1686 paintings show Great Danes on boar hunts. Before the Norman conquest, a similar breed was taken to Great Britain for boar hunting by the Saxons. It's possible the Tibetan Mastiff or the Irish Wolfhound were ancestors of this giant breed, or that the English Mastiff was its principal progenitor. The Greyhound may have been used to increase the Dane's speed and hunting ability. One thing we can verify is that German breeders saw a need for a big, courageous boar- and wolf-hunting dog and the Great Dane is the result. Its claim for antiquity notwithstanding, its personality was molded and its name was changed in the late 1800s by German fanciers to Deutsche Dogge, as it's known in Germany today. The Italian fancier prefers the name Alano, meaning "mastiff," and its club's name is Mastiff Club of Italy. This German giant came to America in the late 1800s and has maintained high-profile popularity since then.

APTITUDE

The Dane needs to be gently socialized with children while still a puppy, and should be accustomed to family pets during puppyhood. Responsive to commands and sensitive to voice intonations, the typical Dane will respond better to training requests than demands. Obedience training should be carried out with consistent and logical commands given in a moderate voice. Although gentleness is paramount and appreciation of the dog's sensitivity is important, this dog must learn its lessons before reaching full growth, and the handler should therefore never allow the clever Dane to reverse roles with the teacher.

APPEARANCE

A Great Dane's minimal height is stated to be greater than 32 inches (81 cm) with no outside limit, providing proper balance is maintained. *Majestic* is the word that might best describe the looks of this giant. Its body is

Original Design

Boars are big, aggressive animals and wolves are nasty-tempered beasts, so naturally the Great Dane originally was designed as a big, powerful, rugged, clever, and intelligent hunter—one that could outsmart and conquer its quarry pound for pound and tooth for tooth.

well muscled, balanced, and athletic, carried with a graceful dignity. It moves with strength and power, giving the impression of speed and endurance. Several colors are accepted, including brindle, fawn, blue, black, and harlequin. Although this dog is beautiful in any color, perhaps the most startling and regal design is the harlequin, a pure white with irregular black patches distributed over the entire body. Its coat is smooth and shiny, requiring little care.

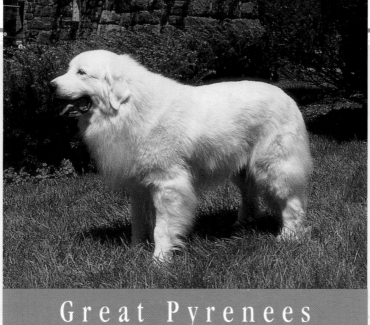

Great Pyrenees

Sometimes called the Pyrenean Mountain Dog or Le Chien des Pyrénées, the Great Pyrenees shares its heritage with the look-alike Pyrenean Mastiff, the Leonberger, Pomeranian Sheepdog, Maremma Shepherd, Kuvasz, Saint Bernard, and Komondor.

This giant white dog has superprotective instincts that are aided by a keen sense of smell and great eyesight.

Said to be a progenitor of the Newfoundland, this enormous dog gained the nickname of "mat dog" because of its propensity for lying outside its owner's cottage door when not busy with farm chores.

Its long, wavy coat requires at least weekly attention with a grooming comb. The coarse hair doesn't mat excessively, but when neglected, it can happen. During shedding, daily coat care is necessary.

Despite or because of its great size, this dog doesn't require excessive exercise, and is usually quite happy with daily walks and backyard romps with its family.

CURRENT FUNCTION

As a companion, no other dog has greater family appreciation. Its giant proportions and fearless attitude, combined with its gentleness with children and amicable personality, have placed it well above many other companion dogs. It prefers the cooler climates, but does well wherever situated. As a pet, it has side benefits of being able to pack its own food on outdoor excursions, pull sleds for small kids, and easily endures endless snowy days. Its courage and senses of smell and sight make it an excellent guard dog.

ATTITUDE

Fearless and loyal, affectionate and protective, this reserved and dignified giant would be much too large to own if it had an ounce of grouchy nature. It's often tolerant of strangers, but is at least wary of visiting dogs and humans, and doesn't happily run to meet strangers with wagging tail. Its confidently calm demeanor is probably the result of years of isolation on

French farms, and its seriousness may be because of one-on-one relationships with lone Basque sheepherders. The Pyrenees is vocal and often sends loud warning signals when it senses visitors afoot. The breed standard lists shyness, nervousness, and aggression as serious faults. Keep these negative characteristics in mind when shopping for a puppy, and if seen in parents, find another breeder!

APTITUDE

Said to be easily trained, this highly intelligent dog may seem independent and strong willed unless the trainer is experienced with giant breeds. The Great Pyrenees is alert and

Original Design

This working dog began as a herd-guarding Mastiff of great courage. Its long, protective coat and greater protective spirit made the Great Pyrenees extremely valuable to stockmen and landlords alike. Frequently wearing a wide, thick collar equipped with numerous long pointed spikes, it changed the minds of wolves and bears that might have preyed upon its charges. Yet with all this physical strength and courage, the Great Pyrenees has no history of being vicious or untrustworthy toward people. Versatility is perhaps the greatest asset of these great dogs that were used as sentries to patrol farms at night, to pull carts to and from market, to carry packs, and to pull sleds and sometimes skiers. Traveling where no customs officers could go, it gained its only black mark (no pun intended) when employed to carry contraband across the French-Spanish border.

Origin

Phoenician traders probably brought the Great Pyrenees or its progenitors from Asia into Spain and France sometime during the Bronze Age (1800 to 1000 B.C.). Recorded in its present form as early as the beginning of A.D. 1500, the breed was nurtured and developed high in the Pyrenean Mountains of France, near the Spanish border. It was adopted as the Royal Dog of France by Louis XIV and became the darling of royal society, but remained the best friend and helper French peasants and farmers could hope for. In America since 1824, the breed became a favorite before its recognition by the AKC in 1933. Until that time, the Great Pyrenees was primarily a sheep-guarding dog and farm companion.

responsive to commands as long as they are logical and consistent. Like many big dogs, the Pyrenees doesn't respond well to force or nagging and gentle training methods must be used early, and continued for life.

APPEARANCE

Standing up to 32 inches (81 cm) tall, the Great Pyrenees is a giant. Well muscled, balanced, and incredibly strong, this breed is amazingly agile. Its long, flat, thick outer coat is coarse and slightly wavy over a fine, wooly undercoat. It may be totally white, or white with markings and mask of badger, reddish brown, or tan. These markings may be distributed as spots or confined to the head.

Greater Swiss Mountain Dog

This biggest Swiss dog is quite similar to the Bernese except for its taller height, smooth coat, and distinctively long tail. It's also is known by the Swiss name, Grosser Schweizer Sennenhund, Great Swiss Mountain Dog, and Butcher Dog.

Its short coat requires only nominal brushing, with added attention to grooming during shedding season.

Exercise requirements are minimal as well because the Greater Swissie's bland attitude adapts to a simple outing or sleepy weekend with its family. Capable of pulling small children in a dogcart, this dog seems to enjoy that mode of exercise. Like other giants, the Greater Swiss needs a large yard and room to move about.

CURRENT FUNCTION

In its home country the Greater Swiss Mountain Dog continues in its farm role. It isn't recognized by the AKC, is in scarce supply, and when found, is usually a family pet and watchdog.

ATTITUDE

Courageous, brave, quiet, calm, and friendly are the terms most often used to describe this tall dog. It's a confident dog, alert and fearless, but quite good-natured, devoted to family, and self-assured with strangers. This big dog bonds tightly with its family and doesn't kennel well. It may become melancholy and lose its spirit if confined away from its family.

APTITUDE

Perhaps not suitable for everyone, the Greater Swiss has a strong character that needs a strong, persistent owner. If consistency, gentleness, and respect are used in training and the rules are kept constant, this dog responds beautifully. Like other strong, silent types, this dog thrives when it grows up in a family environment where fairness is the rule of the day. It is most content with members of its family and is trustworthy, but sometimes is overprotective of children.

APPEARANCE

Standing up to 28½ inches (72 cm), this giant breed is terrifically muscled, well coordinated and moves with assurance and agility. Its soft, intelligent expression is winsome even when puppyhood has passed. It has about the same color and markings as the other Swissies. Its double, weatherproof, flat-lying coat is basically black, with rust-colored and white markings.

Origin

From Switzerland's mountainous regions, the Greater Swiss is the product of cross breeding one of the other Swissies with the shorthaired Saint Bernard. The breed originated during the mid 1800s, the same period as the Bernese Mountain Dog, and bears a definite resemblance to that cousin. The first standard was published by the Swiss Kennel Club in 1939, and this dog served honorably in the Swiss Army in World War II. Though not as popular in America as the Bernese, it was introduced in 1968, and is found scattered over the United States.

Original Design

Developed on Swiss farms as a cattle drover, draft dog, watchdog, and family pet, the Greater Swiss Mountain Dog has served in those capacities for 150 years and continues to do so today. It also pulled the butcher's cart and herded cattle to the slaughterhouse.

Greyhound

Perhaps the fastest dog in the world on a flat track is the Greyhound, whose grace and speed make it one of the best-known dogs on every continent. Its name may have been taken from *Graius,* which means "Greek," because the breed was popular among ancient Greeks. Or it may have originated from *grech* or *greg,* which meant "dog" in the ancient Saxon tongue. Another theory was that the term *gazehound* or *greathound* was corrupted to Greyhound. In any case, Greyhounds enjoy a long life and good health, primarily due to selective breeding that addresses function instead of frills.

Coat care is easily accomplished with a slicker brush or chamois applied biweekly or more often as dead coat is shed.

This breed's need for exercise, though perhaps less than other similar breeds, is sometimes a problem unless owners' yards are large and the family is dedicated to long walks. As is the case with other sight hounds, exercise off-lead may be restricted or banned by community ordinances. These regulations address the danger to small pets chased as quarry. An ever-increasing danger is to the Greyhound that pursues with a single-minded purpose without regard to crossroad traffic.

CURRENT FUNCTION

Meat hunting has given way to racing, wherein a group of purebred Greyhounds chase an uncatchable mechanical lure around a track to the thrill of spectators. Providing the beautiful Greyhounds for this sport includes careful selective breeding, conditioning, and training. Pari-mutual betting increases the interest in this exhibition in America as well as other countries. The Greyhound is still used in lure-coursing events, and because of the availability of beautiful surplus track dogs, this sport has become quite popular in many parts of the country. The Greyhound is being accepted as a companion and family pet as well. As a show dog, this big hound must be a favorite among judges because the official breed standard is so short and understandable, and with its slick coat, its conformation is quite easily viewed.

Origin

Various authors have listed the Greyhound's origin as Greece, Egypt, the Middle East, and England. Among the very oldest breeds in existence and regardless of the country where it was initially developed, the Greyhound's images were found in the Egyptian tombs of the fourth dynasty between 3500 and 4000 B.C., proving the breed's early relationship with pharaohs and kings. This dog was intimately described in the writings of Ovid, who lived from 43 B.C. to A.D. 17. Greyhound images are found upon ancient Assyrian monuments as well. English Greyhound history dates back to the ninth century, when it was kept by kings and noblemen. At that time Greyhound possession was forbidden to common men. One of the earliest canine imports to America, it was probably brought to the New World by the Spanish in the sixteenth century, where it gained popularity and was shown in the 1887 Westminster show.

ATTITUDE

Peaceful, quiet, affable, and sometimes accused of being downright indolent, this dog is nevertheless a bright, affectionate pet. It bonds well with owners and generally has a desirable personality and character. Its propensity to chase small animals may decrease the Greyhound's popularity with cat lovers, but it socializes well with other canine pets. Usually its relationship with children is quite amiable and compatible. The Greyhound often isn't a good guard dog because of its quiet nature and lack of aggressiveness. However, it may be somewhat suspicious of strangers.

APTITUDE

Whereas other sight hounds are less than easily trained, the Greyhound is more accommodating. Indications of the training possible are discovered in early American stories reporting on the Greyhound routinely delivering to hand small game that was killed but not mutilated. Other hounds were trained to bring game to bay and hold it for handlers to dispatch. Compared with other gazehound breeds, the Greyhound is reasonably obedient to commands it's taught, providing the commands are given before the hound espies a moving prey. This breed is easily trained for lure-coursing trials, and its best-known training is for racing.

APPEARANCE

Although no height is given in the AKC standard, other references list 28 to 30 inches (71 to 76 cm) as an average. This big dog appears to be just what it is—a natural athlete. Its color is immaterial, its lean and muscular body is deep chested, and its head is streamlined with small, flat ears. The coat of a Greyhound is short, firm, and smooth, contributing no wind resistance to its speed.

Original Design

Greyhounds were unquestionably bred to hunt by sight, and this propensity lives on today. It has contributed to gene pools of dozens of other breeds in which speed and agility were wanted. It was used to bag a great multitude of animals, including deer, stags, foxes, hare, and in this country, rabbits, coyotes, and some larger game. The Greyhound often supplied meat for American settlers' tables.

Ibizan Hound

This hound has many of the features of the Greyhound, both historical and physical, but it differs in being a gazehound with notable hearing and smelling capacity. The Podenco Ibicenco or Galgo Hound, as it is sometimes known, has in its heritage a heavy-handed selective breeding program that produced extremely sound puppies. Consequently, today it is free of most of the hereditary flaws seen in other breeds.

Coat care depends on the length of hair on the Ibizan. The wirehaired variety requires more combing and brushing, and occasionally tangle repair. The smooth-coated Ibizan is quickly brushed with a rubber slicker or chamois.

As with other hounds, daily exercise is needed to keep this dog in top mental and physical condition. It is perhaps more adaptable in that regard than other sight hounds, and many Ibizans are kept in apartments and suburban environments. Daily jogs, long walks, and big backyards seem to provide adequate exercise for this hunting dog.

CURRENT FUNCTION

The Ibizan Hound's role in America today is primarily that of a pet. Its rarity increases its market value, which in turn maintains its rather low profile as a companion dog. It's gradually gaining in popularity as a show dog. An affectionate, loyal family member, this intelligent dog has other traits that recommend it as well. It has retained its instinctive hunting prowess and sometimes is seen in lure trials.

ATTITUDE

Ibizans are vigilant, affectionate dogs that often make remarkable companions. Usually, they get along well with children and other dogs but are reserved toward strangers, which lends watchdog credibility to their personality. This dog has endless energy and stamina, exhibiting bravery in the bargain. Family house cats often are at risk because the Ibizan's hunting instincts are deeply ingrained and it usually will chase virtually anything that moves.

APTITUDE

Easier to obedience train than other gaze-hounds, the Ibizan is keen to learn, sensitive to its trainer's voice, and focuses well on commands. The Ibizan learns quickly and accepts most training well. They are often taught dog games and can perform competitively at agility and other timed activities.

APPEARANCE

The Ibizan stand up to 27½ inches tall (70 cm) and often slightly taller. Its height and coloration differentiate it from other, possibly related Egyptian dogs such as Pharaoh Hounds. Its body is well muscled, lean, deep chested, and athletic, similar to other gaze-hounds. The principal feature first noticed is the Ibizan's large, pointed, erect ears. The skin is lightly pigmented, and nose rubbers are typically pink or flesh colored. Coats may be either short or wirehaired. Wirehaired Ibizan's coats are one to three inches long (2.5 to 7.5 cm) accentuated by a generous moustache. Ibizans are seen in white or red, which varies from yellowish red to deep red, or in any combination of red and white. Any other color is a disqualification.

Origin

This regal breed claims 3400 B.C. Egypt as the probable place and date of its origin, and numerous statues and painted images of that period attest to this prick-eared dog's presence. The Nile region was undoubtedly the country of this breed's origin, although the Balearic Islands, namely Ibiza, is the site of its recent history. A world traveler, the Ibizan Hound's image graced ancient Roman coins, and Ibizans are said to have accompanied Hannibal when he crossed the Alps. It was probably in Phoenician ships that this hound made its way from Egypt to Ibiza. The isle of Ibiza is now a Spanish possession that has been conquered in the past by Egyptians, Chaldeans, Carthaginians, Romans, and Arabs, and ships from all these countries probably assisted in moving this hound from place to place. The Ibizan Hound was first imported to America in the mid-1900s, and where the breed has flourished here; it was admitted to AKC registry in 1978.

Original Design

The Ibizan's large, erect ears seem to contrast with its sleek, aerodynamic body design. This feature may indicate that it is primarily a gazehound, but one with olfactory ability to hear its quarry as well and to bark when in pursuit. The Ibizan's bloodlines have been kept pure by breeders' isolation on Ibiza Island with no known contamination by other blood.

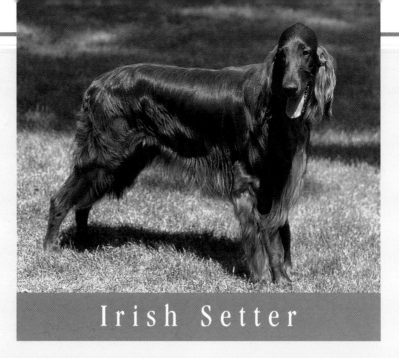

Irish Setter

This uncommonly lovely and interesting breed was founded as a gundog but in America has landed in far more family situations than fields. This beautiful puppy is often bought for its fun-loving, lively personality, and kept it for its longevity and good looks. Originally it was called simply The Red Setter, and by some writers is an extension of the Irish Red and White Setter. An interesting bit of history tells us that the Irish Setter developed a peculiar habit of lying down when its quarry was located. The Irishman continues to be a gundog, and in that capacity is said to lack independence and to follow handler instruction too closely.

Its long, silky red coat requires daily attention to keep it looking good. Some pets are sheared off during the summer, but this isn't recommended by breeders.

Pet Irish Setters demand exercise and without it may develop nuisance vices. An occasional walk around the block is insufficient, and if not given adequate attention, this dog may begin digging tunnels, uprooting garden plants, pacing, and barking. Always seeking a new game or a romp in the park, this breed needs daily exercise to expend its endless energy.

CURRENT FUNCTION

Displaying its pointing and field background every time the opportunity presents itself, the Irish Setter is considered one of the most graceful and beautiful show dogs in America. It takes its place among the top big companion dogs as well. Arriving at what was possibly the pinnacle of show success in the 1970s, the Irish Setter foundered, primarily due to overbreeding, and now rests in a more steady and secure ranking.

ATTITUDE

Gundogs often make admirable companions, and Irish Setters are no exception. Full of fun, lovable, and gentle, the Irish is unaware of its beauty. The lovable red character is forever a puppy with a cheerful, playful personality that usually endures for years. It socializes well with other pets, and often greets strangers with the same enthusiasm as family members. Sometimes offering an initial woof to designate this person as a newly acquired friend, the Irish Setter is rarely reserved with strangers and may extend more amiability than is desired.

APTITUDE

Practically any training is possible if the Irish Setter understands what point is being made. Due to its hunter capacity for thinking on its own, it may decide on another course of action. Sometimes when practicing an off-lead obedience lesson, the noble hunter characteristics spring to the front, and your companion streaks off to follow the scent of a squirrel or bluebird. Because of the propensity to do its own thing, it requires calm, consistent training, but once learned, the lesson isn't easily forgotten.

APPEARANCE

No size limitations are seen in the Irish Setter breed standard, but most males stand about 27 inches tall (68.5 cm). The physical appearance of this breed is strikingly aristocratic. Royal splendor comes to mind when the big red dog strides into the ring. The fluid red,

Original Design

A gundog through and through, the Irish Setter was developed specifically for its ability in the field. It proved its hunting prowess in Ireland and England for many years before being brought to America, where the aristocratic Irishman has held court in more backyards than shooting fields.

Origin

Probably bred from the Red and White Setter, which had blood from the Irish Water Spaniel, mixed with Gordon Setter and Springer Spaniel blood, this breed has its origin in Ireland with roots in Scotland, England, and possibly elsewhere in Europe. Its history extends to early in the nineteenth century, when the self-colored, red dogs were bred independently from the earlier Red and White Setter. Imported to America in mid-1800s, the breed has enjoyed success in the field and family situations.

silky coat seems to flow over the body, ending in long feathers on brisket, belly, legs, ears, and tail. Its gait is graceful and energetic, reaching long strides almost from the first step. Similarity to other setters is seen in general appearance and bone, but the essence of the Irish Setter is singular.

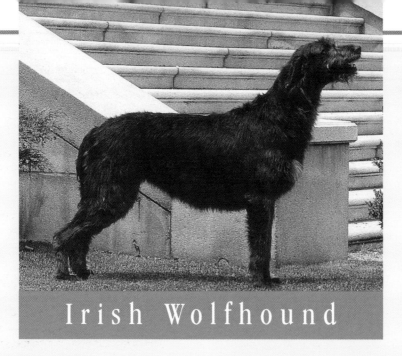

Irish Wolfhound

The archetype of this book is the Irish Wolfhound, with its rugged appearance and graceful manner. This breed has extraordinary height, an imposing appearance, and is variously known as Irish Dog, Big Dog of Ireland, Greyhound of Ireland, Wolfdog of Ireland, and Great Hound of Ireland. The name accepted by the AKC is Irish Wolfhound. Here is a giant in the true sense of the word. Embarking on the responsibilities of Irish Wolfhound ownership is a commitment lasting well beyond puppyhood, beyond the special considerations of the dog's enormous size, extended growth time, special nutrition, and care of a 100-pound (45 kg) puppy that is still cutting permanent teeth at six months of age.

The Irish Wolfhound coat is easily combed and brushed, with few tangles to separate and remove. During shedding season, it should be groomed at least two or three times weekly.

Without question, this breed requires a great deal of thought prior to purchase; an adequately fenced yard and exercise plan is critical. As in all big dogs, moderate exercise is mandated during the Wolfhound's immaturity, because of its rapid bone growth. Too much or *forced* vigorous activity will be detrimental to its health, causing problems that extend into adulthood. Complete development of this dog's physical body requires a full two years, during which it is necessary to concentrate your attention on nutrition and controlled exercise. Confinement to a small home or apartment shouldn't be considered and is unkind, if not abusive, unless accompanied by controlled but frequent walks.

CURRENT FUNCTION

The Irish Wolfhound is the National Dog of Ireland, as one would expect from such a large and strikingly majestic breed, although wolves are rarely hunted there in contemporary times. The absence of Roman circuses, legalized wolf hunting, and elk coursing leaves America's Irish Wolfhound with a rather narrow scope of duties. Although occasionally employed to hunt certain types of wolves and coyotes, the Wolfhound's hunting abilities are used more often in other countries. Lure coursing is a favorite of American Irish Wolfhounds, but the ability to singularly dispatch a wolf quickly and efficiently remains within the modern Wolfhound.

ATTITUDE

The maturing, wagging Irish Wolfhound puppy carries a club at its posterior extremity that with a single stroke can demolish a china cabinet and clear coffee tables of knickknacks and gewgaws. The tail is simply an extension of the pup's ungainly body, capable of causing unconscious demolition when confined to small spaces.

The Irish Wolfhound's nature is reliably pleasant, loyal, and affectionate. This dog is known as a gigantic package of gentle companionship. Thriving on human society, it is a calm, quiet, and friendly pet. Solemn elegance is found in this dog's sweet and intelligent temperament, and it usually displays no shortness of temper when treated gently. The Wolfhound is a poor watchdog, although its impressive size alone should be enough to ward off interlopers. It is customarily kind to children, but during its rapid growing phase, must be treated with care to avoid damaging its developing bones. Barking is rarely a vice, but when surprised, it's known to greet strangers with a single loud roar that is quite impressive and sure to get the visitor's attention. Tranquility is a consistent feature of the Wolfhound, but keep in mind that this patient dog has limits that shouldn't be tested. The courage and agility of an adult Irish Wolfhound should never be forgotten, and when challenged, the response can be awesome!

APTITUDE

Easily trained and quick to understand, the Irish Wolfhound is best suited to gentle, consistent

Origin

Dogs of the general Wolfhound description were reported by the Greek writer Arrian to have been transported to Greece as early as 273 B.C., brought to that country by invading Celts. However, Irish Wolfhound development is positively recorded in Ireland during feudal times of the Middle Ages. Its influence extended well beyond the Irish domain. Letters from Rome indicate that the Irish Wolfhound was known in that city as early as A.D. 391, where it was displayed, appreciated, and perhaps participated in circus sports.

The feudal Middle Ages saw this aristocratic dog rise to well-deserved fame, often finding its way into tales of that time, where wonderful feats of strength, courage, and valor were recorded as factual. Demand for this dog was considerable. The king of Ulster in A.D. 1100 is said to have traded 4,000 cattle for a single Irish Wolfhound.

Later in history, this majestic dog followed the demise of the huge Irish elk and wolves and became nearly unknown. The breed might have become extinct except for the enthusiasm of Captain G. A. Graham, a Scottish officer in the British army. He is said to have used Wolfhounds secured from three different strains, none of which were quite as large as the original Wolfhound. His careful attention to selective breeding and perhaps the introduction of other giant breeds into the gene pool began in 1862 and continued until 1885, when the first Irish Wolfhound breed standard was written.

Original Design

Always favored by nobility, this hound was owned by great lords and kings, and the Irish Wolfhound frequently appears in Celtic literature. The great strength, endurance, and hunting ability of this gazehound are among the chief characteristics qualifying it for distinction in Irish history. Originally developed as a sporting dog with the ability to bring to ground a six-foot-tall Irish elk or the equally awesome if significantly smaller wolf, the great Wolfhound was equal to both tasks.

Over the centuries, the Wolfhound was used to hunt other large game, and served its master as a personal bodyguard during armed conflicts as well. It's possible the Roman contingency of this sporting breed was pitted against other living creatures during circus games. Any dog that will run down and attack a wolf in the wild would probably shine in such conflicts.

handling and training methods. Because of this dog's immense size and strength, routine training should begin as soon as it is in your home, taking note of the previous warnings dealing with overexercise and excessive training during the pup's early development period. Early handling is extremely important to prevent shyness or reticence, neither of which is a usual characteristic of the Wolfhound.

APPEARANCE

The Irish Wolfhound is the tallest purebred dog in America, having a minimum shoulder height of 32 inches (81 cm). Think of it—a family pet whose back rises nearly three feet from the floor, taller than the average kitchen counter or dining table! Under its harsh, somewhat shaggy coat is a sleek, graceful body, similar to that of a Greyhound.

Its body is longer than it is tall. Its movements are easy with its head and neck held high, and its long, well-haired tail is carried with a slight curve. The Wolfhound chest is quite deep and its breast is wide. Its belly is drawn up in the manner of other coursing sight hounds. A Wolfhound's coat is rough and hardy, and especially wiry and long over its eyes and lower jaws. Colors include brindle, gray, red, black, pure white, fawn, or any other color that appears in the Deerhound.

A particularly graphic illustration of this dog's enormous size can be imagined in this way. If you are an adult of average or slightly above average height and you have an adventuresome streak, you might try this exercise. Stand with a tidbit grasped in your hand and extend it straight above your head. Call an adult Wolfhound and encourage it to stand on the ground before you, placing its forefeet on your shoulders. It smells the tidbit, stretches out its neck, and with its cavernous mouth, gently takes the tidbit from your hand.

Komondor

The plural of Komondor is Komondorok—just an interesting bit of trivia to go with this very interesting breed, one of the most ancient and pure breeds in existence.

Its coat may be left natural or separated into long, distinctive cords that often reach the ground by two years of age. Combing and brushing this coat is difficult to say the least, and unless being shown, the Komondor coat is best left alone, with trimming when necessary.

This dog demands little in the way of exercise. Always game for a walk, the Komondor nevertheless meets its exercise needs in a large yard, and is sometimes cast as a lazy or indolent companion. Swimming is rarely used to exercise this heavily coated dog, and bathing is kept at a minimum because of the drying time required.

CURRENT FUNCTION

Owing to the absence of urban and suburban sheep flocks, the Komondor has taken its place as companion and pet in some American family situations. However, sheep continue to be raised in many rural areas, and here the Komondor truly responds to its instinct. Invaluable as a guard dog, absolutely fearless of coyotes, wolves, and bears, this big dog carved a place for itself with flocks, especially where sheep are pastured in the open and might otherwise be at the mercy of predators.

ATTITUDE

Difficult to pet because of its long, tangled coat, the Komondor's character is sober and quiet, calm and balanced. It's reserved and wary of strangers, but makes friends easily with well-intentioned visitors. Sometimes dominant with other dogs, this dog is bright, brave, and determined. In a companion role, it socializes well with the family's children and pets, and is protective of them.

APTITUDE

Uncomplicated or *stable* are terms applied to this great white dog's trainability. It's rarely if ever trained in obedience or for other companion dog tasks, but easily adapts to instinctive flock-guarding duties. Training must be fair, consistent, and approached with respect. Self-confident by nature, the Komondor needs an experienced and confident trainer who understands the breed.

APPEARANCE

The Komondor often reaches a height of 29½ inches (75 cm). Its great stature and rather massive head commands the attention of one and all, and its naturally matted or corded white coat gives it a startling, rather unapproachable appearance. Its muscular and substantial body is symmetric and nearly rectangular, and its leisurely, long gait is characteristic of the breed.

Origin

Magyar sheepherders are said to have brought the Komondor to Hungary from Russia, where it probably descended from the Russian Aftscharka. An instinctive, natural flock-guarding dog of great power and tenacity, this dog has been in existence for at least a thousand years. For centuries, its purebred status was protected by Hungarian shepherds, and about a hundred years ago it was registered with the Ebtenyestok Orzagos Eguselete, the Hungarian version of the AKC. The Komondor spread into other European countries early in the twentieth century. Appearing in America in the mid-1930s, it was accepted to AKC registry in 1937.

Original Design

The Komondor was used exclusively in sheep-guarding duties for many generations and in this vocation became the loyal and dependable companion of herdsmen. Rarely used to drive sheep, this dog accompanied great flocks and protected them from wild animal and human predators. That vocation is instinctive in the Komondor breed and can be seen today without training. When it is introduced to a sheep flock, it will instinctively abide there in all types of weather, in the open, without protection from predators or inclement weather conditions.

Kuvasz

The plural of Kuvasz is Kuvaszok, and both names are corrupted spellings of Turkish or Arabian words meaning "armed guard," or "archer." This dog was originally a giant-sized guardian, owned and bred primarily by the Hungarian ruling classes.

Its thick, double, weather-resistant coat should be combed sparingly but more frequently during heavy seasonal shedding.

In its modern, somewhat smaller stature, the Kuvasz's needs for mental and physical exercise are simple, and should consist of a large yard and daily walks around the neighborhood. It usually patrols the perimeter of its property numerous times daily, and this will furnish fundamental exercise.

CURRENT FUNCTION

Today's assassin usually operates from a distance, flocks are contained within fences, noblemen are at a premium, and vandals are too numerous to count, so the Kuvasz kept in America usually fills the role of family companion and guard dog against trespassers.

ATTITUDE

A very spirited, intelligent watchdog that barks only when necessary, this brave and independent companion dog may be dominant toward other dogs, but proper puppy socialization will reduce that trait. It is tolerant with children of the family, but due to its size alone, shouldn't be left with small tots without supervision. This determined dog often is so protective of its family, it may decide to protect your kiddies from their playmates. Born with an intense curiosity, the Kuvasz has a mind of its own, and may take the initiative to react to a perceived threat to its charges at any time. Typically, this dog isn't overly demonstrative, but is sensitive and devoted to its family.

APTITUDE

A Kuvasz trainer should have a great deal of self-confidence and should be experienced with large dogs. As is the case with other big dogs, a Kuvasz should be socialized with children and small pets while quite young and

Kuvaszok may be closely related to Komondorok, but the two are separate and distinct breeds. This mighty dog was developed in Hungary from progenitors that probably lived in Tibet, the home of many large breeds. Its Turkish name might indicate that it was brought to Hungary from Asia by Turkish invaders or settlers. It also may have been brought from Russia to Hungary by the Magyars to protect their castles during the Industrial Revolution. This breed was well established in Hungary by the mid-1400s, during the reign of King Matthias I. That monarch was constantly threatened and never traveled without at least one Kuvasz for his personal protection. Apparently those dogs were far more trustworthy than the nobles of the king's court. During the Kuvaszok heyday, noblemen hunted these great dogs in packs, and later the big dog was used by commoners for herding sheep and cattle. Claims have been made for the common identity of the Komondor and Kuvasz, with the only difference being coat length. This has been repeatedly disavowed by Komondor fanciers.

trained with kindness. Gentleness and consistency should be employed in training instead of force and nagging. A dog of this breed should be purchased only after a good deal of research and consideration; it usually isn't the dog for inexperienced owners.

APPEARANCE

Standing 28 to 30 inches tall (71 to 76 cm), the Kuvasz is a medium-boned, powerful, athletic, well-muscled dog. This dog's only color is white, and its body has heavily pigmented gray or black skin. Its hair is composed of a thick double coat of coarser guard hair and a fine undercoat that is quite weather resistant. The coat is straight or somewhat wavy, and lies flat.

Original Design

This dog was originally much bigger, and was selectively bred to protect its owners and estates from interlopers, assassins, and vandals. As a secondary role, it was developed as a pack hunter, and later still, it was used to guard flocks from predators. Today, it's still a big dog, not quite reaching giant proportions.

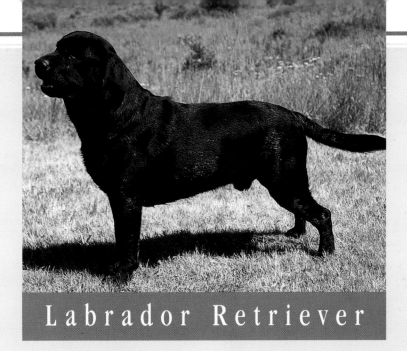

Labrador Retriever

For several years, the Labrador Retriever has been the most popular breed in America for many reasons. A big dog book would not be complete without a brief review of this beautiful and tractable breed. The following discussion is included not because of the Lab's gigantic size, but because of its great American acceptance.

The Lab coat is easily cared for; comb it once a week, and give it more attention during shedding season.

The Labrador Retriever's personality is improved, as is its condition, by regular exercise. Although this adjustable breed usually will settle for what it is given, it responds best to daily playing, leashed walks in the country, and if possible, off-lead exercise and play. A bored Lab is a dog seeking trouble. Join an agility club, try fly-ball training, or give obedience training a go. Keep your Lab busy.

CURRENT FUNCTION

The Labrador Retriever is an excellent gundog. It will retrieve upland birds on land as well as waterfowl from the water. It works from a blind as well as from snow covered ground. The name of the game is retrieving, and that's what Labs are all about. As a bonus, the Lab is a wonderful, undemanding family pet and companion whose talent is displayed in the show arena, obedience trial, search and rescue, assistance work, tracking, backpacking, agility trials, Frisbee contests, and other canine activities.

ATTITUDE

Intelligent, affectionate, and loving to its family, this good-natured dog accepts other pets quite easily, although early socialization is always best. It's friendly and spontaneous, loyal and hardworking, playful and tough. It loves children and is protective of them. Often a viable watchdog, the Lab will signal the appearance of visitors with its loud bark, and if its castle is breached, it has been known to make good its threats.

APTITUDE

Its pliable and sensible attitude makes the Lab easily trained. Always keen to work, the

Labrador invites lessons for the interaction afforded, and is quite proud of its abilities to learn. Water retrieving rarely requires specific training, although its exuberance may require more calming than training. Upland game retrieving may require a bit more training, but is easily accomplished. Training a Lab is similar to training any other big dog. Consistency, focus on the handler, patience, practice, and rewards are the keys. Labs are enthusiastic about obedience training, agility, flyball, Frisbee, tracking, and other activities. It's a crime that more Labradors aren't trained! Instead

Origin

Strangely, the Labrador didn't develop in Labrador, but in Newfoundland. It was unquestionably bred from the same stock that produced the Newfoundland breed and possibly the Chesapeake Bay Retriever. This recently developed breed was still called the St. John's Dog, or Lesser Newfoundland, in the early 1800s. Introduced into England early in the nineteenth century, Labs were gaining popularity by 1835 among devout sportsmen in that country, and in 1837, for some reason became known as Labradors instead of St. John's Dogs. The Lab was crossed with the Flat-Coated and Curly-Coated Retrievers, and possibly with pointers and setters before its breed standard was written by fanciers in 1878. The Labrador Retriever's pedigree was then stabilized, and the dog gained recognition by the English Kennel Club in 1903 and by the AKC in 1917. During the 1930s, numerous imports from England swelled the American ranks of this wonderful dog. It reached the zenith a few years ago and retains a firm foothold.

the tractable, intelligent Lab's talents rest untouched and unappreciated behind a backyard fence.

APPEARANCE

This dog shouldn't be included in this book since the writer arbitrarily set the lowest height as 27 inches for big dogs. Because the most popular breed among American fanciers is so well known, and is so big in heart, it has been

included. Standing at a big 24½ inches (62 cm), the Labrador Retriever is seen in a short, dense, straight, and weatherproof coat of black, chocolate brown, and yellow. It's a well muscled, short coupled, and balanced dog that has been refined and sculptured by selective breeding for many generations. It's otterlike tail is thick, medium length, and unfeathered, and is carried either waving behind or slightly elevated, but never over the back.

Original Design

This dog's swimming ability, webbed toes, waterproof coat, hearty constitution, and easygoing disposition contributed to its original design, but its dedication to retrieving, tenacity, and performance was even more important. Somewhere along the way, the Lab's friendly personality, good nature, and obedient traits were discovered and promoted, and they continue to propagate its popularity.

Leonberger

The giant German Leonberger has many Newfoundland characteristics without the Newfie's tendency to drool.

Its long hair needs weekly brushing to keep it in prime condition.

Exercise is important to this active dog, which loves to swim, hike, and join family outings on any occasion. It survives tolerably in a large backyard with daily walks, and can be kept in apartments, providing it's taken out frequently. Too little exercise will prompt boredom, a surly, reticent attitude, and depression.

CURRENT FUNCTION

The Leonberger hasn't changed much in the past 150 years. It's still an excellent companion and vigilant yet reserved watchdog. Often it's been put to work carrying its own food in backpacks or hauling supplies in carts. Some are taught to track, others prefer obedience, and on occasion, a few are trained for schutzhund trials. Swimming is second nature, and Leonbergers make excellent water rescue dogs.

ATTITUDE

A majestic dog, this peaceful but self-confident pet combines intelligence and vigilance with gentleness. This massive, yet lively and affectionate dog accepts other household pets with little socialization, and usually gets along with other dogs. A Leo will tolerate almost any treatment from children, and when it's had enough, will walk away. This characteristic, however, shouldn't be tested, since an occasional dog of any breed will rebel, and this giant dog can cause serious damage! The Leonberger has a sweet disposition, usually isn't an aggressive watchdog, and barks only once to alert its owner, then makes friends with just about any visitor. A shy, timid, or aggressive Leonberger is rare but dangerous. If considering a pup from parents that display these attributes, leave and don't even look back!

APTITUDE

Leonbergers are quick learners and easily grasp most training lessons with minimal difficulty.

Purposefully bred by the mayor of Leonberg, Germany, this dog was developed between 1840 and 1850. The town's crest featured the likeness of an unknown big dog, and the mayor was inspired to reproduce the dog in the flesh, rather like the reversal of sculpting from a living model. A Saint Bernard was crossed with a Newfoundland, and perhaps the Great Pyrenees, Pyrenean Mastiff, or Greater Swiss Mountain Dog figured into the early breeding. The resultant big dog does resemble the town crest, and naturally was given the name of the place of origin, Leonberg. The breed was nearly lost during World War II, but in 1945, a few specimens were gathered, and the breed was reestablished and continues to thrive throughout Europe. A few Leonbergers were imported to America in 1971, where they were used to guard livestock, among other endeavors.

Trainers and handlers should remember the low-key temperament of this stable, easy going dog, and refrain from pressing or exciting it. As with most big dogs, the Leonberger needs patience, consistency, love, appreciation for lessons learned, and lots of praise when appropriate performance is accomplished. Finally, don't expect instantly perfect responses to your commands; this dog is laid back, and if you're a perfectionist, choose a Sheltie.

APPEARANCE

Standing 29 to 31 inches (74 to 80 cm), this truly is a giant breed. Its coat is soft, of medium length, and with a thick undercoat that is lightly feathered on the legs, ruff, and tail. Its characteristic mane is slow to develop but worth the wait. Most Leos are golden yellow to darker reddish brown, and silver gray. All have a dark, nearly black mask. Its curious, handsome face echoes its happy demeanor. The Leo's attitude belies its muscular build and balanced body, and your Leo may surprise you with a few quick moves when you least expect them.

Original Design

Designed to match an icon, this dog has many attributes, not the least of which is its genteel behavior. The Leonberger was developed as a family companion, a peaceful, trustworthy, and calm pet. In its native land, it is sometimes used for search and rescue.

Mastiff

More legend and folklore surrounds the Mastiff than can be told on these pages. Each old book that mentions the dog reveals another story or two about the origin of the Mastiff or its strength, ferocity, or ability. Mastiff is a name applied to any of a number of breeds and is often used to describe a dog type. The Mastiff of old was a tie dog, or a dog that was used to guard the home, farm, or estate. Often it was tied up during the day and let loose for patrol duties at night. In those days, a Mastiff wasn't regarded as purebred, but was a mongrel or crossbreed. Usually it was giant sized as befitted a guarding dog. The Mastiff breed probably should be called English Mastiff to distinguish it from all the other purebreds and mongrels with the Mastiff name.

Its coat care and grooming needs are minimal because of its short hair. Most Mastiffs thoroughly enjoy grooming, and brushing should be recognized as an excellent bonding technique.

Like other big dogs, the Mastiff's exercise habits should be closely controlled until full growth is attained. As an adult, this dog has no more than average needs for exercise, and often the Mastiff is too dignified to retrieve, play ball, or partake of other means of exercise.

CURRENT FUNCTION

The role of the Mastiff in modern America is guard dog, companion, and well-loved pet. It's an able show dog that moves well on the lead, but isn't exhibited much in obedience trials, and lighter, swifter dogs dominate other canine contests. Possibly the Mastiff's dignity plays a part in its absence from these sports as well.

ATTITUDE

This dog rarely barks, but its instinct is to guard its home, which includes all who live there. A good natured dog, the self-confident, alert, intelligent, and dignified Mastiff is patient with its family, and tolerant with its children— but woe be to the trespasser. It's good-tempered and friendly toward acquaintances, but often will instinctively refuse entry to visitors

The Mastiff-type dog is ancient, probably dating to the Assyrian culture of about 2200 B.C. At that time, icons resembling Mastiffs were carved or made of terra cotta and buried beneath door stoops, probably to ward off evil spirits. About 400 B.C. an unknown Greek artist carved a statue of a huge dog called Molossus, which belonged to Olympias, daughter of King Pyrrhus. This dog is sometimes referred to as the direct ancestor of the Mastiff, but no one knows whether the sculpture was made in the image of a live model or from the artist's recollection or imagination. Roman legions had among their troops a giant dog that carried a goblet of fire strapped to its back. This dog ran under an opponent's horse's belly, producing a Romanesque version of the hot foot. In 1570 the English writer Caius described three kinds of dogs: the Bandogge, the Tydogge, and the Mastyne. The three were closely related and were used in pit fighting, bull baiting, and bear baiting in England during the reign of Henry VIII. *The Four Books of Husbandry*, published in 1586, lists two types of dogs, the Shepherd's Masty, and the House Masty, which might have been a heavy version of a shepherd used for guarding property.

The Mastiff was developed for several purposes, fighting being one. Its fighting role declined in 1835, when bull, bear, and tiger bating and pit fights were outlawed in Britain. For the next twenty years the law was ignored, but when it was enforced, the ferocious dogs that participated in blood sports were lost very quickly. Some Mastiffs remained in guarding roles, and at one time, an ordinance mandated that peasants maintain a few Mastiffs to control wolves and other predators on farms and estates. Few Mastiffs were bred and the breed nearly became extinct. At that time, British sportsmen and noblemen saved the breed for another role, that of gamekeepers' dogs, and yet another role in hunting packs, with quarry being deer and lion. Still later in history, Mastiff breeding was adopted by English fanciers who formed the Old English Mastiff Club in 1883. Although the breed suffered considerable conformation setbacks, breeders eventually corrected its errors. Some of the best English breeding stock was imported to America between the two world wars, and the Mastiff was recognized by the AKC in 1941.

until properly introduced by its master. It socializes easily when young, and usually can be trusted with all family pets. Never shy, timid, or vicious, these serious faults are specifically named in the breed standard.

APTITUDE

Quite intelligent, this dog wants to please its owner, and when applied with consistency,

gentleness, and good humor, training is easily accomplished. The trainer should have a calm approach and encourage performance with love, understanding, and some special treats. The Mastiff is rarely exhibited in obedience, but obedience commands should be taught for control. Because of its size, Canine Good Citizen training is a must for your Mastiff's acceptance into the neighborhood.

Original Design

The Mastiff of today is no doubt an English descendant of the big dogs of the world and a beautiful representative of its type. All the above designs considered, the fact remains that sometime during the past century or two, the British developed a huge guarding dog that could be recognized as a true breed, and that dog was the English Mastiff.

APPEARANCE

The minimum stance for the Mastiff is 30 inches (76 cm), and the height should come from the body depth rather than leg length. This dog has great substance, is massive, heavily boned, and bears heavy musculature. Its coat is straight, coarse, and moderately short. Double-coated, the dog's undercoat is dense and short. Colors include fawn, apricot, or brindle, and all have a darkly pigmented facial mask.

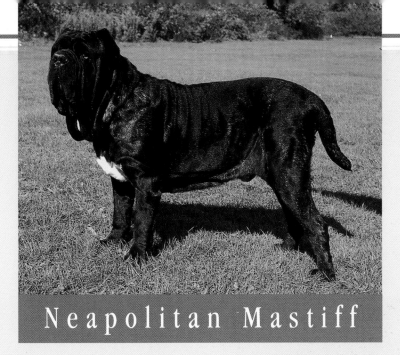

Neapolitan Mastiff

Mastino Napoletano or Neopolitan Mastiff are other names for this massive Mastiff-type breed.

Originating in Italy, this dog is said to have been Caesar's bodyguard, Michelangelo's friend, and Alexander the Great's companion. Stories of the Neapolitan Mastiff are found everywhere dog lore is found.

Rubber brushes rather than combs are used to remove dead hair from the coat of a Neapolitan, with more attention needed during seasonal shedding. The Neapolitan enjoys creature comforts, such as a soft and draft-free place to sleep. One further point should be made regarding its wrinkly face. These deep folds and furrows should be routinely examined for local skin infections that may appear in the deep crevices.

Not one to encourage participation sports, this gigantic, unique-appearing dog has a similar attitude about exercise. Moderate leashed walks, an occasional trip to the park, and a regular romp in the backyard will suffice.

CURRENT FUNCTION

The Neapolitan Mastiff's enormous strength makes it a valuable guard dog, its compatibility and good nature make it an excellent family companion, and its friendly, nonaggressive nature tends to make finicky neighbors accept it more easily.

ATTITUDE

The Neapolitan is not aggressive by nature, but he's all business when employed as a defender of property. A steady, even-tempered dog that isn't apt to bite or attack without provocation or command, this giant dotes on its owner and family, and is a trustworthy, affectionate companion. Somewhat dominant around other dogs, this is an intelligent, peaceful dog, one whose bravery and determination is unquestioned.

APTITUDE

As is the case with all large breeds, consistency in training will pay off. Nagging is usually ignored, and gentle balance is best used when teaching lessons. Not for beginners, this dog is best suited to a calm handler with easygoing leadership skills. Since it is an instinctive guard dog, additional training in this regard may be contraindicated.

APPEARANCE

Often standing about 29½ inches (75 cm), this breed is superbly muscled as would be expected of a guard dog. His color ranges from gray or blue to black, and mahogany. The most outstanding characteristic of this breed is its massive wrinkled head and neck.

Original Design

Originally bred for utility rather than beauty, this breed was developed as a fighter and guard dog. The Neapolitan Mastiff's massive head with its prominent skin folds probably was intended for protection in the fighting pits. The aggressiveness of a fighting dog was selectively bred out, and the remaining guard features were retained. Additionally, this dog has been used at various times to carry packs and pull carts.

Origin

This ancient breed, like other Mastiffs, may trace its ancestors to several thousand years before Christ. Similarities are seen in carvings and figures associated with wars and cultures of Egypt, Persia, and Asia, thence to the Greek Molossus sculpture and the dogs that fit the Mastiff's general description. Breeders in the Neapolitan region of southern Italy bred their Mastiffs to guard homes and estates, and in that locality the unique features of the Neapolitan were developed. One claim of this breed that seems to be undisputed regards its extinction or near-extinction sometime during the early 1900s. Rediscovered in several Italian villages in 1942, the Neapolitan underwent extensive, careful breeding, made its resurgence, and has been multiplying ever since. It was first exhibited in Naples in 1946, had its first standard written, and was recognized by the Federation Cynologique Internationale in 1949. By mid-1970, it had been introduced into other European countries and America, and the Neapolitan Mastiff Club of America was formed in 1973. Pedigrees are scrupulously kept by this club, and the breed standard has been recognized by the AKC, one step toward AKC breed registration. Meanwhile, the breed is gaining in popularity with owners and fanciers, and there are an estimated six thousand Neapolitan Mastiffs in America, mostly along the Eastern seaboard.

Newfoundland

The Newfoundland is a relatively new breed, probably a distant descendant of Mastiffs and other giant breeds.

A child's pet disguised as a giant working dog, this great dogs' attributes include impeccable character and gentleness.

Its coat is massive and will take considerable routine combing and brushing to maintain it without tangles, and more during shedding season.

Typical of a big dog, the Newfoundland's exercise must be curtailed during its growing phase, and its adult requirements are nominal. A large yard and regular excursions outside the yard will suffice to keep the Newfie trim and mentally satisfied.

Once it is fully grown, however, this dog can participate in many activities.

CURRENT FUNCTION

Newfoundlands in America are children's pets, carting and packing dogs, obedience competitors, assistance dogs, and in nearly every case, well-loved companions.

ATTITUDE

Possessing a wonderful sense of humor, this dog is sociable, good-natured, affectionate, and tractable. It's friendly to other dogs, people, and smaller pets. A Newfie is more likely to be found splashing around in the backyard pool than standing guard. It welcomes those who are recognized as friends, and protects its family when intruders are found. This wonderful dog is a consummate companion and is considered totally devoted to its children.

APTITUDE

Sensitive to voice modulations and inflections, the Newfie is relatively easy to train. Most owners advise beginning its training early, because a Newfie pup is a quick study. Like other large dogs, care must be taken to be consistent and gentle in all cases and to reward accomplishments emphatically. This dog will try practically anything it's asked to do, including assistance work, retrieving, obedience,

Some writers speculate that the original Newfie was a cross between a native Newfoundland dog (or wolf) and a dog kept aboard a ship plying its trade on the Newfoundland coast. The puppies of the cross were shipped to England, where the line was developed into today's Newfie. Pure conjecture, of course, but with some credibility, since early settlers of the Newfoundland island failed to identify the presence of such an outstanding great dog. Much later, in 1830, a visitor to Newfoundland reported the presence of a black and tan dog of great stature. Regardless of the circumstances, the Newfoundland was well suited to its island, where it was a natural swimmer and equipped with a dense, water-resistant coat.

Newfoundland heritage is about water. It has been known to rescue people who have found themselves in the icy northern sea as victims of boating accidents, shipwrecks, or long walks on short piers. These adventures led to Newfoundland lifesaving trials, which turned out to be no more than staged exhibitions but were fantastic evidence of this great dog's intelligence, capability, and strength.

weight pulling, carting, packing, skijoring, and other such endeavors.

APPEARANCE

Standing an average of 28 inches (71 cm), the Newfoundland often is much taller. Heavily muscled with great strength in its legs, it's capable of strenuous work. Its heavy coat accentuates its massive body, and its expression is one of benevolence and dignity. The Newfie is solid black, brown, or gray, or solid colors with white markings on the chin, chest, toes, and tip of tail. The Landseer Newfie has a white base coat with black markings.

Original Design

Whether or not the Newfoundland truly is a dog developed exclusively in Newfoundland, or English influence is partially responsible for its blueprint, the original Newfie design is problematic. Obviously the Newfoundland's gigantic webbed feet are handy when it is crossing the marshes of its native island. A thick coat confers protection against the cold water. Great courage and intelligence coexist with water rescue, but this dog seems to possess and surpass those characteristics. Lord Byron summed up the Newfie's original design when he penned the epitaph that labels his beloved Newfoundland companion, Boatswain, as "one who possessed beauty without vanity, strength without insolence, courage without ferocity, and all the virtues of man without his vices."

Otterhound

This big pack-running hound might be described as a shaggy Bloodhound with a clownlike face. The Otterhound is a large ambitious dog that is all business in the field. Otters are aquatic animals, and as one might expect, the Otterhound is well equipped for water work, having a double, oily, water-resistant coat.

Coat care presents a problem for busy families, yet the Otterhound's rough coat needs attention. Mats will form in the long shaggy coat and must be combed out or split and removed. The undercoat must be combed during shedding season, and hours will be spent in this endeavor.

Its exercise requirements are significant, and to prevent lawsuits, exercising this 100 pound (45 kg) dog on-lead is a chore. However, if the Otterhound isn't exercised on a regular basis or put to work in the hunting field, it will become melancholy and bored, which may lead to personality problems. Exercise off-lead usually isn't practical since its tendency to chase small animals is instinctive. Join a tracking club or train your Otterhound for search and rescue.

CURRENT FUNCTION

Although bred to work, the Otterhound in America has taken the role of show dog and companion. It retains its wonderful sense of smell, and can be trained to track virtually any animal that walks. It's one of the least popular breeds registered by the AKC, as well as the UKC, although not because of its personality.

ATTITUDE

Cheerful and intelligent, affectionate and affable, boisterous and independent, the Otterhound makes a wonderful pet if you don't insist on strict obedience and easy care. This dog is friendly to a fault, loving other pets, children, and people in general, family and strangers alike. Their coats are difficult to manage, and this influences their acceptability as pets.

APTITUDE

Training requires consistent soft handling and persistence. Not necessarily obedient, they require consistency, patience, and love to get a

An authority surmised that the Otterhound was developed by crossing the English Foxhound or Harrier with the Water Spaniel, perhaps including the hardiness and tenacity of the Bulldog. The Southern Hound and Welsh Harrier also are said to be Otterhound progenitors. However, the most believable probability puts the Bloodhound, crossed with Foxhounds or Southern Hounds, as the ancestors of this curious breed. Though the true heredity of this dog remains in doubt, it was developed during the reign of King Edward II between 1307 and 1327.

rectangular body are covered with a natural shaggy coat that is made up of a dense, rough outer coat and a short, wooly, and oily undercoat. Any color or color combination is accepted. Its sad-eyed expression is sure to get your attention, and its friendly personality seals the bargain.

This dog was designed for the singular purpose of bringing to bay the hated otter that preyed on fish in English waterways. The aquatic otter was scent tracked to its den by Otterhound packs, and then a terrier was sent into the den to flush out or kill the pesky otter. As the other population diminished, the Otterhound population did likewise. In England, otter hunting continued as a sport because otters were the only game to hunt between April and September.

point across. They tend to have a mind of their own, and stubbornness may be one of their faults. This dog was bred for years as a pack hound and gets along well with other like dogs.

APPEARANCE

Standing up to 27 inches (68.5 cm) in height, this is a big hound. Its large head and bulky,

Pointer

The Pointer is an old sporting breed prized for its phenomenal sense of smell. It was and is one of the great hunting breeds of all time. Neither flowing, luxurious coat nor flashing color is claimed by this agile athlete. The Pointer is a gundog with clean lines and a muscular body and is bred for nose, intelligence, speed, and endurance. It's capable of hunting hard day after day for its owner or an owner's friend, since its thoughts are principally of game, not human society. Its physical development comes to a relatively young age, as do its hunting instincts. Some critics of the Pointer say its greatest fault is the dust raised when it slides to a halt to keep from overrunning game. That's how hard this fellow concentrates on scent.

Coat care is simple. Occasional brushing with a slicker or chamois cloth is required, with more attention during shedding season.

Relatively few of this breed are kept as family pets, and these must be exercised energetically to provide them with a means of expending their energy. The kenneled Pointer

that is taken out several times a week for hunting receives sufficient exercise, but in a backyard, it easily becomes bored and lethargic. It is best suited to active, energetic families or weekend sportsmen.

CURRENT FUNCTION

Although Pointers can make excellent companions, that role doesn't receive the attention given to some of the sporting breeds. This dog was and is primarily a working bird dog dedicated to the shooting sport. Bench show dogs are certainly visible, beautiful, and appreciated by many fanciers, but birds are what Pointers are all about.

ATTITUDE

A Pointer puppy has a sweet temperament and gentle nature, but as it matures, its thoughts turn to the field and its instinctive business of pointing birds. A dedicated athlete, this dog thinks hunting most of the time. Cases have been recorded that indicate this propensity has almost reached overkill status—instances in which a Pointer has held a point for hours on end, seemingly without moving a muscle or blinking an eye. A pet Pointer is often rambunctious and energetic, although it tolerates children well and loves to play games with the younger set. When out for a walk, it never misses a chance to find an interesting trail of a game animal. Only an average guard dog, it often greets owner and stranger alike with a friendly attitude.

APTITUDE

A quick learner, a Pointer is easily trained because of its intelligence and the singular purpose for which it is bred. It's clever and understands commands well. Often kenneled,

Origin

The Pointer comes from England, possibly from progenitors in Spain and France. In fact various pointers seemed to have cropped up in many European countries at about the same time, but this English dog undoubtedly developed in the British Isles. Early 1600s is the approximate date the Pointer appeared, and that preceded the advent of shotgun harvesting game birds. Possible ancestors of the Pointer include the Foxhound, Greyhound, and Bloodhound, and probably one or more spaniels such as the Spanish Pointer.

Original Design

The Pointer's original design was well defined: Run fast, hunt well, make few mistakes, and turn in a near perfect scorecard! Bred with a terrifically competitive spirit, the Pointer is a surefire contestant in field trials. Its size, balance, and muscling are intended to support its hard-running ability, and originally less attention was paid to its personality.

it has the ability to get along well with other dogs in its stable.

APPEARANCE

Standing up to 28 inches tall (71 cm), this strong, well-muscled dog is the epitome of a field athlete. A short, dense, smooth coat helps to display its musculature and hard physical condition. Color range is wide, and the breed standard states that a "good Pointer can't be a bad color." Usually appearing in white with ticks and spots of liver, lemon, black, and orange, these dogs have been bred for conformation without regard to color. The Pointer moves with power, its tail swaying back and forth in time to its pace. The description of this breed emphasizes strength, balance, and agility, "dressed in working clothes."

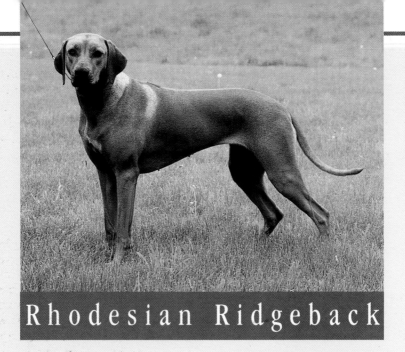

Rhodesian Ridgeback

The Rhodesian Ridgeback, also known as Dog of Zimbabwe or Rhodesian Lion Dog, is an intelligent hound of great strength that withstands weather extremes, hunts virtually every type of game from partridge to lions, and is a trustworthy companion.

Caring for this shorthaired big dog's coat is no problem, and requires only occasional brisk brushing with a rubber slicker.

Its mental and physical exercise needs are substantial and at the minimum, a large yard and daily long walks are required. Some Rhodesians like to carry packs, making camping and hiking trips an excellent means of exercise. This dog sometimes is entered in gazehound and tracking events, which give other options for needed exercise.

CURRENT FUNCTION

The Rhodesian Ridgeback hunts by sight and scent, and these qualities are still present in this breed though infrequently put to use in America. Serving quite well in the companion role, the Ridgeback is an excellent guard dog as well.

ATTITUDE

The Ridgeback is trustworthy, loyal, and exceedingly protective of its human families, but has a trace of independence remaining from its hunter heritage. Known to be vigilant and reserved toward strangers, this dog is good with children, though sometimes more rambunctious than necessary. If introduced to other pets early in life, the Ridgeback is sociable with them, but without proper obedience training and socialization, it may be aggressive toward other dogs and animals.

APTITUDE

This powerful dog exhibits intelligence and cunning and learns quickly. It has a tendency to be stubborn and strong willed, and must receive consistent training by an authoritative handler.

APPEARANCE

A Rhodesian Ridgeback stands up to 27 inches (68.5 cm) tall. All are similarly colored, red

Theoretically, an interesting dog called the Phu Quoc was introduced by Phoenician trading ships to the African Veldt from an island in the Siamese Gulf. The Phu Quoc was the only dog known to have a peculiar ridge of hair growing in the opposite direction from the rest of the coat. The ridge extends down its back from withers to tail. It's assumed that this was the half-wild hunting dog kept by the Hottentots, a native race of people in the area. Boer farmers, settlers of Rhodesia, may have bred this half-wild, ridge-backed hunting dog with dogs brought to South Africa by emigrants from elsewhere in Europe. Dogs that could figure in the Ridgeback's heritage include Mastiffs, Great Danes, Bloodhounds, and Pointers, among others. Immigration was closed for 100 years beginning in 1707 and it was during this time that the Ridgeback was developed. In 1870, the dog was taken to Rhodesia (now Zimbabwe) to hunt, and was an immediate success. It was imported to Great Britain in 1930, to America in 1950, and registered by the AKC in 1955.

wheaten to light wheaten. Its short coat is dense, and is accented by the characteristic ridge of hair standing along the spine. This ridge is well defined, symmetrical, and tapering from shoulder to hip. Its muscular body gives the impression of power and agility.

Original Design

The Boers' design included a tough hunting dog that would fill the need for a partridge dog, as well as a deer and lion dog. They needed a big dog that would back down from neither vandals nor marauding wild animals. Their design addressed a shorthaired dog that could easily be examined or treated for external parasites, and one that would bond with and protect their families.

209

Rottweiler

A favorite Mastiff-type dog in America, the Rottweiler recently has been among the most popular breeds registered by the AKC. Having served in various roles throughout history, the Rottweiler has filled many needs, and is given credit for being a progenitor of the Doberman Pinscher.

The Rottie's coarse coat is relatively easily cared for, and needs routine brushing with a rubber brush or slicker.

Its exercise demands are significant, and an adult Rottweiler will appreciate frequent walks in open country. When looking for a means of entertaining and exercising a Rottie, don't forget its packing and carting history. Not a dog to ignore or keep kenneled, this dog retrieves naturally and loves to swim.

CURRENT FUNCTION

Most Rotties in America are primarily pets and family companions, and secondarily fill the watchdog vocation quite well. It's an outstanding show dog, an able obedience competitor, and a great schutzhund.

ATTITUDE

Confident, bold, clever, intelligent, and obedient to its owner, the Rottweiler is devoted to its family and has a protective attitude that surpasses all else. This vigilant and brave dog has a strong, jealous temperament that puts itself between its family and danger, and has been known to sacrifice its life for its owner. This dog will become a great playmate, but is needful of careful puppy socialization, both with small children and household pets. Affectionate but somewhat undemonstrative except when playing with its children, this dog seems always to be thinking.

APTITUDE

Somewhat dominant in nature, the Rottie is easily trained by a patient, consistent, and calm handler. The trainer should have total confidence in himself and the dog, and above all else, be fair and logical. Trainers who practice harsh discipline or negative reinforcement will usually fail with this strong-willed dog, and

Origin

The Rottweiler's origin isn't well documented. Legend has it that about 1,900 years ago Rome conquered Rottweil, an important cultural and trade city in Wurttemberg, South Germany. In the wake of the Roman soldiers came the cattle that were used for food for the journey, driven and guarded by fearless descendants of herd dogs and Mastiffs. When the Roman troops advanced from Rottweil, some of their dogs remained behind and thereafter were called Rottweilers. The sturdy herding and guarding dog assumed another role and became a butcher's draft dog that willingly defended the purses of those vendors. When donkeys replaced the Rottie in that endeavor, it found another niche in German police work. The Rottweiler broke into show-dog ranks during the first two decades of the twentieth century, and was imported to America and recognized by the AKC in 1931, when it rapidly became a family companion, and worthy competitor in many canine events.

usually, those who nag suffer the same defeat. The trainer who treats this dog with gentle persuasion, giving rewards at the proper times, is most apt to succeed. Dominance training and expert leadership is required by the Rottweiler owner throughout this dog's life.

APPEARANCE

Standing up to 27 inches (68.5 cm), the Rottweiler is a massive dog with musculature to match its big attitude. It has the looks of a much larger dog, and is often described as gigantic by passersby. Its balanced, athletic build has great substance, and it moves with drive and authority. Its black and tan coat is straight, coarse, dense, and of medium length.

Original Design

The Rottweiler probably descended from the Roman Molossus and was crossed with herding dogs early in history. It found its fame as a German butcher dog, police dog, and guardian of property and families, but it lives on primarily in that ultimate design, the important role of companion.

Saarloos Wolfhound

The Saarloos is a little-known breed named for its original breeder, Mr. Leendert Saarloos, a Dutch geneticist. Also known as the Saarloos Wolf Dog, this healthy, big dog is said to live an average of thirteen to fourteen years, and apparently has few if any of the genetic diseases that often affect other large and giant breeds.

The wolflike coat of the Saarloos is easy to care for, with weekly combing and brushing increased twofold during shedding season.

Its exercise demand isn't much different than other hounds, and probably is less than typical of sight hounds.

CURRENT FUNCTION

Dutch references describe this dog as a family pet that is patient with children, but other countries' books describe the breed as shy and independent, used primarily to improve other dogs' breeding stock.

ATTITUDE

The Saarloos is reported to be intelligent, alert, and apparently is affectionate toward its handler or owner. It's sociable with other dogs if introduction is accomplished very early in life. Socialization with people should begin before the pup is ten weeks old, and this intensive training should continue for life. The Saarloos is cautious of strangers, new situations, and other pets. It retains a strong wolflike pack instinct and needs firm handling. Strong willed and wary, it is often aggressive toward other dogs and people, and needs decisive, firm handling by its owner.

APTITUDE

A Saarloos definitely isn't the dog for inexperienced owners. It can be an excellent guard dog when well trained, but is not a particularly obedient dog. The breed is not well known outside its native country, and little is published about its aptitude and personality.

Origin

The Saarloos Wolfhound originated in the Netherlands in about 1945 and was the result of a single man's breeding effort. Its ancestors were the wolf and the German Shepherd, and the Saarloos was developed in an effort to eliminate the genetic flaws occurring in purebred Shepherds. The breed was recognized by the Dutch Kennel Club in 1975, but hasn't proven popular outside its native land.

APPEARANCE

The Saarloos stands up to 29½ inches (75 cm) at the shoulder. Being a wolf cross, the Saarloos naturally resembles a wolf in many ways, both in phenotype and genotype. It has a wolflike head with high-set triangular ears, almond-shaped eyes, a coat that is short and dense, and a muscular body. Colors range from wolf gray to brown, cream, and white.

Original Design

This dog is the result of a genetic experiment that is apparently partially successful and may in the future be more accepted by the general public. The Saarloos is specifically designed to eliminate hereditary diseases such as Canine Hip Dysplasia (CHD). Whether or not the dog will at some time be superior to the German Shepherd in any other traits remains to be seen. Little is published to indicate that Mr. Saarloos was striving for equal intelligence, herding ability, olfactory capability, temperament, personality, trainability, or any of the other well-defined German Shepherd Dog characteristics.

Saint Bernard

Legend and folklore surround this mighty dog and permeate its history. Its grand place in the annals of dogdom is seldom challenged, and its bravery, stamina, and devotion to mankind is second to none. The stories of its determined alpine rescues have been written and made into movies, but they hardly do justice to reality.

The Saint's coat must be groomed regularly to prevent tangles and matting unless the dog is a shorthaired variety, which requires only minimal combing but more attention during shedding season.

Exercise requirements are minimal for this giant, and it gets along well with romps in a large backyard, with regular walks around the neighborhood for a change of scene.

CURRENT FUNCTION

Currently, the Saint Bernard is invariably put to work as family pet and big companion, although it retains the qualities of a competent mountain rescue dog.

ATTITUDE

The Saint is blessed with a superb sense of humor, intelligence, a friendly attitude, and biddable personality, with just a tiny streak of stubbornness, as befits its huge size. One of its greatest attributes is being a kids' dog. Children love the Saint, and it reciprocates wholeheartedly. Be sure to monitor all play involving your good-natured, child-loving Saint and his favorite child. When an immature big dog puppy is playing with a young child, disaster is just around the corner. These oversized puppies look like sturdy trucks, but are quite easily injured. Re-read the warning on page 16 of Chapter 2. The Saint is loyal to its family and will defend its home when necessary. Easily socialized with other pets, the Saint Bernard is a fun-loving, equable companion.

APTITUDE

The Saint sometimes is seen competing in obedience trials and occasionally is entered in tracking contests. The best of the Saint

Origin

This massive dog is reported to be the result of crossing native Swiss dogs with the Asian Molosser that accompanied Roman soldiers on their invasions of the Alps. The period of development was during the first two centuries A.D. For the next few hundreds of years, the Saint Bernard was used for draft duties, guarding, herding, and finally as the great mountain rescue dogs of the hospice, which served as refuge for travelers between Switzerland and Italy. The Saint Bernard was named for Archdeacon Bernard de Menthon, the originator of that famous Swiss hospice, or to be more exact, the dog was named for the hospice or the pass that carried Saint Bernard's name. The dog was bred by the monks as a hospice dog for three centuries, and is believed to have saved more than 2,000 lives. By 1810, the Saint Bernard was known in England and was imported to Germany, where it was called the Alpendog. Later in the nineteenth century, it was imported to other European countries and to America.

Original Design

This mighty dog was designed for work. It carried packs, pulled carts, guarded flocks, and probably served in other roles as well on its Swiss farms. The Saint's pathfinding and scenting ability were proven while a hospice dog, and its instinctive ability to sense avalanches is legendary.

Bernards make excellent show dogs when handled properly, but if not trained when young, they tend to reverse roles with their handlers. Usually quite easily trained, this dog may show a bit of stubborn behavior, which is best treated with love and consistency, an occasional treat, and a great deal of praise.

APPEARANCE

A minimum height of 27½ inches (70 cm) is set by the breed standard, but most Saints range well above that size. *Powerful* is the term best used to describe this great dog. It's a tall, muscular dog exuding great strength and power. Its head is massively impressive to match its gigantic body. This dog is seen in two coat types, shorthaired and longhaired. Its color is white with red or red with white, accompanied by brindle markings. Brownish yellow is also accepted, but no solid color is accepted without white markings.

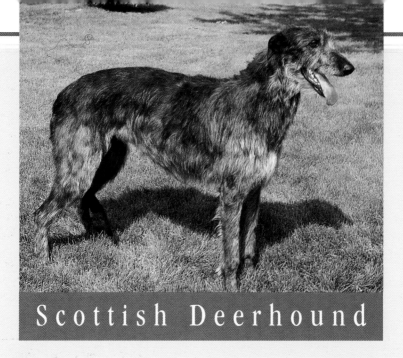

Scottish Deerhound

Historically, this gazehound is a dog of nobility, at one time possessed by no one with lower rank than an earl. The Scottish Deerhound always has been a valuable investment, and stories abound related to the amount of gold required to purchase a single specimen. It has come close to extinction because of the value placed upon it by chieftains and lords. The stately carriage and graceful bearing of the Scottish Deerhound fairly exudes wealth, position, and aristocracy in every move. In its history, it has had numerous other names such as the Royal Dog of Scotland, Irish Wolf Dog, Scotch Greyhound, Highland Deerhound, Rough Highland Greyhound, and Staghound, many of which confuse the specific origin and progenitors of this great dog.

Combing this dog's wiry coat presents little problem, and adds to the bonding between groomer and companion. Tangles are infrequent, and are easily split and combed out.

A true athlete, the adult Deerhound requires a great deal of exercise that can't possibly be afforded by a walk around the block.

As is the case with many other gazehounds, it is often banned by ordinance from being exercised off-lead due to its propensity to chase small pets.

CURRENT FUNCTION

Today, the tall, regal Scottish Deerhound is a superb family pet, and if tried, would probably race to bring down a deer for your table. The dog also has been successfully trained to course coyotes, wolves, and small game. The magic of dog shows has lured this breed as well, and they have competed with honor in this endeavor. The primary use of the average Deerhound is companionship, and because they are easily taught, competitive obedience takes a secondary role.

ATTITUDE

The personality of this royal dog of Scotland is exemplary, although hunting instincts occasionally distract from it. This hound is typically friendly, gentle, intelligent, and kind to children. It's born with good sense and amiability. It is a tractable pet that asks little of its family except exercise and love.

APTITUDE

Quite trainable, the Scottish Deerhound is a quick study for most exercises. Its behavior around other dogs rarely presents a problem, but cats and other small pets may call up hunting instincts, much to the dismay of those pets. This gazehound is blessed with a good nose as well, and is often found to be a fine tracker. Obedience training is usually easy to accomplish because the dog is focused upon its handler.

Original Design

This powerful creature was bred to course and bring down Scottish deer that sometimes reach a weight of 250 pounds. The Scottish Deerhound's companionship is equally valued both historically and at present; this indeed was and is a faithful and obedient friend.

Origin

Regardless of its earliest ancestry, of one thing we can be sure. The Scottish Deerhound of today is the same dog that was identified in the mid 1700s. It was in the Scottish Highlands when the big stag made its last appearance in goodly numbers that the Deerhound was developed. Because of the value assigned to this dog, its numbers ebbed until about 1825, when the breed made a resurgence with the help of fanciers who bred it again.

APPEARANCE

This tall, shaggy dog stands upward from 30 inches (76 cm) and is usually colored blue gray or darker and lighter grays or brindles. Its coat is 3 to 4 inches long (7.5 to 10 cm) and is hard and wiry except on the head, breast, and belly, where it is softer. It has the general confirmation of a Greyhound, but is of larger bone. A long neck, narrow head, and arched loin is indicative of the speed and endurance of this dog.

Tibetan Mastiff

Tibet, that cold, unique, faraway country of fewer than 500,000 square miles, perched between India and Nepal, claims the title of highest region on Earth. Its elevation, averaging 12,000 feet above sea level, is, strangely enough, the origin of a number of dogs. Isolated from the world by enormous mountain ranges and surviving under Communist Chinese rule since 1965, this land is home to the massive Tibetan Mastiff.

As would be expected, this mountain dog's all-weather coat requires regular grooming and care, sometimes up to half an hour daily when seasonal shedding begins.

The Tibetan Mastiff's demand for exercise is only average, and a walk or two each day will usually suffice if its yard is sufficiently large.

CURRENT FUNCTION

Today, the Tibetan Mastiff is an excellent but strong-willed family pet, a willing companion that is best placed with families who are experienced with giant breeds of formidable size and stubborn dispositions.

ATTITUDE

The Tibetan's character features include great strength and initiative, courage tempered by gentleness and patience, and independence but loyalty to its family. The Tibetan Mastiff is generally good-natured, intelligent, and curious, loving with children of the family but reserved with strangers. Its deep lionlike warning bark is resonant and loud, and will discourage most predators and thieves before their trespassing plans can materialize. Socialization with small family pets during the Tibetan's puppyhood is a must, and puppy kindergarten and monitored exposure to neighborhood children and pets is an excellent plan. This dog is said to have a strong will that goes beyond independence, and dominance training should be started early in puppyhood and continued for life.

APTITUDE

The Tibetan Mastiff is quite at home with guarding responsibilities; it's been a practitioner in that role for centuries and needs no special lessons. Training in other endeavors is problematic; the breed has been making its own decisions for thousands of years. This intelligent giant may excel at obedience work if training is introduced quietly and with respect. Consistency and persistence balanced with gentleness and rewards will win the training program. Corporal punishment and force will never work, not only because of this dog's high pain threshold, but also because of its tendency to stubbornly ignore the trainer who attempts to use such tactics.

APPEARANCE

The Tibetan Mastiff breed standard lists 28 inches (71 cm) as the minimum stature for a male, with no outer limits stated. Often pictured with a red yak's-hair collar as a sign of its status, this Mastiff differs from others in many ways, but its coat is the first noticeable feature. This dog's covering is designed to withstand the severest weather. Its outer coat is thick and full, and the undercoat is profuse and wool-like. The Tibetan is seen in black, black and tan, brown, gold,

Origin

If the origin of many of today's Mastiff predecessors lies in Tibet, then the Tibetan Mastiff must be a very proud dog. Indeed, this easygoing giant is a very proud and dignified dog, self-confident and dominant. It's said to be among the progenitors of other Mastiff breeds that have come out of the Tibetan mountains and monasteries. It's a primitive dog that matures very slowly, with females often beginning their estrous cycles between three and four years of age, and males reaching maturity between three and five years.

gray, or gray and tan, and its tail is high set and carried forward over the back. Its head is cleaner with fewer wrinkles and folds than some other Mastiffs. The Tibetan has the appearance of great power and excellent proportion.

Original Design

For several centuries the Tibetan Mastiff has been the guardian of Tibetan livestock and homes. It was bred and maintained to ward off wolves, tigers, and bears that threatened its families and flocks. Its instincts have been attuned to action without commands being given, and therefore this Tibetan giant has developed its instinctive independence.

Index

Afghan Hound, 111–113
Age considerations, 8–9,
    12–13, 105
Aggression, 42
Akita, 114–115
Alaskan Malamute, 116–118
Amino acids, 93
Anatolian Shepherd Dog,
    119–121
Antigenicity, 67
Artificial respiration, 75
Atopy, 58–59
Azawakh, 122–123

Beauceron, 124–125
Begging, 39
Behavioral problems, 36–42
    aggression, 42
    begging, 39
    biting, 37, 41
    compulsive disorder,
        37–38
    chasing, 44–45
    chewing, 39–40
    coprophagia, 40
    digging, 43–44
    growling, 37
    jumping up, 38–39
    leadership training, 42–43
    mouthing, 39–40
    predatory activities,
        36–37
    roaming, 41–42
    separation anxiety, 37–38
Bernese Mountain Dog,
    126–128
Biting, 37, 41
Bloodhound, 130–132
Boarding kennels, 21–22
Bonding, 24–26

Bones, 96
    cancer, 64–65
Borrelia burgdorferi, 72
Borzoi, 133–135
Bouvier des Flandres,
    136–137
Breeders, 5–7
Breeding, 100–104
Breeds, 110–219
Briard, 138–139
Bullmastiff, 140–141

Calluses, 52
Canine:
    compulsive disorder, 37–38
    distemper, 71
    hepatitis, 71
Carbohydrates, 95
Cardiopulmonary resuscita-
    tion, 75
Castration, 104
Caucasian Owtcharka,
    142–143
Chasing, 44–45
Chesapeake Bay Retriever,
    144–146
Chewing, 39–40
Children, interactions with,
    16
Coccidioidomycosis, 57
Collars, 15
"Come" command, 35–36
Coonhound, black and tan,
    128–129
Coprophagia, 40
Corona virus, 71
Crates, 18, 27–28
Crossbred dogs, 7–8
Curly-Coated Retriever,
    147–148

Decubital ulcers, 52
Degenerative joint disease, 63
Delayed maturation, 101–102
Diabetes mellitus, 57
Digestive problems, 84–91
    air swallowing, 89
    bloat, 87–89
    flatus, 89
    food quality, 84–85
    gastric torsion, 87–89
    hiccups, 85–86
    hunger, 84
    impaction, 87
    obesity, 90–91
    pancreatitis, 86–87
    vomiting, 90
    weight loss, 91
Digging, 43–44
Diseases, preventable, 71–72
Doberman Pinscher,
    149–151
Dogo Argentino, 152–153
Dogue de Bordeaux, 154–155
Dystocias, 102

Ectropion, 60
Elbow:
    dysplasia, 64
    hygroma, 51–52
Emergencies, 73–83
    artificial respiration, 75
    automobile accidents,
        76–77
    cardiopulmonary resuscita-
        tion, 75
    first aid kit, 73
    heatstroke, 77–78
    nosebleeds, 81
    poisoning, 78–79
    porcupine quills, 81–82

shock, 75–76
    skunks, 82–83
    snakebite, 81
    vital signs, normal, 74
    wounds, 79–80
English Setter, 156–158
Entropion, 59
Epilepsy, 55–56
Equipment, 15, 17–18
Estrela Mountain Dog,
    159–160
Euthanasia, 106–108
Exercise, 29–33

Fat, 94
Fatty acids, 93
Feeding, 92–99
    bones, 96
    meat, 96
    nutrition, 92–96
    overfeeding, 98–99
    schedule, 29
    treats, 98
Fila Brasileiro, 161–162
First aid kit, 73
Flatus, 89
Food, 84–85, 93–94, 97

Gastric:
    dilation and volvulus,
        87–89
    torsion, 87–89
Gender considerations,
    5
German Shepherd Dog,
    163–165
Giant Schnauzer, 166–167
Gordon Setter, 168–169
Great Dane, 170–172
Great Pyrenees, 173–174

Greater Swiss Mountain Dog, 175–176
Greyhound, 177–179
Growling, 37
Guarding, 42

Halters, 15
Handling, 23–24
Hazards, 18–19
Head collars, 15
Health considerations, 10–12, 46–65
  antigenicity, 67
  common disorders, 52–65
  digestive problems, 84–91
  diseases, preventable, 71–72
  emergencies, 73–82
  immunity, 66–70
  laboratory tests, 48–50
  preventive medicine, 66–72
  vaccinations, 68–70
  veterinarian, 46–51
Heart diseases, 56
Heatstroke, 77–78
Hemorrhage, 80
Hiccups, 85–86
Hip dysplasia, 62–63
Homecoming, 23–45
  bonding, 24–26
  crates, 27–28
  exercise, 29–33
  feeding schedule, 29
  handling, 23–24
  housebreaking, 27–28
  identification, 33
  lifting, 23–24
  manners, 33–34
  obedience, 25–26
  socialization, 24–26
  training, 25–26, 34
Housebreaking, 27–28
Houseplants, 78–79
Hunger, 84
Hypothyroidism, 58

Ibizan Hound, 180–181
Identification, 33
Immunity, 66–70
Impaction, 87

Insurance, 15–16
Irish Setter, 182–183
Irish Wolfhound, 184–186

Joint anatomy, 61
Jumping up, 38–39

Kennel cough, 71
Kennels, 17–18, 21–22
Kidney disease, 56
Komondor, 187–188
Kuvasz, 189–190

Laboratory tests, 48–50
Labrador Retriever, 191–193
Leadership training, 42–43
Leonberger, 194–195
Leptospirosis, 71
Lifting, 23–24
Longevity, 105–108
Lyme disease, 71–72

Male maturation, delayed, 102
Mastiff, 196–198
Mastitis, 102
Minerals, 95
Mixed breed dogs, 7–8
Mouthing, 39–40
Muzzle, 76

Name, learning, 35
Neapolitan Mastiff, 199–200
Neutering, 104
Newfoundland, 201–202
Nosebleeds, 81
Nutrition, 92–96
  bones, 96
  carbohydrates, 95
  fat, 94
  meat, 96
  minerals, 95
  overfeeding, 98–99
  protein, 94–95
  supplements, 96
  vitamins, 95–96
  water, 94

Obedience, 25–26
Obesity, 54–55, 90–91

Osteoarthritis, 63
Osteosarcoma, 64–65
Otterhound, 203–204
Overfeeding, 98–99

Pancreatitis, 86–87
Parasites, 98
Parvovirus, 71
Pens, 27–28
Personality assessing, 9–10
Pointer, 205–207
Poisoning, 19, 78–79
Porcupine quills, 81–82
Predatory activities, 36–37
Preparations, 14–22
  children, interactions with, 16
  crates, 18
  insurance, 15–16
  neighbors' considerations, 14–15
  puppy-proofing, 18–21
Preventive medicine, 66–72
  antigenicity, 67
  diseases, preventable, 71–72
  immunity, 66–70
  vaccinations, 68–70
Progressive Retinal Atrophy, 59
Protein, 94–95
Pseudocyesis, 103–104
Puppy:
  mills, 6
  -proofing, 18–19
  raising, 104
Pyometra, 102

Rabies, 72
Recall, 35–36
Rescue dogs, 13
Rewards, 34
Rhodesian Ridgeback, 208–209
Rottweiler, 210–211

Saarloos Wolfhound, 212–213
Saint Bernard, 214–215
Scottish Deerhound, 216–217

Selection considerations, 1–13
  age considerations, 8–9, 12–13
  breed considerations, 1, 7–8
  breeders, 5–7
  gender considerations, 5
  health check, 10–12
  impulse purchases, 4–5
  intelligence, 3–4
  personality assessing, 9–10
  rescue dogs, 13
  sources, 5–7
  timing, 4
Separation anxiety, 37–38
Shock, 75–76
"Sit" command, 36
Skeletal problems, 60–61
Socialization, 24–26
Sources, 5–7
Space requirements, 17
Spaying, 104
Supplements, 96

Tail beating, 52–54
Tattoos, 33
Therapy, 50–51
Tibetan Mastiff, 218–219
Training, 25–26, 34
  behavioral problems, 36–42
  commands, 35–36
  leadership, 42–43
  name, learning, 35
  rewards, 34
Treats, 98

Uterine inertia, 103

Vaccinations, 68–70
Veterinarian, 46–51
Vital signs, normal, 74
Vitamins, 95–96
Vomiting, 90
Von Willebrand's Disease, 57–58

Water, 94
Weight loss, 91
Wounds, 79–80